C Y
I N

Carole Saint-Laurent

ULYSSES
TRAVEL PUBLICATIONS
Travel better... enjoy more

Series Director
Claude Morneau

Project Supervisor
Pascale Couture

*Research and
Composition*
Carole Saint-Laurent

English Translation
Tracy Kendrick
Sarah Kresh
Felicity Munn

English Editor
Jennifer McMorran

Cartography
Colour atlas
IGN
Diagrams
André Duchesne

Layout
Christian Roy
Stéphane G. Marceau

Collaboration
Daniel Desjardins
Lorette Pierson

Artistic Director
Patrick Farei
Atoll Direction

Photography
Cover
Gaétan Fontaine

Special thanks to: Alain Cuny, Simon Plouffe, Luce Saint-Laurent, Christine Carrière, Francine Landry, France Saint-Laurent, Jacqueline Goulet, Ginette Bélanger, Suzanne Barsalo, Anne Cyr, Carl Martin, Jacqueline Ouellette, Gislaine Provost and all the tourist office representatives who were so friendly and helpful.

Ulysses would like to thank: SODEC (Québec government) and the Canadian Heritage Minister for their financial support.

Distributors

AUSTRALIA:
Little Hills Press
11/37-43 Alexander St.
Crows Nest NSW 2065
☎ (612) 437-6995
Fax: (612) 438-5762

BELGIUM AND LUXEMBOURG:
Vander
Vrijwilligerlaan 321
B-1150 Brussel
☎ (02) 762 98 04
Fax: (02) 762 06 62

CANADA:
Ulysses Books & Maps
4176 Saint-Denis
Montréal, Québec
H2W 2M5
☎ (514) 843-9882, ext.2232
Fax: 514-843-9448
http://www.ulysse.ca

GERMANY AND AUSTRIA:
Brettschneider
Fernreisebedarf
Feldfirchner Strasse 2
D-85551 Heimstetten
München
☎ 89-99 02 03 30
Fax: 89-99 02 03 31

GREAT BRITAIN AND
IRELAND:
World Leisure Marketing
9 Downing Road
West Meadows, Derby
UK DE21 6HA
☎ 1 332 34 33 32
Fax: 1 332 34 04 64

ITALY:
Edizioni del Riccio
Via di Soffiano 164 A
50143 Firenze
☎ (055) 71 33 33
Fax: (055) 71 63 50

NETHERLANDS:
Nilsson & Lamm
Pampuslaan 212-214
1380 AD Weesp (NL)
☎ 0294-465044
Fax: 0294-415054

SCANDINAVIA:
Scanvik
Esplanaden 8B
1263 Copenhagen K
DK
☎ (45) 33.12.77.66
Fax: (45) 33.91.28.82

SPAIN:
Altaïr
Balmes 69
E-08007 Barcelona
☎ 454 29 66
Fax: 451 25 59

SWITZERLAND:
OLF
P.O. Box 1061
CH-1701 Fribourg
☎ (026) 467.51.11
Fax: (026) 467.54.66

U.S.A.:
The Globe Pequot Press
6 Business Park Road
P.O. Box 833
Old Saybrook, CT 06475
☎ 1-800-243-0495
Fax: 1-800-820-2329

Other countries, contact Ulysses Books & Maps (Montréal), Fax (514) 843-9448
No part of this publication may be reproduced in any form or by any means, including photocopying, without the written permission of the publisher.
© May 1997, Ulysses Travel Publications
All rights reserved
ISBN 2-89464-008-0
Printed in Canada
Canadian Cataloguing in Press see p 4

"C'est de là que je vous écris, ma porte grande ouverte, au bon soleil. Un joli bois de pins tout étincelant de lumière dégringole devant moi jusqu'au bas de la côte. À l'horizon, les Alpilles découpent leur crêtes fines... Pas de bruit... À peine, de loin en loin, un son de fifre, un courlis dans les lavandes, un grelot de mules sur la route..."

"It is from there that I write you, my door wide open to the good sun. Before me, a lovely pine forest, sparkling with light, tumbles all the way down the hill. The crests of the Alpilles cut a fine figure on the horizon... No sound... Barely perceptible from here and there, the sound of a fife, a curlew in the lavender, a mule bell on the road..."

Alphonse Daudet (1840-1897)
Lettres de mon moulin

ABOUT THE AUTHOR

Carole Saint-Laurent is an avid cyclist who has been organizing bicycle tours for ten years. She has lead groups along the roads of Italy, Switzerland, Greece, Portugal and, of course, France.

Each cyclist who has followed his or her dream by joining one of Carole's tours has contributed to the preparation of this guide. Thanks to them, she is able to share her passion for Europe and France while enjoying the wonderful adventure that is bicycle touring.

Help make Ulysses Guides even better!

The information contained in this guide was correct at press time. However, mistakes can slip in, omissions are always possible, places can disappear, etc. The authors and publisher hereby disclaim any liability for loss or damage resulting from omissions or errors.

We value your comments, corrections and suggestions, as they allow us to keep each guide up to date. The best contributions will be rewarded with a free book from Ulysses Travel Publications. All you have to do is write us at the following address and indicate which title you would be interested in receiving (see the list at end of guide).

Ulysses Travel Publications
4176 Rue Saint-Denis
Montréal, Québec
Canada H2W 2M5
http://www.ulysse.ca
E-mail: guiduly@ulysse.ca

Canadian Cataloguing in Publication Data
Saint-Laurent, Carole, 1954
     Cycling in France
     (Ulysses Green Escapes)
     Translation of: Cyclotourisme en France
     Includes index
     ISBN 2-89464-008-0
     1. Bicycle touring - France - Guidebooks. 2. France - Guidebooks.
I.Title. II. Series.
GV1046.F8S2413 1997   796.6'4'0944   C97-940032-5

TABLE OF CONTENTS

How to use this guide

First off, you will notice that each region includes one or several tours, which consist of one or several legs. Each route is clearly explained in the text, including many details to help you get oriented. You'll find precise and simple directions, for example: "Turn right on the small winding road".

Next, each route is outlined on black and white diagrams, which you'll find in each chapter. These diagrams have been included to help you visualize the route you will be following. They only show the roads you will following. You'll find the road number and the names of the towns and cities you will cross as well as a clear reference to the tour you have chosen, for example: 1. Grand Tour of the Camargue; Leg from Nîmes to Grau-du-Roi.

Finally, you will find, at the end of the guide, an atlas made from maps provided by the Institut Géographique National Français (IGN). These colour maps will help to familiarize you with the terrain you'll be covering, to take note of the topography of the route, to locate important cities nearby, bodies of water, etc. Each map covers only the immediate surroundings of the tours described in this guide. As with the diagrams, each map refers to the tour it covers. Note that the pages of the atlas are numbered from 1 to 32, preceded by *A*.

To find out where to find the specific diagram and map of your tour, refer to the tables on pages 8 and 9. All the page references are clearly indicated. As well, in the text, at the beginning of each new tour, the pages where you'll find the diagram(s) and colour map(s) are clearly indicated. For example: Diagram p 26, Map A3 indicates that the black and white diagram is on page 26 and the colour map is on page 3 of the atlas.

Good ride!

Where is France ?

France

Capital: Paris
Language: French
Population: 56,000,000 inhab.
Area: 550,000 km²

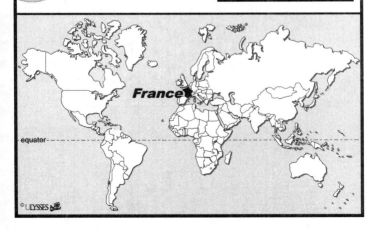

		Cities	Description page	Diagram page	Colour Map page
	PROVENCE				
1	Grand Tour of the Camargue	Nîmes, Grau-du-Roi, Saintes-Maries-de-la-Mer, Arles	36	37	A2, A3
2	Grand Tour of the Gard	Nîmes, Alès, Uzès, Bagnols-sur-Cèze, Barjac	45	49	A3, A4
3	Heart of the Garrigues	Nîmes, Uzès	54	55	A3
4	Gard to Vaucluse	Nîmes, Avignon	56	69	A5
5	Gard to Alpilles	Nîmes, Saint-Rémy-de-Provence, Arles	58	69	A5
6	Alpilles Loop	Arles, Saint-Rémy-de-Provence	60	60	A5
7	Grand Tour of the Vaucluse	Avignon, Carpentras, Orange	67	69	A5
	BURGUNDY				
8	Loop Dijon - Vallée de l'Ouche - Dijon	Dijon, Gevrey-Chambertin	79	81	A6
9	Dijon to Beaune	Dijon, Beaune, Vougeot	82	81	A6, A7
10	Loop Beaune - La Rochepot - Beaune	Beaune, La Rochepot	84	87	A7
11	Loop Beaune - Bouilland - Beaune	Beaune, Bouilland	88	87	A7
	FRANCHE-COMTÉ				
12	Saône Plain	Beaune, Dole, Auxonne	94	95	A7, A8
13	The Jura	Dole, Salins-les-Bains	97	95	A8
14	The Doubs	Dole, Besançon, Rougemont	100	95, 103	A8, A9
15	The Haute-Saône	Rougemont, Giromagny	105	103	A9, A10

		Cities	Description page	Diagram page	Colour Map page
	ALSACE				
16	Alsace Tour	Giromagny, Thann, Turckheim, Barr, Strasbourg	110	113, 117	A10 to A12
	NORMANDY				
17	Grand Tour of Calvados	Bayeux, Ouistreham, Saint-Pierre-sur-Dives, Thury-Harcourt	124	125	A13
18	Tour of La Manche	Bayeux, Isigny-sur-Mer, Coutances, Granville, Avranches, Pontorson	135	139, 141	A14, A15
	BRITTANY				
19	Haute-Bretagne	Rennes, Pontorson, Saint-Malo, Dinan, Sables-d'Or-les-Pins, Ploeuc-sur-Lié, Pontivy	153	155, 163	A16 to A18
20	Pontivy to Quimper	Pontivy, Quimperlé, Quimper	168	163, 171	A19, A20
21	The Côte-sud	Quimper, Forêt-Fouesnant, Pont-Aven, Lorient, Auray, Muzillac, Guérande, Savenay, Nantes	173	171, 181, 185	A20 to A23
	THE LOIRE VALLEY				
22	Tour of the Loire Valley	Nantes, Saint-Florent-le-Vieil, Angers, Saumur, Chinon, Azay-le-Rideau, Loches, Amboise, Blois	195	197, 203, 211, 216	A24 to A28
	PÉRIGORD AND QUERCY				
23	Grand Tour of Périgord and Quercy	Bergerac, le Bugue, Montignac, Sarlat-la-Canéda, Souillac, Gramat, Figeac, Saint-Cirq-Lapopie, Cahors, Villefranche-du-Périgord	221	223, 237, 243	A29 to A32

CYCLING IN FRANCE

France is renowned among bicycle travellers as "the" destination. It offers small, quiet roads, hospitable, pretty villages, a wide range of accommodation, major historic sites, diverse scenery and, of course, legendary cuisine and wines!

This book explores France's deep-rooted charms. The suggested tours each depart from the big cities, with their artwork and fabulous history, and each lead through the overlooked nooks and crannies, and the lovely towns of France. Pedaling your bicycle along the back roads, you can take the time to observe nature around you, to breathe in the heady scent of the countryside and to savour the local specialties you'll find all along the way.

Whatever your reasons for travelling by bicycle, whether to get in touch with nature or to satisfy a taste for adventure, your expectations will be met and even surpassed. Neophyte or seasoned cyclist, you'll be satisfied all along the hundreds of kilometres there are to travel. The 20 suggested tours wind through many different regions of France. These scenic routes were selected because they are among the best for bicycle touring. And they were chosen based on my own experience. I've pedaled them all, alone or with a group.

THE TOURS

You can choose which of the various tours is best for you depending on the time of year, the amount of time you have, the level of difficulty, your personal taste, etc. The routes follow small secondary roads (departmental and community roads), except on the way in to and out of some of the large cities where it's impossible to avoid the Routes Nationales. Generally speaking, the pavement is in good condition and well-maintained; you'll find it's like rolling along on velvet!

In some cases, the tour is a loop that ends where it started, allowing for a "grand tour" of a particular region. In other cases, the tour does not come back to the departure point, allowing you continue on to the next tour. Each tour goes through at least one good-sized city where you can find bicycle shops (consult the practical information chart for each route). Small villages and towns are very close to one another. If the route seems too long, you can always stop and find lodging and food practically anywhere (although this is less easy in July and August).

THE REGIONS

Provence lies in the south of the country, basking under a sun that puts a smile on everyone's lips. The wild Camargue coast, the many Roman sites of Gard, the majesty of the Alpilles and the fantastic spring flowers of the Vaucluse await. So that you won't miss anything, different tours routes are suggested out of Nîmes, Avignon, Saint-Rémy-de-Provence and Carpentras.

An expedition towards the east, between Dijon and Strasbourg, will enchant cyclists with plenty of time. The Côte d'Or in Burgundy (*Bourgogne*) is home to the prestigious Route des Grands Crus (great vintages route) and countless small roads where you're rarely bothered by car traffic. From Burgundy, you can return to Alsace via the Franche-Comté, by following the winding Doubs and then pedaling through the Jura and Vosges mountain ranges. In Alsace, the Route des Vins (wine route) and flower-bedecked villages will lead you to the European capital of Strasbourg.

Normandy in the north offers lush countryside where wood-frame manors nestle in the greenery; this is an area of dairy farms and apple trees. The coast is etched with roads and dotted with beaches of fine sand and fishing villages with granite houses.

At the western extremity is Brittany (*Bretagne*), original, authentic, mystic... An absolutely unforgettable bicycle trip from Rennes to Nantes, along a thousand kilometres of roads that run through Armor, the coastal area, and Argoat, the interior.

Also in the west, the Loire Valley landscape beckons dreamily along both sides of its grand river. The route runs among the wineries of Nantes and Anjou, and sometimes leaves the Loire to explore some of its tributaries. On the shores of the Indre or the Cher, in Touraine, you can admire magnificent Renaissance châteaux. The route returns to the Loire and ends in Blois, a beautiful city with centuries of colourful history.

The route through the heart of Périgord and Quercy is fascinating. It snakes along the valleys of the Dordogne, Vézère and Lot, abundant with ancient grottos. The itinerary, a large loop, starts and ends in Bergerac, adoptive home of the famous musketeer poet Cyrano.

All these beautiful areas of France await with a network of small roads that will take you from manor to château, from medieval city to historic site, from small fishing port to seaside resort. The only thing left to do is organize your trip through one or several of these regions, depending on how much time you have and on the choice of sites that most appeal to you.

THE DESCRIPTIONS

For each tour, a text precedes the description of the route itself. It includes history and tourist information that will help you figure out which region is best suited to your taste. The information familiarizes you with the towns along the way and allows you to better prepare for the trip. Each chapter also features a practical information chart with additional facts about the towns along the way plus useful telephone numbers. Read the route description carefully before departure, and you'll cycle with peace of mind.

The description of each region covers villages, natural sites (grottos, rivers, beaches), heritage, scenery and, when challenging, the change in altitude. Art and history lovers can learn more by toting regional cultural guides or by stopping at a tourist information office in towns along the way, where you can also obtain items such as a map of the town and listings of lodging possibilities. In most villages, the offices are open from 9am to noon and from 2pm to 7pm In some big towns, they are open all day as well as on Sundays.

In order not to lose your way, I recommend a careful reading of the text that describes the route as you go along. It includes precise markers that don't necessarily appear on maps or road signs. If you wish, you can also trace the route on the IGN map of the region with the help of the description (the map numbers are given in the practical information chart); this will allow you to thoroughly review each leg of the trip.

ACCOMMODATIONS

France has an extensive and wide selection of accommodations.

> Hotels of all categories: Classified with 1 to 4 stars depending on their comfort.
> Châteaux: Converted to luxury hotels.
> *Chambres d'hôtes*: French-style bed and breakfasts.
> *Gîtes d'étapes*: Country dormitory (in Brittany).
> Youth hostels: Membership card required.
> Campgrounds: Classified with 1 to 4 stars.

Directories of the different types of accommodations can be found in various guides available in specialized bookstores along the way or at the town's tourist information bureau.

A FEW TIPS

Distances

The total distance provided for each leg of the trip does not include ground you might cover in town, visits off the route and extra kilometres pedaled because you took the wrong road! It's important to keep this in mind if you're the type who is curious or easily distracted. You can easily add 10 km to the total for the day. The difficulty of a route can sometimes make you decide to shorten that leg of the trip, to rest more frequently or to walk your bicycle, nevertheless, these tours are generally accessible to all cyclists who are in good physical condition. To learn the level of difficulty, number of legs and the total distance of each route, consult the table on page 31.

Training

Good preparation is necessary before departure. Here are some tips to help you. You don't have to be a veteran cyclist to go on a cycling trip, but a minimum level of knowledge and technique is required. Read some specialized books; they're crammed with tips and good advice. As soon as you decide you're going to go bicycle touring, there's no time to lose. Start training immediately!

In winter, go cross-country skiing and skating, both of which improve the cardiovascular system and sense of balance. Try to do something physical every day, whether it's walking instead of taking the car of using a staircase instead of an elevator. Watch your diet and try to shed any excess weight.

When spring arrives, begin bicycle training. To start with, go on short rides, but do so frequently. Avoid stiffness and injuries (cramps and tendinitis). Try not to come back from rides too exhausted, so that you'll want to do it again within the next few days. If you live in a big city and can't easily get around by bicycle, do some other kind of exercise, whether at a gym, in a pool, or jogging outdoors, for example.

On weekends, go on longer bike trips. Try to vary the destination (through rolling countryside, through a mountainous region...). Establish a training routine and follow it right up until departure day. That way, by the time you're actually on the trip, your body will be accustomed to daily workouts. Finally, go on an outing with all your equipment (firmly attached). There's no better way for you to get a sense of the weight, the volume, the balance and the overall comfort.

Many people are happy owners of 21-speed bicycles, but don't know how to use them. To get to know your bicycle, practise on hilly terrain so that you can use the different gears. Good equipment, good clothing and good physical conditioning are the major requirements to enjoying travel by bicycle. Test them all before your vacation.

On the Trip

A long trip starts slowly. Don't expend all your energy the first few days by covering too much distance, setting your gears too high and not taking breaks. Beware the heat. Never pass a water fountain without drinking from it. It's best to get going early in the morning, when it's still cool, and to cover more than half the day's scheduled distance before noon. (When booking lodging, check what time they begin serving breakfast). Stop every 15 to 20 kilometres. Some people will want to stop more often than that. It's up to you. Just don't overestimate your capabilities.

In order to appreciate and contemplate the scenery, you have to be able to forget the effort you're making and be comfortable on your bicycle. Shift position on the handlebars frequently, and stand up from the seat from time to time. Whatever type of bicycle you're using on your trip (I recommend a touring or hybrid bike), it must be adjusted to your size to be comfortable and safe. The frame should be the right size for you. Invest in a good seat. The bicycle should have good-quality derailleur and a good range of gears (15, 18 or 21 speeds). Bicycle touring should never be one long voyage of suffering on an inadequate bicycle. Consult your bike shop and specialized books and magazines on this subject.

Food

Always carry lots of water; don't wait until you're completely out of water before looking for more. You should have two water bottles on your bike at all times. If you can't find sources of water along the route (which shouldn't happen very often), make a detour. Practically every village in France has a water fountain, often near the main square, for example. If not, ask someone. Water is an essential part of bicycle touring, especially when the weather's hot. Food and water replenish your energy.

Eat small amounts of food at a time, but frequently (cereal bars, dry fruit, bread, etc.) A varied diet produces energy; a day of cycling requires a huge number of calories. Take advantage of the fact that you're in France! You should be eating carbohydrates, lipids (oil, butter, cheese), proteins, vitamins and minerals every day. Avoid big meals just before heading out, and avoid drinking alcohol with your noon meal. Don't drink ice water when it's hot. And of course, don't litter.

Safety

In the event of an emergency, the number to call is **18**. Write it down somewhere where you can find it quickly; in a panic situation, you may not remember the number.

I'd like to pass on my observations about traffic in general, to help you prevent accidents, avoid possible conflicts and earn the respect of drivers. In France, cyclists use the roads as much as cars do, and drivers are used to cyclists. Naturally, along with everyone else using the road, cyclists must obey traffic rules.

Since there is no shoulder on most departmental roads, you must ride right in the traffic. Most falls occur when a cyclist, having left the pavement, tries to return to it, and runs into the edge of the road. A classic! If you leave the pavement, come to a full stop on the side. Then get back out onto the road carefully. For the sake of safety, take up as much as a third of the road when you're going downhill, always on the right hand side, of course.

Generally speaking, French drivers are fairly courteous towards cyclists. If a driver honks, it's usually to call attention to his presence and indicate to you that he is about to pass you. That's what truckers do. So don't be offended by it; it's simply a matter of safety.

On small country roads, you can pedal along side-by-side when the lane is clear. But get into single file as soon as a car approaches. Always signal your turns by pointing your arm in the direction you're turning to; use your right arm for turning right and your left arm for turning left. This signal should be highly visible and maintained until you're into the turn.

Going downhill, always maintain control of your speed. Be ready to stop at any instant by keeping your hands close to the brakes, your pedals parallel to the ground and by sitting as far back as possible on the seat. On the Routes Nationales, watch out for trucks, always travel in single file and be ready to react by getting onto the shoulder. On bridges, it's best to take the sidewalk and walk your bicycle across. At traffic circles, be doubly careful, for cars zip in and out very rapidly.

As you get near big cities, you will be forced to bicycle in heavy traffic. Be vigilant. You can ride bicycles in big cities, but stay alert. You should always pedal safely; respect traffic direction, signal your turns, and make sure you've been seen (watch out for doors of parked cars opening suddenly). Try to establish visual contact with pedestrians and drivers.

At intersections, the rule is **the right has right-of-way**, unless a traffic sign indicates otherwise. Once you've left the big boulevards and are on small pedestrian streets of old neigborhoods, be polite to people and do what they're doing – walk. Use bicycle paths in city centres if you can, and bicycle lanes on roads.

Before setting out each day, take the time to thoroughly inspect your bicycle (spokes, tires, brakes, cables, bolts) and make sure no elastic or bungee cord is stuck between the tire spokes or, worse, in the freewheel. Tie your shoe laces securely. One last tip: When checking maps for a place or a road, come to a complete stop.

THINGS TO KNOW

Road Signs

Directional highway and road signs come in specific colors. Thus, in city squares, along roads and at big interchanges, directional signs are on blue, green and white backgrounds. When there are several together, they generally are blue, green and white from top to bottom.

A blue sign refers to the highway system. It contains the highway number. These roads are generally toll roads and strictly off-limits to cyclists. Example: A20.

A green sign refers to the national system of roads. Most of these roads are two lanes. The speed limit is 50 kph in urban areas and 90 kph elsewhere. The signs contain the road number and the destination. Example: N113 ARLES.

A white sign refers to the regional system, consisting of departmental roads (*routes départementales*), town roads (*voies communales*) and by-ways (*chemins vicinaux*). These signs are often in the shape of an arrow. They contain the name of the village and the distance to it.

Examples:

> departmental road, D13 Générac 11 km;
> town road, C4 Mialet 6 km;
> by-way, V1 Castel-Merle 3 km.

Signs don't always contain road numbers. The number is marked on boundary markers along roads.

An orange sign indicates a detour (roadwork, accidents...).

A red-and-white triangular sign indicates traffic circles and intersections at which cars already there have priority. Except for urban areas, the principal of the right having the right-of-way always applies, unless a sign indicates otherwise. Generally, the priority is in order of arrival.

When to Go

Spring and autumn are the best seasons for a bicycle trip in France. The weather is pleasant, roads are less busy and hotels and campgrounds less crowded. In the south, you can bicycle comfortably starting in May right through to November. Remember, though, that the days are longer in spring than in autumn.

In summertime, the temperature can climb to 30° C or 35° C in some areas, like in Provence and in the Périgord. Try to avoid scheduling a trip in August, especially along the coast. August is official vacation time for most of France. If you must travel in August, then make hotel reservations well ahead of time and be prepared to share the road with scores of vacationers.

Group Tours

You'd like to go on a bicycle trip, but the thought of organizing it seems too much? Join a cycling club and participate in some group trips for a season. You'll learn to bicycle better, you'll learn new tricks and you'll swap vacation ideas with other cyclists. Contact the cycling association in your region; it can provide a list of clubs or other groups that offer bicycle outings near you.

Early in the season, cycling clubs usually organize an outing for newcomers in order to introduce them to group bicycling. The day is fairly technical. The goal is not to make you into a Tour de France competitor, but to learn and practise the basic rules. On a group outing, you must be aware at all times that another cyclist is following close behind you. Avoid sudden movements (bad braking, irregular pedaling rhythm, contact, etc.).

Cycling in single file (6 to 10 cyclists) lets each cyclist take a turn at resting. After a predetermined period, the lead cyclist drops off to the left, out of the line. The second cyclist goes ahead without changing cadence. The rotating cyclist is the one who slows down until he or she is at the back of the line. By taking advantage of the strength of each cyclist, this technique of shadowing another cyclist allows you to pedal into the wind without becoming over-tired. The cyclist at the head of the line must make clear signals when he or she is going to turn, slow down, stop or leave his position.

There are other techniques for group cycling, such as bunching up, or travelling in a fan formation, etc. But for cyclists with luggage travelling on busy roads, single file is the safest way to travel in a group.

Bicycle Tours

On your first bicycle trip, you may prefer to have it organized for you, or to go with a small group led by a guide. Here is a list of agencies offering bicycle tours in France.

In Canada

Les Voyages du Tour de l'Îles
1251 Rue Rachel Est
Montreal, Que.
H2J 2J9
☎ (514) 521-8356
Package tours of Provence and Burgundy.

Expéditions Monde
1705 Rue Saint-Denis
Montreal, Que.
H2X 3K4
☎ (514) 844-6364
or
78 George Street
Ottawa, Ont.
K1N 5W1
☎ (613) 241-2700 or
1-800-567-2216

Package tours of Provence, the Loire Valley, Burgundy, Champagne and Bordelais.

Voyage Découverte
365 Rue Émery
Montreal, Que.
H2X 1J2
☎ (514) 848-1974
Packages combine barge tours and cycling in Provence.

Club Aventure
1221 Rue Saint-Hubert
Montreal, Que.
H2L 3Y8
☎ (514) 990-9290
or 935 Chemin Sainte-Foy
Quebec, Que.
G1S 2L3
☎ (418) 687-9043 or
1-800-361-9043
Cycling tour of the Pyrenees. Also custom tours for private groups.

Trek Holidays
8412-109 Street
Edmonton, Alta.
☎ 1-800-661-7265
Package tours of Provence and the Loire Valley.

In the United States

Vermont Bicycle Touring
P.O. Box 711
Bristol, Vermont
05445
☎ 1-800-245-3868
Specializes in bicycle trips, one-week packages in Bordelais, Provence, Burgundy, Alsace and the Loire Valley. Also offers custom tours for private groups.

Backroads
1516 5th Street
Suite R207
Berkeley, Calif.
94710-9861
☎ 1-800-462-2848
Specializes in bicycle trips, hotel and camping packages in the Loire Valley, Dordogne and Provence.

In France

Terre d'aventure
5 Rue Saint-Victor
75005 Paris
☎ 01 40 46 87 65
Specializes in walking tours, also offers mountain-biking trips.

Loire Valley Travel
5 Rue de la Paix
41000 Blois
☎ 02 54 78 62 52
Tours in the Loire Valley and in Brittany.

ATM Voyages
15 Place C. Blaze
84302 Cavaillon Cedex
☎ 04 90 71 37 66
One-week package tours in the Luberon.

Arc Naturel des Vosges du Nord
Maison du Parc
67290 La Petite Pierre
☎ 03 88 70 46 55
One-week package tours in the Parc des Vosges du Nord.

CDT Aveyron-Service Loisirs Accueil
Carrefour de l'Agriculture
12026 Rodez Cedex 9
☎ 05 65 73 77 33
One-week package tours in the Lot Valley.

CDT Haute-Vienne-Service Loisirs Accueil
4 Place Denis Dussoubs
87000 Limoges
☎ 05 55 79 04 04
One week tours in Limousin.

Les Huttes de France
46 Boul. Pasteur, B.P. 360
63010 Clermont-Ferrand
☎ 04 73 34 18 48
One-week tours in Haute Auvergne.

EQUIPMENT

Hotel- or inn-based bicycle tours require less equipment than camping bicycle trips. Consult this list of clothing when it comes time to pack.

Clothing and Accessories

---

3 pairs of cotton or poly-cotton socks (they dry faster)
3 pairs of cotton or poly-cotton underwear
long underwear (depending on the season)
1 pair pyjamas
2 pairs lycra racing shorts with natural or synthetic chamois skin (pay attention to hygiene, for bacteria love chamois and cause irritation, pimples etc.)
3 or 4 t-shirts or singlets
a warm, fleecy long-sleeved shirt
a pair of sweat pants or long tights (depending on the season)

a pair of shoes with rigid soles for biking (if you travel with a single pair of shoes and ride in the rain, you're doomed to wear soaked shoes from morning 'til night)
a pair of walking shoes
clothing for the city (avoid clothes that crease and are heavy)
a bathing suit
a beach towel (thin, so it'll dry faster)
rainwear
a pair of cycling gloves
a bicycle helmet

Never carry a bag on you! And remember that everything on your bicycle will be with you as you ride into the wind and climb hills. Don't hesitate to reduce the amount of luggage you're taking (no more than 13 or 14 kg, or 18 to 20 kg for campers); if you discover later on you're missing something, you can always buy whatever it is. After all, you're not heading into the wilderness.

It's best to dress comfortably, in clothes that allow you to move and are brightly coloured and therefore highly visible; **on a bicycle, it's vital that you be visible!** Always carry a windbreaker or rainwear, because the weather can change abruptly. Always wear a helmet. Gloves are very comfortable over long distances and protect your hands in the event of a fall.

A few other indispensable items:

Toiletry bag
Sunglasses
Sun block
Hat or cap
First-aid kit
Bottle opener and corkscrew (or Swiss-Army knife)
Picnic utensils
Camera
Flashlight
Pen, travel journal and address book
Small bag for your walks in towns
Road maps (Michelin or IGN)
All necessary camping equipment (for campers!)
Guidebook for hotels, B & Bs, etc.

Bicycle Accessories

Obviously, you have to tune up your bike before departure. Take the opportunity to "standardize" it; make sure for example, that one screwdriver fits all the screws. In France, everything is metric, including wheels and tires. Are you?

Your repair kit should contain items to repair flats, tire levers, a screwdriver, a hexagonal wrench, a monkey wrench, an open-end wrench (for the pedals), a vice-grip, a spoke tightener, a chain tool, brass wire and adhesive tape (for electric wires).

As well, you should travel with:

2 inner tubes
a tire (optional if your wheels are metric)
a pump
a gear cable
a brake cable
a light lubricant.

A day's worth of mechanical training will give you confidence and self-sufficiency. Check with your association or cycling club to find out about their courses. There are also many books on bicycle mechanics. Don't let mechanical problems spoil your vacation. Relax, for in the event of a major breakdown, you'll always be able to find someone competent to repair your bicycle. This is the land of the Tour de France, after all!

Finally, you should bring along (if two of you are travelling together, make sure you're not doubling up):

bungee cords
rope
a combination-lock anti-theft device (with a cable is more practical than a U-shaped one, and in the countryside there are more trees than parking meters)
2 water bottles (with 2 water-carriers)
a handlebar bag (with shoulder strap to carry it on walking tours)
a good-quality baggage rack
2 rear panniers (that can be easily carried by hand)

2 front panniers (for campers or for those who are embarking on a long trip, otherwise two rear panniers and one handlebar bag are sufficient)
a rear-view mirror
fenders
big plastic bags to put inside your panniers (when it's pouring rain, no pannier is truly 100% waterproof, so don't risk it).

TRANSPORTING YOUR BICYCLE

By Plane

The first thing to do is check with the airline to find out about its policy on transporting bicycles. Some carriers sell cardboard boxes or plastic bags that you can obtain at the airport just before departure. So get there early! These boxes are big; all you have to do is take off the bicycle pedals, turn the handlebars and deflate the tires. We strongly recommend putting your name and address on the bicycle and on the box.

The other option is to ask your bike shop to give you a box. It will be smaller, so you'll have to take your bike apart. That means removing the handlebars, seat, front wheel and pedals. It's important to firmly attach all these bicycle parts. Be sure to cover the two holes in the box that serve as handles, because they can tear during transit and you could lose some parts. Use rope to transport the box.

Your bicycle isn't protected from shocks in either case. With a minimum of tools, you can prepare padded packing material to reduce the chances of getting a nasty surprise once at your final destination. Don't wait until the last minute; it can take more time than you'd think! Ask for advice at your bike shop, or ask them to pack it for you. Your bicycle is important!

Once at your final destination, what to do with the box? If you have friends with whom you can leave it, that's great! If you're starting and ending your tour in the same city, you can always politely ask your hotelier or innkeeper to keep it for you. You can also get rid of the box and hope you can find one at a bike shop at the end of your trip. You still have the option of buying one at the airport; check with the various airlines. As a last resort, your bicycle can travel unpackaged.

Aéroport Roissy Charles-de-Gaulle
Information:
☎ 03 28 62 22 80

Aéroport d'Orly
Information:
☎ 01 49 75 15 15

By Train

The TGV (*train à grande vitesse*) is the fastest way to get to different areas of France. However, the TGV doesn't serve all regions and, in some places, you must take the regular train. Depending on your destination, you leave from one of four train stations in Paris. Taxis at the airport (Orly or Roissy) occasionally refuse to take passengers who have bicycles. You can use the Air France shuttle or take the RER (commuter train). For the brave-hearted, there is a bicycle path from Orly airport into Paris. You then have to thread your way through traffic in the narrow streets of downtown Paris. Roissy now has a TGV station that lets you avoid Paris. Note that there is no counter to register luggage (or bicycles) at the train station at Roissy Charles-de-Gaulle airport. So you can't travel with your bicycle out of that station.

You'll have to take a train at least twice during your visit, at the start and at the end. It's very easy to take a train with your bicycle; you just have to know the basic rules. When you register your bicycle at the unaccompanied-baggage counter, you must have with you your ticket or your rail pass. Note that on the main railway lines, bicycles are supposed to be shipped several days ahead.

The Société nationale des chemins de fer français (S.N.C.F.) guarantees delivery at the destination within 72 hours and, in peak season, in less than five days. In my experience, if you show up 24 hours prior to your departure and check with the baggage clerk to find out which train your bicycle will be on, the chances are good that your bike will be waiting for you on your arrival the next day. For your flight back home, don't take any chances. Allow for the minimum time guaranteed by the S.N.C.F., or else rent a car.

In the big train stations in Paris, the luggage counter is often located in a remote area that's hard to get to (the stairs!). Remember that you will have to cover some distance with your luggage and your bicycle box. If there are two of you, it's easier. If your bicycle can be wheeled, it's easier still. Don't leave anything attached to the bike that can fall off, like the water bottle, odometer, pump and bags. You can also protect your bicycle from scratches by putting it in a box that the

S.N.C.F. sells. Fill out the registration tag clearly (name, address, etc.) and guard your receipt carefully. It costs 150 FF to transport a bicycle.

On some trains, you're allowed to take your bicycle on board at no charge. Check the schedule with the S.N.C.F. All you have to do is be on the platform when the train comes into the station, and get to the baggage car quickly (but it's hard to predict whether it'll be near the front or the back of the train!). You must be ready to get off with your bicycle as soon as the train stops in the station. One last piece of advice: When picking up your bike from the luggage counter, make sure it's in good condition before leaving the station. You can't make a claim later on.

Rail Europe
General information:
In Canada
☎ 1-800-361-7245
⇌ (905) 602-4198
In the United States
☎ 1-800-848-7245
⇌ (303) 444-4587
www.raileurope.com

S.N.C.F. Paris
General information:
☎ 01 45 82 50 50

RENTING BICYCLES

Paris-Vélo
2 Rue du Fer à Moulin
Paris 75005
☎ 01 43 37 59 22
⇌ 01 47 07 67 45

Paris By Cycle
99 Rue de la Jonquière
Paris 75017
☎ 01 42 63 36 63

Bicy Club de France
8 Place de la Porte Champerret
Paris 75017
☎ 01 47 66 55 92

Fédération française de
cyclotourisme
8 Rue Jean-Marie Jégo
75013 Paris
☎ 01 44 16 88 88
⇌ 01 44 16 88 99

The S.N.C.F. rents bicycles in some trains stations in France. According to the Fédération français de cyclotourisme, this service isn't always available. It's therefore impossible to provide a reliable list of stations where you can rent bicycles.

TOURIST INFORMATION

In Australia
Maison de la France
BNP Building 12th Floor
12 Castlereagh Street
Sydney, Australia
NSW 2000
☎ (2) 231-5244
≈ (2) 221-8682

In Belgium
Maison de la France
21 Avenue de la Toison d'Or
Brussels, Belgium
1060
☎ (2) 513-0762
≈ (2) 514-3375

In Canada
Maison de la France
1981 McGill College Ave.
Suite 490
Montreal, Que. H3A 2W9
☎ (514) 288-4264
≈ (514) 845-4868

Maison de la France
30 St. Patrick Street, Suite 700
Toronto, Ont. M5T 3A3
☎ (416) 593-4723
≈ (416) 979-7587

In Germany
Maison de la France
Westendstrasse 47
Postfach 2927
Frankfurt Main 1, Germany
D 60325
☎ (69) 75.60.83.30

In Great Britain
Maison de la France
178 Piccadilly
London, Great Britain
W1V OAL
☎ (71) 493-5576
≈ (71) 493-6594

In the Netherlands
Maison de la France
Prinsengracht 670
Amsterdam, Netherlands
1017 KX
☎ (20) 627-3318
≈ (20) 620-3339

In Switzerland
Maison de la France
Löwerstrasse 59
Postfach 7226
Zurich, Switzerland
8023
☎ (1) 221-3578
≈ (1) 212-1644

In the United States
Maison de la France
676 N. Michigan Ave.,
Suite 3360
Chicago, IL 60611-2836
☎ (312) 271-7838
≈ (312) 337-6339

Maison de la France
9454 Wilshire Blvd, Suite 715
Beverly Hills, CA 90212-2967
☎ (310) 271-7838
≈ (310) 276-2835

Maison de la France
444 Madison Ave.
New York, NY 10020-2452
☎ (212) 838-7800
⇤ (212) 838-7855

Paris
Maison de la France
8 Avenue de l'Opéra
75001 Paris
☎ 01 42 96 10 23
⇤ 01 42 86 08 94

Opening Hours

Stores

Generally speaking, shops close between noon and 2pm in towns and villages. If you want to have a picnic, schedule a stop in a village before noon to buy food. In the evenings, shops close around 7pm. In big cities, supermarkets remain open over the lunch hour. Bakeries and delicatessens are open on Sunday mornings. Many bike shops are closed on Mondays.

Restaurants

If you want to eat in a restaurant, bear in mind that most open at noon and serve until 2pm. Then they re-open from 7pm to 9pm. They offer both fixed-price *menu du jour* meals and *à-la-carte* meals. Outside opening hours, you can grab a sandwich in cafés or in bars. (I often bicycle during those two hours, because there's a lot less traffic on the roads.)

Banks

Banks are open on weekdays from 9am to noon and from 2pm to 4pm or 6pm, except on Mondays. They're closed on Sundays. You can use credit cards in automatic teller machines in banks, post offices and trains stations. Make sure your credit card has a code (p.i.n.) that enables you to use it at automatic teller machines. You can also withdraw cash from your bank account by using Plus or Cirrus bank cards. Travellers' cheques can be cashed at banks or post offices (charges apply). Stores rarely accept them.

Mail

Post offices open at 8am or 9am and close at 6pm or 7pm on weekdays. On Saturdays, they're open from 8am to noon. Stamps are also sold in tobacconists, marked with a red diamond sign.

Telephones

Public telephones are operated by *télécartes* (telephone cards) sold in post offices and tobacconists. Some telephones in small villages and in restaurants and cafés still take coins.

Museums and Government Offices

There's no general rule as to museums' opening hours, except that they all close on Tuesdays. Check opening hours with each museum or at the tourist information bureau. Government offices are open Monday to Friday, from 8am to noon and from 2pm to 6pm.

TOUR CLASSIFICATIONS

Degrees of Difficulty

The tours are classified into three levels of difficulty specific to this guidebook: easy, somewhat difficult, difficult. They are represented with this icon: 🚲.

🚲 (easy): The route runs over flat terrain. There may be a few gentle rises.

🚲 🚲 (somewhat difficult): The route runs over slightly rolling terrain with a few steep inclines.

🚲 🚲 🚲 (difficult): The route is over hilly terrain with numerous climbs (or strong winds).

	Number of legs (or days)	Difficulty	Distance	Page
Provence				
Camargue	4	🚲	190 km	36
Gard	6	🚲 🚲	275 km	45
Gard (Garrigues)	2	🚲 🚲	80 km	54
Gard to Vaucluse	1	🚲 🚲	70 km	56
Gard to Alpilles	1	🚲 🚲	50 km	58
Alpilles	3	🚲 🚲	155 km	60
Vaucluse	3	🚲 🚲	170 or 185 km	67
Burgundy				
Dijon-Vallée de l'Ouche	1	🚲 🚲	55 km	79
Dijon-Beaune	1	🚲 🚲	65 km	82
Beaune-La Rochepot	1	🚲 🚲	40 km	84
Beaune-Bouilland	1	🚲 🚲	50 km	88
Franche-Comté				
Saône Plain	1	🚲	75 km	94
Jura	2	🚲 🚲	100 km	97
Doubs	2	🚲 🚲	130 km	100
Haute-Saône	1	🚲 🚲 🚲	60 km	104
Alsace	4	🚲 🚲 🚲	195 km	110
Normandy				
Calvados	4	🚲 🚲	240 km	124
Manche	5	🚲 🚲	230 km	135
Brittany				
Haute-Bretagne	6	🚲 🚲 🚲	355 km	153
Pontivy to Quimper	3	🚲 🚲 🚲	120 km	168
Côte-Sud	9	🚲 🚲	525 km	173
The Loire Valley	9	🚲 🚲	490 km	195
Périgord-Quercy	10	🚲 🚲	540 km	221

PROVENCE

The art of Provençal living and the region's incredible heritage are just two of the treasures you'll discover in Provence. In this chapter, the area is defined by the **Cévennes**, the shores of the **Ardèche**, **Mont Ventoux**, the **Vaucluse** plateau, the **Camargue** and the Mediterranean. During your visit, you'll explore the many facets of the Gard region, the marshy expanses of the Camargue and the *garrigues* and small woods around Nîmes and the Cévennes. One route runs through the Bouches-du-Rhône area, where the Alpilles range stands. A short exloration at the base of the mountains will turn up all sorts of marvels; the region is a fantastic outdoor playground for cyclists. Finally, you can ride deep into the interior to tour the rich Vaucluse area, planted with vineyards and fruit trees.

THE CAMARGUE

To begin your bicycle tour of Provence, I suggest a trip through an area where the sun sparkles on saltwater marshes and bogs, beats down on the sea and the sand, suffuses orchards and vineyards with colour and turns the stones of Roman temples and medieval ramparts gold. It is also a region of festivals where bulls, horses and their *gardians* (herdsmen) are heros. *Occitans* at heart and language, handsome, independent, proud of their land, the people of Camargue have always had their own distinct personality.

Camargue Vocabulary

Gardian: Cowboy-like herdsman who watches over the Camargue's herds of bulls and horses.

Mas: Farm or country house.

Manade: A herd and everything related to raising bulls.

Féria: Spanish festival including corridas, bull races, street parties and impromptu gatherings.

Bodegas: Improvised bars (basements, garages, houses) where you drink pastis, sangria, white wine from Spain or tequila, to the strains of Spanish music.

Abrivado: A bull-related event, a bull-run through the streets.

Encierro: A Spanish tradition, a bull-run through the streets.

To stay in the Midi is to take the time to savour life. **Nîmes** is a café where pastis flows, a game of *pétanque* beneath the plane trees, Roman sites, the Jardins de la Fontaine, an *abrivado* on the boulevards, corridas in the bullrings. Sounds too clichéd? Wait and see. You'll succumb to its Latin charms too.

Another Roman town, **Arles** boasts terraced bullrings that have accommodated 80 generations of *Arlésiens*. They also gathered at Alycamps, an ancient cemetery once located in the middle of a marsh that had a spiritual reputation and became part of Vincent Van Gogh's art. Another universe familiar to the artist and the people of Arles is the Boulevard des Lices, lined with outdoor cafés beneath plane trees. On Saturdays, market day, this is the place to buy fruit, vegetables, spices, flowers, local products and bric-à-brac in a convivial, colourful ambience that will recharge your batteries.

The tour begins in Nîmes and leads into **Petite Camargue**. En route, you will traverse farm towns and vineyards that produce the Costière de Nîmes vintage. These villages are festive in summertime. Perhaps you'll see an *abrivado* or an *encierro*! The streets are barricaded, the bulls are let off a truck and herded by *gardiens* on horseback through the village to the arena. Youths, at once enthusiastic and fearful, try to take the bulls by the tail... In short, get off your bike if you hear a commotion coming your way... where there is one bull there are many others!

The ancient fortified town of **Aigues-Mortes** lies in the heart of the Petite Camargue. The town was founded to protect King Louis IX's fleet of ships. King Louis embarked on the Seventh Crusade from here in 1248. The town's magnificent ramparts (1,650 metres long) are remarkably well-preserved. Inside the walls, the old city was built as a fortified town, its streets meeting at right angles. Nowadays, Aigues-Mortes is a farming town whose economy is based on growing asparagus and *"pays de sables"* wine, fishing and traditional cattle rearing, reed harvests and salt production.

If you want beaches and water sports, continue on to **Grau-du-Roi** and **Port-Camargue**, a traditional fishing village, modern seaside resort and the largest pleasure-craft port on the Mediterranean. There you can visit the Listel wine cellar, where the famous *"pays de sables"* wine is produced. Between the vines, the sun shines on the Midi salt works, the region's oldest commerce. Take off your sunglasses to see the true colours of the countryside around you; it shifts from pink to mauve or violet, depending on the time of day and the time of year. You'll also notice little pink areas that are colonies of flamingos!

The route next goes through the Basse Camargue, a mosaic of marshes and salty expanses. Half water, half earth, this is an area where the famous Camargue bulls and horses roam free. To plump the secrets of its untamed beauty, get off your bicycle and explore on foot with binoculars. These prairies are a refuge for pink flamingos, herons and ducks. The plants that grow here, like the saltwort, the *saladelle* (a small mauve flower), rushes and reeds, are impervious to salt.

Imagine the magnificent Camarguais scenery in a storm. You're on your bike, a strong wind pushing against you, nature's colours darkening, birds wheeling above a *manade* of bulls, the *gardians* galloping for their *mas*...

The sea and its fine-sand beaches lie at the end of the route, in Saintes-Maries-de-la-Mer. Marie-Jacobé, the legendary sister of the Virgin Mary, and Marie-Salomé, alleged mother of the apostles John and James, landed on the beach where the church now stands after being chased out of Judea. The church building was fortified at the end of the Middle Ages, making for a striking exterior. Today, this seaside resort is invaded in late May by *gitans* (gypsies) on an annual pilgrimage. It's very colourful with dancing, music, costumes and parades. Together, the gypsies, the *gardians* and the fishermen create a bewitching atmosphere that blends piety and freedom.

The Camargue agricultural zone is in the Arles region near the Grand Rhône. Peaches, apricots, almonds and vegetables are grown around vast plains planted with wheat and rice. In a tableau of typical Provençal farms, magnificent farmhouses melt into the landscape beneath shady parasol pines. The Camargue offers cyclists of all abilities a fascinating natural spectacle. Cyclists who love the ocean, festivals and flat roads will love this tour.

---

1. Grand Tour of the Camargue

Total distance:	190 km
Number of legs:	4
Level of difficulty:	🚲
Diagram:	p 37
Map:	A2, A3

Leg from Nîmes to Grau-du-Roi: 45 km

The **Nîmes** train station is on Avenue Feuchères in the south of the city. The avenue leads to the bullring. From there, you can get to the centre of the old part of town along small alleyways. It is said of Nîmes that it evokes both tradition and modernity. Montrealers, who know all about covered stadiums, may be interested to know that in Nîmes, too, the arenas are covered. In wintertime they're covered with a detachable bubble, which turns the amphitheatre (built in the 1st century) into a remarkable performance area and a symbol of the marriage of archaeology and modern life. In the heart of the city's historic centre, this union is further symbolized by the Masion Carrée, a Roman monument, and the Carré d'Art, a high-tech monument.

Spanish revelers, take note: For five days in early June, all regular activity in Nîmes comes to a halt for a *féria* with bullfighters, corridas, *bodegas*, flamenco... ¡ole!

Go to the train station to leave Nîmes. Your back to the station, head left and ride towards Saint-Gilles, Caissargues and the airport. Ride

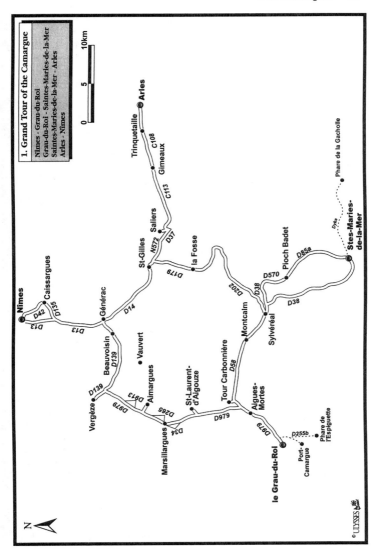

1. Grand Tour of the Camargue

Nîmes - Grau-du-Roi
Grau-du-Roi - Saintes-Maries-de-la-Mer
Saintes-Maries-de-la-Mer - Arles
Arles - Nîmes

under a viaduct and leave the city via Rue du Planas. Make sure you leave Nîmes on the D42. Continue to the traffic circle and take the D135. Stay on it until the second traffic circle and then take the D13 toward Générac. The route goes through a region of vineyards and orchards.

PRACTICAL INFORMATION ON NÎMES

Population
140,000 *Nîmois*

? **Tourist office:** 6 Rue Auguste, 30,000 Nîmes, ☎ 04 66 67 29 11, ⇒ 04 66 21 81 04

Bicycle Shops: Tendil Cycles, 6 Boul. Am. Coubet, ☎ 04 66 67 28 27 Cycles Rebour, 42 Av. Jean-Jaurès, ☎ 04 66 62 20 39

Market
Tuesdays

Major events: Féria de la Pentecôte; Féria des Vendanges (grape harvest; September)

Specialties: *Brandade de morue* (salt cod with garlic, oil and cream), olive *tapenade*, Nîmes paté, Costières de Nîmes wine, Clairette de Bellegarde wine

Access from Paris: Autoroute du Soleil, the Languedocienne, the N86; TGV, Gare de Lyon to Nîmes

Map
IGN no. 66

From **Générac**, take the D139 for Beauvoisin and Vauvert. In **Beauvoisin**, follow the signs for Vergèze, Vestric and Candiac, still on the D139. Did you know that the Perrier source is near here? Technology makes this ultramodern complex *(open from 9am; 30310 Vergèze, ☎ 04 66 87 62 97)* unique in the world. Audiovisual presentations and tastings are held at pre-set hours. In order not to waste time, check the schedule before leaving Nîmes.

Then take the D979 toward Aimargues. Cross the Route Nationale, follow the D913 and then take the D265 towards Grau-du-Roi and the Château de Taillan. Continue to Vidourle and ride into **Marsillargues**.

PRACTICAL INFORMATION ON AIGUES-MORTES

Population
5,570 *Aiguemortains*

 Tourist office: Porte de la Gardette-BP 32, 30220 Aigues-Mortes, ☎ 04 66 43 73 00, ⚏ 04 66 53 65 94

Market
Wednesdays and Sundays

Major events: Fêtes de la Saint-Louis (August 26-27)

Specialties: Fish, *tellines* (shellfish), Listel *"pays des sables"* wine

Map
IGN no. 66

Get back on the D34 for Aigues-Mortes (*aigues* for "water"), cross the Vidourle once again and take the D979 to **Aigues-Mortes**. You are now in Petite Camargue. Follow the bicycle lane right to the ramparts.

Visiting the old town is easier without your bicycle because the streets are narrow and crowded in peak season. Find some place out in the open to padlock your bike, near the gate in the wall or the parking lot, for instance. Old villagers often settle at the Gardette gate to watch the comings-and-goings.

Go back to the D979 and continue on the bike lane to **Grau-du-Roi**. This seaside resort is split by an ocean channel, the Grande Roubine. The traditional fishing port is on one side (with more than 100 fishing boats), while the beach, boutiques and hotels are on the other side.

To get to **Port-Camargue**, return to the D62b at the entrance to the village. This unusual pleasure port was created in 1969. It's the biggest in Europe, with 4,350 berths. You can take an excursion to the **Phare de l'Espiguette**, a lighthouse further south, where huge beaches edged with dunes invite visitors to linger and relax. This excursion adds an extra 20 kilometres

Leg from Grau-Du-Roi to Saintes-Maries-de-la-Mer: 40 km

Return to **Aigues-Mortes** along the same road, the D979, again cycling between the **Salines du Midi** and the Grande Roubine (the canal) and passing the Listel winery en route. The winery, in operation ever since the Middle Ages, is open to visitors; you can go into the cellars and taste the wine. This road offers a magnificent view over Aigues-Mortes' ancient fortifications. Great photo opportunity!

At the intersection, continue straight through towards Arles and Saintes-Maries-de-la-Mer, then take the D48 towards the **Tour Carbonnière**. It dates from the 14th century and served as a relay stop for Aigues-Mortes on the road that came from the north. You'll likely spot bulls roaming free along this road, as far as Saint-Laurent-d'Aigouze.

PRACTICAL INFORMATION ON SAINTES-MARIES-DE-LA-MER

Population
3,050 *Saintois*

 Tourist office: 5 Avenue Van-Gogh-BP 34, 13460 Saintes-Maries-de-la-Mer, ☎ 04 90 97 82 55, ⊷ 04 90 97 71 15

 Bicycle shops
Camargue Vélo, 27 Rue Frédéric-Mistral, ☎ 04 90 97 94 55
Le Vélociste, 1 Place des Remparts, ☎ 04 90 97 83 26
Le Vélo Saintois, 8 Route de Cacharel, ☎ 04 90 97 74 56

 Market
Tuesdays

 Major events: Gypsy pilgrimage (May 24-25); Fête des Gardians (October)

 Specialties: Bouillabaisse, *tellines* (shellfish), beef *à la gardianne*, Bouches-du-Rhône wine.

Maps
IGN no. 66

To get to Saintes-Maries-de-la-Mer, you have to get back to the D58, then go past the Listel winery and on to **Montcalm**. Stay on the D58 as far as the Sylveréal bridge and the D38. There are signs for the ferry to Saintes-Maries. It's an option, but note that there is a ferry only every half-hour. Continue along the D38 to **Saintes-Maries-de-la-Mer**, with its nature park, small fishing port, resort, museums, restaurants, boutiques and 30 kilometres of fine sand. If you're on a mountain bike, a short side trip to the **Phare de la Gacholle** is possible via the dike.

Leg from Saintes-Maries-de-la-Mer to Arles: 60 km

Leave Saintes-Maries-de-la-Mer on the D85a via **Cacharel**. Follow the road to the D570. Ride for a few kilometres, then take the D38 for Aigues-Mortes. Cross the Petit Rhône and, right after the bridge, take the D202 through rice paddies along the Petit Rhône, bordered with reeds. You'll see birds (herons, egrets, ducks, wading birds) and bulls. Follow this road to the **Fosse** and the D179.

Head north on the D179 to Saint-Gilles. At the intersection, turn right and leave Saint-Gilles on the N572, heading for Arles (you can visit Saint-Gilles on the way back). Cross the Petit Rhône. Be careful on the wooden bridge. Get back on the D37 for Saliers. Don't go into Saliers. Take the next road on the left, for **Gimaux**, via the C113 (the Arles road). Follow it through fields of grain, *saladelle* (small purple flowers) and reeds. At the traffic circle, head toward **Trinquetaille** and cross the other bridge to Arles, thereby avoiding the Route Nationale. Continue along Rue de la République to the tourist office.

Leg from Arles to Nîmes: 45 km

Arles, whose rich history is reflected in its architecture, wears its Latin identity proudly. To truly experience it, all you have to do is wander its streets, terraces, gardens, museums, Roman sites...

Leave the city the same way you came into it, via the Trinquetaille bridge over the Rhône. At the traffic circle, take the Arles road again, towards Gimaux on the C108. Follow this road to **Saliers**. Proceed on the D37 and cross the Petit Rhône via the same wooden bridge. Enter **Saint-Gilles** on the N572.

PRACTICAL INFORMATION ON ARLES

Population
52,500 *Arlésiens*

? **Tourist office:** 35 Place de la République, 13 200 Arles, ☎ 04 90 18 41 20, ☏ 04 90 93 17 17

Bicycle shops
Peugeot, 15 Rue du Pont, ☎ 04 90 96 03 77
Dall'Oppio, Rue Portagnel, ☎ 04 90 96 46 83
Hélios Aventure, Place Lamartine, ☎ 04 90 49 50 09

Market
Wednesdays and Saturdays

Major events: Fêtes des Gardians (May 1); the Pégoulado, a big nighttime folklore parade (early July); Fête des Prémices du Riz (early rice harvest; mid-September)

Specialties: Little sausages, rice, Bouches du Rhône wine

Access from Paris: A7, A9, A54; TGV, Gare Lyon to Avignon, connection for Arles; return to Paris from June to September: TGV Arles-Paris

Map
IGN no. 66

A pilgrimage site on the road between Saint-Jacques de Compostelle and St. Peters in Rome, Saint-Gilles was founded in the 7th century. The ancient Benedictine monastery is famous for its Romanesque façade, the largest in the south of France. It's also a "triumphant" façade, for its design was based on that of the Roman arch. It's a definite must-see! In the same neighbourhood, you can also visit the Maison Romane, the house where Pope Clement IV was born and which is now a museum. Saint-Gilles is also the departure point for cruises in Camargue; check them out.

Go towards the tourist office and take the street to its left to leave Saint-Gilles for Générac on the D14. This pretty road runs through a landscape of gently rolling hills, covered in orchards, vineyards and magnificent parasol pines. From **Générac**, head for Nîmes on the D13 until you hit the D135. Follow the D135 towards Caissargues and Nîmes. Then take the D13 into Nîmes.

PRACTICAL INFORMATION ON SAINT-GILLES

Population
12,000 *Saint-Gillois*

? **Tourist office:** 1 Place Frédéric-Mistral, 30800 Saint-Gilles, ☎ 04 66 87 33 75, ✆ 04 66 87 16 28

Market
Thursdays and Sundays

Major events: Bullfights (May to November); Fête de Saint-Gilles, pilgrimage to the Baume (September 1)

Specialties: Beef *à la gardianne*, waterfowl, local wine

Map
IGN no. 66

THE GARD

This tour through unspoiled nature is one of my favourites. People who appreciate wild beauty will delight in the varied landscape of hills covered in evergreen oak trees, vineyards and orchards, plateaus and scrubland, rivers and canyons. The route begins in **Nîmes** and runs along Gard roads through the Anduze and Alès regions at the foot of the **Cévennes** mountain range, to Uzès, Remoulins, and the Gardon in the heart of the fragrant garrigue. You can't avoid the unavoidable in this area – the **Pont du Gard**. A majestic Roman aqueduct, the only one of its type, the Pont du Gard has spanned the Gardon for 20 centuries. It carried water from the Fontaine de l'Eure, near Uzès, to Nîmes. It is an immense monument, a magnificent site that makes for an unforgettable visit.

The gorges of the Gardon offer up a fascinating spectacle: a dry, barren landscape filled with the sound of cicadas. At noon hour, it's stupefying! In summer, the arid air makes the heat bearable... as long as you have enough water with you. Many of the roads are narrow and winding, crossing sun-bathed garrigues – hills and plateaus of bleached rocks covered in thistles, kermes oak and herbs that mingle with cultivated plants like olive trees, vines and lavender.

Leaving **Anduze**, the "Gateway to the Cévennes" you'll be amazed by the Asian appearance of unusual Prafrance park. Created in 1850, this forest of giant bamboo trees is unique in Europe. Nearby, **Alès** nestles in a bend of the Gardon. The centre of Protestantism in the 16th century, Alès developed thanks to the silkworm industry. Pasteur spent four years there in search of a remedy that would arrest the mysterious epidemic of 1847. Today, the traditional Cévennes silk work is being revived.

The charming town of **Uzès** stands on a plateau overlooking the Alzon valley. The Uzès trail leads to a lovely picnic area with a view of the town and its tiled roofs. And you might try your hand at *boules* (a game which resembles lawn-bowling). Men from the village congregate at the end of the chestnut-tree-lined avenue to play all afternoon. Uzès is best known for having been the first duchy in France, and for its Saturday market, which scents the streets with the aroma of Provençal herbs. A great place to stock up on provisions!

After leaving Uzès, the route heads for **Bagnols-sur-Cèze**, the only major city on this itinerary. Most of the populace works at the Marcoule atomic energy plant. Thirteenth-century houses and a fine museum of modern art are found in the city's old quarter.

The Gard roads next take you through unspoiled scenery along the shores of the Rivière Cèze. Far from major tourist centres, the roads here are as peaceful as they are spectacular. Aside from a few farm towns and medieval villages perched on the hills, you're pedaling through wilderness-like scenery. The route follows roads that let you visit such natural sites as gorges, grottos and natural springs. But the magnificent panoramas in the region between the Ardèche and Cèze rivers don't come without pain. Many of those spectacular viewpoints lie uphill!

The old villages of **La Roque-sur-Cèze, Cornillon** and **Castillon** are perched in the hills. To get to them, you have to leave your bike behind; the narrow streets, paved with large cobblestones, rise too steeply for a bicycle to navigate. **Aven d'Orgnac** is an enchanting stop, especially if you missed the **Grotte de Trabuc**, equally amazing but harder to get to by bicycle. A guided visit takes you into an entrancing underground world. This grotto, with it natural vertical opening, giant stalagmites and red-hued chambers, is renowned as one of the most interesting grottos in France.

If you're ready to climb a few hills and pedal a little further, you'll delight in a short detour to the **Concluses** nature site. In summer, when the rocky bed of the Rivière Aiguillon is dry, it's possible to walk on it. On the La Roque-sur-Cèze side, take the Cascade du Sautadet trail to see the Cèze up close and wade in it. In the village of Goudargues, springs and fountains, the fragrance of a flower-bedecked canal and shady plane trees all make for a lovely atmosphere. You'll be tempted to linger and recharge your batteries awhile before resuming the tour.

2. Grand Tour of the Gard

Total distance: 275 km
Number of legs: 6
Level of difficulty: 🚲 🚲
Diagram: p 49
Map: A3, A4

This tour has relatively short legs to allow for time to visit the numerous natural sites (grottos, waterfalls, gardens) along the way. So as not to miss anything and to get the most out of your expedition, plan your days carefully. A few telephone calls can save you a few kilometres of pedaling.

Leg from Nîmes to Alès: 55 km

To get out of Nîmes (see p 38 for practical information on Nîmes), head for the Jardins de la Fontaine at the end of Avenue Jean-Jaurès. Follow the signs for Alès. Make sure you leave Nîmes on the D926. Follow the D926 to the N106 junction. Ride a few kilometres along the N106 and then turn left onto the D907 for Lédignan. Be careful leaving Nîmes, because traffic is heavy and pretty unpleasant.

Continue along the D907, through vineyards and the scrubland. Pass the village of **Fons**. Stay on the D907 until **Lédignan**, where you go through the Lens woods. The **Cévennes** mountains are visible in the background, omnipresent. The ride is steep as far as Montagnac; take a break under the cool shade of parasol pines.

Proceed on the D907 to Anduze and Alès. Enter **Anduze**, a small town
built in the shape of an amphitheatre on the shores of the Gardon,
along two limestone walls. Lock your bicycle and head out on foot to
see three historic monuments that evoke the area's past – the Tour de
l'Horloge, or clock tower (left over from an ancient rampart), the
Fontaine Pagode, or pagoda fountain (dating from the era of silk-worm
cultivation) and the Protestant Temple (one of the largest in France).
Anduze is famous for its glazed pottery, a technique passed down
from the 18th century.

Leave Anduze by crossing the Gardon and take the D129 towards the
Bambouseraie de Prafrance (*every day from 9:30am, except in winter;
Générargues, 3010 Anduze,* ☎ *04 66 61 70 47*). This jungle, created
in 1850, contains not just bamboo trees but 100-year-old sequoia
trees, rare greenhouse plants, a water garden, boutiques selling
bamboo items, etc. Take a little trip to the Orient in the Cévennes!

Continue towards **Générargues**; the road number changes, becoming
the D50.

I recommend a side-trip, well worth the detour, to see the famous
Grotte de Trabuc (*Conservateur des Grottes de Trabuc, 30140 Mialet-
Anduze,* ☎ *04 66 85 03 28*), the largest grotto in the Cévennes. It's
also known as "the grotto of 100,000 soldiers" because of its
formations, unique in the world. En route, history buffs will want to
stop at the Musée du Désert, which recounts the history of the
Huguenots and the war of Camisards. After Générargues, veer to the
left and follow the D50 to Mialet and the Grotte de Trabuc (6 km). The
road climbs the mountain and offers a lovely view of the area. A
guided tour of the grotto takes a good hour. Remember to bring warm
clothes!

After visiting the grotto, there are two options for getting back to the
road to Alès. You can retrace your route by going back down to
Générargues (easier) and the D50, or you can go up to the top of the
mountain on the **Puech** road. I recommend the latter only for
experienced cyclists on mountain bikes who aren't carrying a lot of
gear. The road surface isn't very good and to get to the summit you
have to ride four kilometres over an extremely narrow road. It's not
easy being a cyclist... but you'll be overwhelmed with a sense of
freedom at the top of the rugged garrigue; it's as if you've discovered
a lost world. Palpitations are guaranteed during the five-kilometre
descent into the valley. Be careful!

PRACTICAL INFORMATION ON ANDUZE

Population
3,000 *Andusiens*

 Tourist office: Place de Brie-BP 6, 30140 Anduze, ☎ 04 66 61 98 17

 Market
Thursdays

 Map
IGN no. 66

If you decide on the climb, follow the Puech road from the grotto. At the intersection, turn right; don't turn left towards the village, because it's a dead end. Descend to **Le Ranc** and continue along the D50 to **Saint-Jean-du-Pin**.

Continue on the D50 for Alès. Follow the signs for downtown, where you cross the Gardon. The tourist office is along the dock on Place Gabriel-Péri.

Leg from Alès to Uzès: 35 km

Alès is famous for the mineralogical and paleontological museum at the École des Mines. The Mine Témoin, an underground museum with 650 metres of galleries, recounts the history of miners from Zola on. The Musée du Colombier is home to paintings ranging from the 16th century to the present, including two Bruegel de Velours canvasses.

To get out of Alès, start with your back to the tourist office and take Avenue Carnot to the right, towards Uzès and the N106. Leave Alès on the D981, the Uzès road. Stay on the D981 for about 20 kilometres, until you reach **Baron** and the D114 (watch carefully along the right-hand side of the road so you do not miss the turnoff). Leave the D981 to get into Baron. Stay on the D114 until it intersects with the D120 at **Collorgues**. Follow the D120 for Uzès, **Aubussargues** and **Arpaillargues**, and then take the D982. On your right, you pass the Musée 1900, part of a farming operation. It showcases old working farm machines, cars, motorcycles, bicycles, photo and movies cameras and other items bound to please "retro" enthusiasts. Cross the Seynes and climb to Uzès.

PRACTICAL INFORMATION ON ALÈS-EN-CÉVENNES

Population
45,500 *Alésiens*

Tourist office: Place Gabriel-Péri, 30100 Alès-en-Cévennes, ☎ 04 66 52 32 15, ⌨ 04 66 52 57 09

Bicycle shops
Peugeot Cycle, 18 Rue E. D'Orves, ☎ 04 66 30 4241
Run Cycles, 19 Rue Guynemer, ☎ 04 66 86 60 84

Market
Sundays and Mondays

Major events: Féria des Mangetripes (Ascension Day); Fête Nationale (July 14); bull games (July and August).

Specialties: Tripes *à l'alésienne*, game, cepe mushrooms, *pélardon* (goat's cheese), Gard region wines

Map
IGN no. 66

Leg from Uzès to Bagnols-sur-Cèze: 35 km

Uzès is a charming Provençal village. The approach is along a pleasant avenue lined with plane trees that leads to a ring road around the town. Devote some time to this part of the trip. The heyday of Uzès, a ducal and Episcopal town, was in the 17th century. Take a look at the duchess in the château overlooking town. The Tour Fenestrelle, fashioned in the Italian bell-tower style, is part of the remains of a 12th-century Romanesque cathedral. The tower is 42 metres high and is unique in France.

To leave Uzès, go to the side of the cathedral and the Tour Fenestrelle. Just after the parking lot, take the D982 for Bagnols-sur-Cèze. Then take the D5 towards Vallabrix (on the left). Stay on the D5 as far as **Vallabrix**. Continue on the D5. At the crossroads, get off the D5 and turn left on the D166 for **Pougnadoresse** and Cavillargues. The scenic road rises and falls through woodlands.

Stay on the D166 until **Cavillargues**. At the intersection, take the D9 to the right, for Bagnols, and then immediately the D166 for **Mégier**.

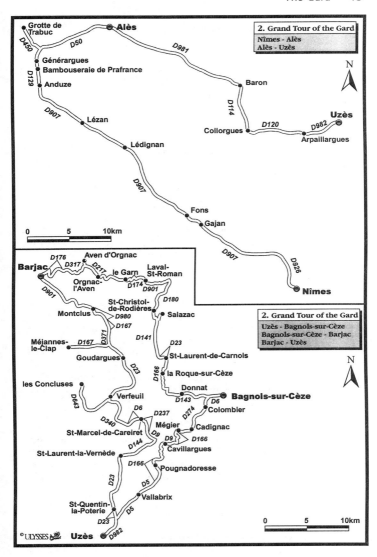

©ULYSSES

PRACTICAL INFORMATION ON UZÈS

Population
8,800 *Uzétiens*

 Tourist office: Avenue de la Libération, 30700 Uzès, ☎ 04 66 22 68 88, ⚬ 04 66 22 95 19

Market
Saturdays

Major events: Festival Les Nuits Musicales d'Uzès et de Uzege (music festival, late July)

Map
IGN no. 66

Take the D274 for **Cadignac**, **Colombier** and Bagnols-sur-Cèze. A lovely downhill ride takes you to the D6. Turn right onto the D6 for **Bagnols-sur-Cèze**. Go into town and follow the boulevards that lead to the tourist office.

Leg from Bagnols-sur-Cèze to Barjac: 50 km

Get out of the heavy traffic on Bagnols' boulevards and ride instead along the old streets and Place Mallet, site of the Musée Albert-André, where there are Renoirs, Matisses, Bonnards, Van Dongens and more.

Be aware that the route between Roque-sur-Cèze and Orgnac is along virtually deserted roads that have long climbs and descents. There are very few villages en route. So be sure to carry plenty of water and provisions!

Leave Bagnols-sur-Cèze on the D6 for Alès. Leave the D6 and turn right for Donnat, La Roque-sur-Cèze and the D143. Then take the D166 to **La Roque-sur-Cèze**, a medieval city perched on a mountain peak. To visit the village, cycle to the parking lot and lock your bike. If you're wearing cycling shoes, change into regular shoes because the streets are steep and cobblestoned. Must-sees include a pretty Romanesque chapel, a château and an art gallery.

After your walk, get back on the bike and return to the D166. Cross the bridge and take the little trail that leads to the **Cascade du**

PRACTICAL INFORMATION ON BAGNOLS-SUR-CÈZE

Population
18,180 *Bagnolais*

? **Tourist office:** Espace Saint-Gilles, Av. Léon-Blum, 30200 Bagnols-sur-Cèze, ☎ 04 66 89 54 61, ⌨ 04 66 89 83 38

Bicycle shops
La Roue Libre, 10 Av. Léon-Blum, ☎ 04 66 89 91 79
Pro Cycle, 305 Av. De la Mayre, ☎ 04 66 89 83 23

Market
Wednesdays

Major events: Fête de la Saint-Jean; Bagnols Blues (early July); Fête Votive (2nd week of September).

Specialty: Côtes-du-Rhône wines

Map
IGN no. 66

Sautadet. It's quite an astonishing site! You can walk along the limestone rocks known as the "Marmites de géants" (potholes). Despite the signs that say swimming is prohibited, locals seem to have no qualms about frolicking in the Cèze whirlpools. Do so at your own risk; if you get caught, you could face a hefty fine. This spot is a perfect place to stop for a picnic.

Get back on the D166 and continue towards Barjac. At the D980 junction, turn left and then immediately right to **Saint-Laurent-de-Carnols** via the D166. Leave Saint-Laurent-de-Carnols on the D23 for Barjac. Keep going until the D141 and follow the signs on the right for **Salazac.** Continue until the D180, fork left and ride towards **Saint-Christol-de-Rodières** and **Laval-Saint-Roman**.

Stay on the D180 as far as the D901. Turn left onto the D901 and follow it to Laval-Saint-Roman. Take the D174 towards **Le Garn** and Aven d'Orgnac. Then take the D217 for the village of **Orgnac-l'Aven,** which you'll encounter near **Aven d'Orgnac.** Dress warmly before going into this immense cavern *(everyday 9:30am, except in winter; 07150 Vallon Pont D'arc,* ☎ *04 75 38 62 51)*. The guided visit lasts about an hour and the temperature in the grotto is 13° C. Dry, warm clothing is a must if you've been perspiring on a bicycle. In 1995, the 60th anniversary of Robert de Joly's discovery of the swallowhole was celebrated. A giant pit, enchanting forms and colours, enormous chambers and many types of stalagmites and stalactites flash beneath floodlights. You see about one-tenth of the grotto on the well-organized tours. The commentary is spiced with lots of humour.

Afterwards, continue on the D317 and the D176. The road drops into a magnificent evergreen oak forest and thence to Barjac.

Leg from Barjac to Uzès: 50 km

Barjac, a charming village that lies in the heart of garrigue and lavender country, offers a nice architectural mix with its 17th-century château and its Renaissance church. Leave Barjac on the D901 towards Bagnols-sur-Cèze and Laval-Saint-Roman. Ride through vineyards and lavender fields as far as the D980 junction. In August, you can visit the lavender distillery on the Monteils road. From the D980, there's a pretty view of the old village of **Montclus**, built on a rock that overlooks the river.

PRACTICAL INFORMATION ON BARJAC

Population
1,385 *Barjacois*

Tourist office: Place du 8 Mai-BP 23, 30430 Barjac, ☎ 04 66 24 53 44, ≈ 04 66 60 23 08

Bicycle shop
Garage Brugier, Rue des Glycines, ☎ 04 66 24 54 70

Market
Fridays

Major event: Antiques fair (Easter and August 15)

Specialties: Lavender, wine

Map
IGN no. 59

Keep going along the D980, along the gorges of the Rivière Cèze, to the bridge and the D167 (canoe-kayak rentals available). Cross the bridge and keep going towards Méjannes-le-Clap. At the first intersection, fork to the left to **Goudargues** and the D371. Take the time to tour this attractive village, nicknamed "the Venice of Gard". An old abbey church (9th to 11th century) dominates the village. You might also want to pick up provisions in the few cafés, restaurants and shops that line the canal.

Leave Goudargues on the D23 for **La Bastide** and **Verfeuil**. At the D143 intersection, turn right towards Verfeuil.

The **Concluses** are worth a detour for those who are interested in natural curiosities. Count on at least a two-hour visit – plus a few hills! From Verfeuil, take the D143 and then the D643, from which a magnificent avenue of towering box trees leads to the parking lot. Find a spot to lock your bike and take the marked trail towards the "Portail". Wear good walking shoes and carry lots of water. Remember that this walk along the bottom of the gorges is on a dry river bed. Retrace your steps on the return trip.

After the visit, take the D340 towards Saint-Marcel-de-Careiret. At the D6 intersection, turn left. Ride along the D6 as far as **Saint-Marcel-de-Careiret** and then go through the village.

Stay on the D237, then turn left onto the D9 towards Cavillargues. At the fork, take the D144 to the right, as far as **Saint-Laurent-la-Vernède**. Follow the D23 towards **Saint-Quentin-la-Poterie**. As its name suggests, this village is renowned for its ceramics and pottery, along with its art galleries, fairs and exhibits. Continue along the D23 and the D5 to the D982, which leads into **Uzès**.

Leg from Uzès to Nîmes: 50 km

Leave Uzès by taking its ring road as far as Avenue Foch, towards Nîmes and Avignon. Make sure you exit Uzès on the D981, heading for the Pont du Gard. Stay on the D981 as far as the D3b for **Argilliers** (to the left), then continue straight ahead, following the signs for **Vers**.

Get out of Vers on the D192 and carry on to **Castillon-du-Gard** (despite its elevated location, don't miss this medieval jewel) and **Saint-Hilaire**. Ride a few metres along the N86 and then veer left towards Avignon. Enter **Remoulins** on the D792. At the intersection, continue straight ahead, through the village, across the Gardon and along the avenue of plane trees that leads to the Pont du Gard, that symbol of Roman genius (1.5 million visitors a year!).

Continue to the site on the D981. If there's enough water in the Gardon, you can go for a dip! In 1989, a year when the river was exceptionally dry, spectators sat in the river bed to watch a sound and light show. After thoroughly exploring the Roman masterpiece, leave the Pont du Gard by pedaling along the south shore of the river and back onto the D981 for Uzès and Collias. Ride for about three kilometres on the D981 and then turn left onto the D112 and the D3 for Collias.

In **Collias**, you can go canoeing, either by going down to the Pont du Gard or higher up near the Pont Saint-Nicolas. Both bridges span the Gardon's magnificent gorges. Or you can simply stroll the riverbanks, listening to the cicadas' carefree chirping.

Continue on the D3 to **Cabrières**, where there's a fabulous panorama. Stay on the D3 and cross over the highway. In **Saint-Gervasy**, take the D3a to the right, and then the N86 as far as **Marguerites** and Nîmes. Be careful! Traffic is very fast for 10 kilometres.

---

3. The Heart of the Garrigues

Total distance: 80 km
Number of legs: 2
Level of difficulty: 🚲 🚲
Diagram: p 55
Map: A3

If you haven't got enough time for the "Grand Tour of the Gard", consider this easier, shorter loop out of Nîmes. It winds through a landscape of garrigues where oaks mix with thyme, vineyards and orchards. It runs along a narrow road, at times overhanging canyons, alongside the gorges of the Rivière Gardon. You'll explore old *Gardois* villages and the charming town of Uzès.

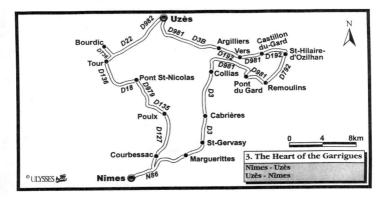

3. The Heart of the Garrigues
Nîmes - Uzès
Uzès - Nîmes

Leg from Nîmes to Uzès: 30 km

To get out of Nîmes, head for the train station and follow the signs for Avignon and the N86. Ride cautiously on the N86 for a few kilometres, then head for **Courbessac** on the D127. The road climbs steadily en route to **Poulx** and affords a lovely view of the surroundings.

From Poulx, take the D135 towards Uzès and the **Pont Saint-Nicolas** as far as the D979 intersection. Turn right onto the D979 towards Uzès. Cross the bridge (slowly, for this 18th-century structure is worth admiring) and turn left at the D18 towards Aubarne. At the fork, take the D136 towards Bourdic and ride as far as the D22 junction on the right. Take the D22, cross the Seynes, turn right and go into Uzès on the D982. Continue straight ahead and follow the signs for downtown and the tourist office on Avenue de la Libération.

After your visit, take the ring road to Avenue Foch, towards Nîmes. Make sure you leave Uzès on the D981 towards the Pont du Gard.

Leg from Uzès to Nîmes: 50 km

To return to Nîmes, follow the directions for the Uzès to Nîmes leg in the "Grand Tour of the Gard" section, on p 53.

4. From the Gard to the Vaucluse

Total distance: 70 km
Number of legs: 1
Level of difficulty: 🚲 🚲
Diagram: p 69
Map: A5

Leg from Nîmes to Avignon: 70 km

This route leads to Avignon in the Vaucluse. Along the way, you can explore an abbey carved out of the rock in Saint-Romain, medieval châteaux in Beaucaire and Tarascon and the Saint-Michel-de-Frigolet abbey in Barbentane.

To get out of Nîmes, take Rue de Beaucaire from Place Gabriel-Péri and pass beneath the viaduct. Make sure you leave Nîmes on the D999. Keep going to Rodilhan. Leave the D999 to enter **Rodilhan**. Take the D546 to **Manduel**. Go through the village and exit it on the D403, heading towards the Château Campuget, and then take the D163 for Jonquières-Saint-Vincent. Keep an eye out for some of the road signs in these villages; they warn you to watch out for crossing bulls... Imagine!

PRACTICAL INFORMATION ON BEAUCAIRE

Population
13,200 *Beaucairois*

Tourist office: 24 Cours Gambetta-BP 106, 30302 Beaucaire Cédex, ☎ 04 66 59 26 57, ✉ 04 66 59 51 64

Market
Thursdays and Sundays

Major events: Ascension fair; Les Estivales (summer festival, late July)

Map
IGN no. 66

In **Jonquières-Saint-Vincent**, continue towards Beaucaire on the D999 (careful, traffic is fast). The **Abbaye Troglodytique de Saint-Romain** is about four kilometres before Beaucaire. This 5th-century abbey, carved out of the rock, is among the oldest monasteries in France. To reach it, get off the D999 and take the road to the left, sign-posted for the abbey. The road climbs over one kilometre to the driveway that leads to the parking lot. Lock your bike and take the paved path leading to the abbey (roughly a 15-minute walk). After your visit, you can walk to the top of Mont Aiguille. Follow the markers.

Get back onto the D999 to enter **Beaucaire**. Follow the signs for the château and Tarascon. As a river crossing on the Rhône, the former border between Provence and Occitanie, Beaucaire was well-known for its big international fair, an event that kept it prosperous for many centuries. Nearly all the houses in its preserved neighbourhood are classified as historic monuments. Numerous hotels date from the 17th and 18th centuries. The 11th-century Château Royal stands across from its Tarascon rival. If you're in Beaucaire in July, you'll see acrobats, musicians, horses and bulls, all taking part in the "Estivales" festival.

PRACTICAL INFORMATION ON TARASCON

Population
11,500 *Tarasconnais*

Tourist office: 59 Rue des Halles, 13150 Tarascon, ☎ 04 90 91 03 52, ↔ 04 90 91 22 96

Bicycle shops
Cycles Christophe, 70 Boul. Itam, ☎ 04 90 91 25 85
Cycles MBK, 1 Rue E. Pelletan, ☎ 04 90 91 42 32

Market
Tuesdays

Major events: Fêtes de la Tarasque (late June); Festival d'Expression Provençale (early July); Journées du Patrimoine (heritage days; 2nd week of September)

Specialties: The *tarasque* (a big chocolate cake), the *tartarinade* (small cherries dipped in chocolate)

Map
IGN no. 66

Cross the Rhône to enter **Tarascon**. King René's château is on the left. This medieval castle is one of the most beautiful in France. The tourist office on Rue des Halles is hidden behind the Sainte-Marthe church (12th and 13th century).

Leave town on Boulevard Victor-Hugo. Ride under the viaduct. At the intersection, take the D80 towards Maillane. Cross the Route Nationale and continue across the Petite Crau to **Maillane**. This small, typical Provençal village is home to a museum dedicated to the poet Frédéric Mistral, winner of the Nobel prize for literature in 1904. The "Museon" is in his former home.

From Maillane, take the D5 to **Graveson**, at the foot of the Montagnette. Next, you must return towards Tarascon for a few kilometres on the N570 in order to take the D81, which climbs the Montagnette to the Abbaye de Saint-Michel-de-Frigolet. The monastery, founded in the 10th century by the monks of Montmajour, was the setting for Alphonse Daudet's tale of *L'Élixir du Révérend Père Gaucher*. It's only a story, but the liqueur actually exists. It's a yellow chartreuse whose base consists of plants gathered from the surrounding hills.

Then take the D35E, which drops through a magnificent pine forest to **Barbentane**. Before leaving the village, you may want to visit the castle that's nicknamed *"Le petit Trianon du Soleil"*. Continue on the D35 and then the N570 towards Avignon. Cross the Pont de la Durance (carefully). Entering **Avignon**, proceed cautiously to the ring roads and the gates of the city.

---

5. From the Gard to the Alpilles

Total distance: 50 km
Number of legs: 1
Level of difficulty: 🚲 🚲
Diagram: p 69
Map: A5

Leg from Nîmes to Saint-Rémy-de-Provence: 50 km

You can get to Saint-Rémy-de-Provence and join up with the Alpilles tour by following the previous itinerary as far as Maillane. From there, take the D5 to Saint-Rémy-de-Provence.

THE ALPILLES

This route takes you through the Provence of Alphonse Daudet, Frédéric Mistral and Vincent Van Gogh. The limestone mountains of the **Alpilles** (or Little Alps) form its backbone. The tour winds through pine forests, olive groves, copses of evergreen oaks and fields of wheat, where you'll discover the luminous sunlight that flooded Van Gogh's life and art.

The tour starts in **Arles**, in the flat terrain of the Petite Crau's rice paddies and wheat fields. Van Gogh turned out about 200 paintings during the 15 months he lived in the area. A good number of them are indisputable masterpieces, and all exude light, colour and energy.

Montmajour and the ruins of its 10th-century abbey lie just a few kilometres from Arles. A little further on, the windmill that inspired Alphonse Daudet stands in the **Fontvieille** hills. These hills were covered in windmills in Maître Cornille's day, Maître Cornille being a character in Daudet's stories. "He worked with the mistral and the tramontana," which he described as "the breath of God." Cyclists, on the other hand, tend to agree with Van Gogh, who as he painted said of the winds "they are of an annoying contrariness."

I recommend a pilgrimage to the **Maillane** coast in this fertile countyside in the heart of the Petite Crau. Maillane is a small, typical Provençal village with a museum dedicated to the poet Frédéric Mistral, an ardent defender of the Provençal language.

The climb to **Baux-de-Provence** is one of the trip's high points. Built in a eyrie, Baux (derived from "baou", or rock) is a blend of ruins and white stone, a mineral world carved by erosion. The village-fortress stands on a magnificent site in a strange environment. It is mostly uphill, at times steeper than others, and whether you ride your bicycle or push it, the only way is up.

Saint-Rémy-de-Provence lies at the foot of the unusual Baux limestone massif. Its landscapes seem mournful in Van Gogh's works, painted during his stay at the Saint-Paul asylum. While there were Roman ruins around, he was never interested in them. Still, it's well worth your while to linger in the inspiring and elaborate ancient town of **Glanum**.

From Saint-Rémy-de-Provence, a circular tour runs eastwards along the base of the Alpilles to Cavaillon. With its olive groves, orchards, vineyards and pastures for sheep and goats, this region is reminiscent of Greece. Next, head back to Saint-Rémy, typically Provençal with its avenues lined with plane trees and its outdoor cafés, and treat yourself to a refreshing pastis. This apéritif, highly prized by the *Méridionaux*, relaxes the tongue as well as the muscles!

---

6. The Alpilles Tour

Total distance: 155 km
Number of legs: 3
Level of difficulty: 🚲 🚲
Diagram: p 60
Map: A5

Leg from Arles to Saint-Rémy-de-Provence: 40 km

To get out of Arles (see p 42 for practical information on Arles), go the Porte de la Cavalerie (gate) in the north of the city. Continue until you reach a traffic circle. Take the exit for Baux-de-Provence. Pass under the viaduct. Pedal for two kilometres towards **Avignon** on the N570. At the next traffic circle, take the D17 towards Fontvieille and immediately cross the bridge. Stay on the D17 as far as the **Abbaye de Montmajour.** You can visit the remains of the abbey, founded in the 10th century up on a hill in the middle of a marshy expanse. There's a terrific panorama from the top of the abbey tower.

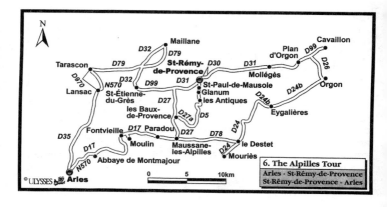

Keep going along the D17 to the D82 junction, from whence you can get to the **aqueducts** (1st and 2nd centuries) and the **Meunerie Romaine** (Roman flour mill) at **Barbegal**. From the D82, turn left onto the D33 for the **Moulin d'Alphonse Daudet**, a small museum dedicated to the writer who so lovingly evoked the Midi. His story, *La Chèvre de Monsieur Séguin*, was set in the region around this windmill.

Then proceed to the village of Fontvieille. Take the D17 towards **Paradou** and **Maussane**. Don't go into the centre of Maussane; just before the village, take the D27, which climbs to **Les Baux-de-Provence**. The road rises gently out of the olive groves; in any event, it's the easiest of all of them.

To visit Baux, head for the parking lot. Padlock your bike near the guard's post. Follow the route marked on the city map. It leads along trails and laneways to the fortified château, remnant of the proud line of the Baux seigneurs.

PRACTICAL INFORMATION ON LES BAUX-DE-PROVENCE

Population
450 *Baussencs*

Tourist office: Impasse du Château, 13520 Les Baux-de-Provence, ☎ 04 90 54 34 39, ⊷ 04 90 54 51 15

Major events: Green olives festival at Mourières (September)

Specialties: Olives, goat cheese, Baux-de-Provence wines

Map
IGN no. 66

Before leaving Les Baux, don't miss the Cathédrale d'Images located in an old quarry. To get there, get back on your bike and continue along the D27 towards Maillane. The cathedral is on your right, about 500 metres outside Les Baux. After your visit, go back towards the village and follow the signs for Saint-Rémy. Leave Les Baux-de-Provence on the D27a. Keep going to the D5 intersection. Turn left and take the D5, which leads to Saint-Rémy-de-Provence via the ancient site of Glanum.

The **Glanum dig**, site of both an ancient Greek city (Glanon) and an ancient Roman city (Glanum), lies about 1.5 kilometres before Saint-Rémy. Leave your bike at the entrance to the site. After your visit (about an hour), bicycle to the **Antiques** archaeological site, where there's a triumphal arch and a Roman mausoleum. Nearby, to the right, is the former Romanesque monastery of **Saint-Paul-de-Mausole**, which later became a health facility where Van Gogh spent a year.

Take the D5 straight to the tourist office. Van Gogh fans should ask about *"Promendade sur les lieux peints par Van Gogh"*, a guided tour of the places he painted. It's an interesting walk that takes you right into the painter's world. You'll view the scenery with new eyes.

Saint-Rémy is a good place to treat yourself to a rest after all your efforts. Stretch out in the shade of a pine tree, or hurry to an outdoor café beneath the leaves of a plane tree.

PRACTICAL INFORMATION
ON SAINT-RÉMY-DE-PROVENCE

Population
8,900 *Saint-Rémois*

Tourist office: Place Jean-Jaurès, 13210 Saint-Rémy-de-Provence, ☎ 04 90 92 05 22, ⇆ 04 90 92 38 52

Bicycle shops
Bruno Ferri, Av. De la Libération, ☎ 04 90 92 10 88

Market
Wednesdays

Major events: Fête de la Transhumance (Pentecost Monday); Fête de la Saint-Jean (June 21); Féria (3rd week of August); Fête Votive (last week of September)

Specialties: Herbs, olives, olive oil, candied fruit

Map
IGN no. 66

Alpilles Loop: 70 km

To get out of Saint-Rémy, start from the Place de la République and take Avenue Fauconnet towards Tarascon. On the left, you'll see the D31 leading to Saint-Étienne-du-Grès. Follow it as far as the D27 junction. Turn left on the D27 for **Les Baux-de-Provence**.

This route to Les Baux-de-Provence is the most spectacular of all. The climb is tough; take the time to breathe, and drink lots of water. On arrival, you'll be justly rewarded with a magnificent view of the village and its arid, ruin-like setting. Keep going on the D27. Pass the Cathédrale d'Images (on the left) and, at the intersection, go towards Arles. Stay on the D27 towards Maussane. The region around Les Baux is covered with olive groves.

Exit Maussane on the D17 for Mouriès. Immediately take the D5 on the left, towards Destet and Eygalières. Be careful not to confuse the towns of Eygalières and Eguières.

Take the D78 to **Destet**. The road rises and offers a pretty view of small Mont Opies. Turn left onto the D24 for Eygalières. From the hill, you'll be able to see the crest of the Caume. On the right, take the D24b to get into **Eygalières**.

This charming village of stone houses sits on a hill. If you feel like it, get off your bike and climb up into the old keep, from whence there is a splendid view. Continue along the D24b towards Orgon. The Romanesque Saint-Sixte chapel stands to the right of the road.

Enter **Orgon**. There's a terrific panoramic view of the Durance valley from the Notre-Dame-de-Bearegard chapel park (follow the signs, pass the cemetery and climb the hill). Leave Orgon on the D26 towards Cavaillon.

Note that from Cavaillon, you can join the Vaucluse tour. Take the D24 for Fontaine-de-Vaucluse and then the D31 to Isle-sur-la-Sorgue (about 12 km). Follow the Vaucluse tour from Velleron (see p 67).

Enter **Cavaillon** on the D99. Be doubly careful! Go over the highway and across the bridge over the Durance. Keep going along the Avenue du Pont and follow the signs for the tourist office on Place François-Tourelle.

Cavaillon, a river town at the foot of the Saint-Jacques hill, is located right in the middle of market-gardening territory (France's largest trade). Don't leave the area without sampling its famous melon!

PRACTICAL INFORMATION ON CAVAILLON

Population
23,470 *Cavaillonnais*

? **Tourist office:** Place François-Tourel BP 176, 84305 Cavaillon, ☎ 04 90 71 32 01, ↝ 04 90 71 42 99

Bicycle shops
Cycles Rieu, 25 Av. Du Maréchel Joffre, ☎ 04 90 71 45 55
Cavaillon 2 Roues, 166 Cours Gambetta, ☎ 04 90 78 07 06

Market
Mondays

Major events: Festival International de Folklore (July and August); Semaines Estivales du Luberon (summer weeks of Luberon)

Specialties: Melon, *melonette* (chocolate-melon ganache), melon-based jams, liqueurs and candies, Luberon wines

Map
IGN no. 66

From the old quarter, follow the *"Sentier de Découverte de Cavaillon"* (Cavaillon discovery trail) to see one of Europe's most beautiful 18th-century synagogues as well as a 12th-century cathedral. A path from Place François-Tourel leads to the Saint-Jacques chapel, built in the 12th century. From the hill, there's a vast panorama of Cavaillon and the surroundings. This pleasant walk will take about 45 minutes.

To get out of Cavaillon, return to the bridge and take the D99. Ride carefully! Go over the highway and carry on to **Plan d'Orgon**. Follow the D99 to the D31 junction. Turn right towards **Mollégès** and Saint-Rémy. Continue along the D30 to enter **Saint-Rémy-de-Provence**.

Leg from Saint-Rémy-de-Provence to Arles: 45 km

To get out of Saint-Rémy, start at Place de la République and take Avenue Fauconnet towards Tarascon. On the left, you'll see the D31 leading to Saint-Étienne-du-Grès. Follow it as far as the D99 intersection. Take the D99 towards Saint-Étienne-du-Grès. Continue on the D32 for Maillane until you get to the D79.

You can make a small detour for an intellectual pilgrimage to Maillane, the birthplace of Frédéric Mistral, the famous Provençal poet who won the 1904 Nobel prize for literature. Visit the "Museon," a museum in the writer's home, and stop by his mausoleum in the cemetery. It's a copy of the Pavillon de la Reine Jeanne des Baux-de-Provence.

After your visit, return to the D79 and peddle to Tarascon (see p 57 for practical information on Tarascon). The tourist office is on Rue des Halles, behind the Sainte-Marthe church (12th and 13th centuries), right near the château. The impressive medieval castle, which locals call the "château du Roi René", or King René's castle, is one of the most exquisite in France.

To get out of Tarascon, take Boulevard Victor-Hugo and go under the viaduct. Continue on Boulevard Jules-Ferry and exit Tarascon on the D970, heading for Arles. Stay on the D970 until the intersection. Take the N570 and immediately turn right onto the D35 for **Lansac**. Stay on it until you get to Arles.

THE VAUCLUSE

The Comtat Venaissin, located between the Rhône, the Durance and **Mont Ventoux**, has seen a succession of Greeks, Romans, counts and popes. This tour in the heart of "Jardin de France" (garden of France) leads to villages perched high in the hills and ancient towns that have witnessed the passge of time.

One of them, **Avignon**, home to the famous bridge, overlooks the Rhône. Selected by popes, the town reached a pinnacle of prosperity in the 14th century. Courtisans, the bourgeoisie, merchants, artists, poets and painters came from far and wide. The **Palais des Papes**, a reminder of the days when popes ruled the city, is at once fortress and palace, a magnificent example of military Gothic architecture. Before getting back on your bike and leaving the walled part of the city, stroll through the **Jardin du Rocher des Doms**. This enchanting garden offers a splendid view of the surrounding landscape.

France's most luxuriant garden, the Comtat Venaissin (derived from "Vénasque", the first capital of the county), spreads out from

Avignon. Irrigated by the waters of the Durance and a network of channels called *roubines*, the land produces succulent fruits and vegetables. Small roads snake through orchards and gardens (apricots, peaches, cherries, strawberries, melons, tomatoes, etc.) to the attractive town of **Carpentras**, which has been a commercial centre for what seems like forever. The Greeks, the Romans, the popes and the Jewish community all left historic and artistic treasures there.

The rest of the area is the Provence of hillside villages, with their fountains, public washhouses and colourful, fragrant outdoor markets. And never miss a chance to climb to the top of the roads that zigzag across the hills; you'll be well-rewarded!

Leaving Carpentras, you have a choice between two routes to **Vaison-la-Romaine**. The first is easy, via the Route des Vins and **Beaumes-de-Venise**. This village, known for its delicious muscat, sits in the foothills of a mountain range sculpted by erosion, attractively named the **"Dentelles de Montmirail"** (literally, "Montmirail lace"). Magnificent views of these lacy stone formations are to be found along the route, which leads to **Vacqueyras**, **Gigondas**, **Cairanne** and **Rasteau**, all of which produce renowned wine.

You can't miss **Mont Ventoux**, whose 1,909-metre peak towers over the Comtat. The second route takes you to the foot of this *"Géant de Provence"* (Giant of Provence), a nickname that evokes an image of Tour de France participants, clinging to their bikes, grimacing as they tackle one of the most difficult segments of the race. If you, too, want to conquer the mountain, you have to do so via Bédoin!

This much tougher route begins in Carpentras, goes through the villages of **Crillon-le-Brave**, **Bédoin** and **Barroux**, climbs the Dentelles de Montmirail range, through the **Col Saint-Amand** and then drops dizzily to **Malaucène** and Vaison-la-Romaine. It's a splendid route made especially for climbers.

Finally, the route takes on a gastronomic flavour by running though the Côte-du-Rhône vineyard region, which you reach via **Orange**. Riding along these roads, you'll pass the most illustrious winery of all, **Châteauneuf-du-Pape**. The ground is covered with thousands of pebbles that contribute to the quality and originality of this great wine by retaining daytime heat and throwing it back up at the vines come nighttime. It makes for very sweet grapes. *"In this place blessed by the gods, the popes plant vineyards..."* Treat yourself to a wonderful tasting! The wine route next takes you along the left bank of the river at the foot of the garrigues. The landscape is dominated by the **Tavel** and **Lirac** vineyards, which have produced excellent rosés since the time of Philippe Le Bel. Be sure to stop at the village cooperative.

It was on this side of the Rhône, in **Villeneuve-lès-Avignon**, that the cardinals built their new quarters. The view over Avignon is spectacular. In fact Villeneuve offers several fabulous viewpoints, including from the Philippe le Bel tower and the terrace of the Fort Saint-André. It is said that King Philippe wanted to keep an eye on the neighbouring papal city!

7. Grand Tour of the Vaucluse

Total distance:	170 km or 185 km
Number of legs:	3
Level of difficulty:	🚲 🚲
Diagram:	p 69
Maps:	A4, A5

Leg from Avignon to Carpentras: 50 km

In summer, **Avignon**'s dramatic-arts festival attracts hoards of visitors. The lively and merry streets are reminiscent of the popular festivals of the Middle Ages. Make hotel reservations well ahead if you plan to stay in the walled portion of the city during the festival.

To get out of Avignon, take the ring road that runs around the ramparts. Be careful, because there's always lots of traffic on it. Follow the signs for Morières and Isle-sur-la-Sorgue. Make sure you leave Avignon on the N100. At the intersection, take the D28 for Saint-Saturnin and Pernes-les-Fontaines. Go over the highway and into **Saint-Saturnin-les-Avignon**. Stay on the D28 until you get to the D16. Turn right onto the D16 towards the **Grotte de Thouson** (which you can visit), the château and **Le Thor**.

Then take the D1 for **Velleron**. Take the D938 into the village of **Pernes-les-Fontaines**. It's a delightful little place with numerous fountains, and well worth exploring on foot. Stroll the banks of the Nesque and take a break near one of the romantic fountains.

PRACTICAL INFORMATION ON AVIGNON

Population
91,474 *Avignonnais*

? **Tourist office:** 41 Cours Jean-Jaurès, 84000 Avignon, ☎ 04 90 82 65 11, ⚬ 04 90 82 95 03

Bicycle shops
Cycles Peugeot, 80 Rue Guillaume-Puy, ☎ 04 90 86 32 49
Dépot Sport, 15 Av. De l'Orme Fourchu, ☎ 04 90 89 77 77
Vélomania, 1 Rue de l'Amelier, ☎ 04 90 82 06 98

Market
Saturdays and Sundays

Major events: Rencontres du Cinéma Franco-Américain (Franco-American film festival, late July); Festival d'Art Dramatique (drama festival, July and August); Festival Provençal (July)

Specialties: Côtes-du-Rhône wines, *Paplines* (sweets)

Access from Paris: A6, A7, N580; by train TGV Gare de Lyon to Avignon.

Map
IGN no. 66

To leave, take the D28 for **Saint-Didier**. You're now at the base of the Vaucluse plateau. Continue on the D28, and then the D4, to **Vénasque**. Comtat Venaissin got its name from the ancient "Venasca", a natural fortress 320 metres in height. Be sure to climb to the top for the view of vineyards, orchards and farm fields. And don't miss the baptistry that dates from the 6th century!

Leave Vénasque on the D4 for **Notre-Dame de Vie** and Carpentras. Continue as far as the D77. Turn right onto the D77 for **Malemort-du-Comtat**. Stay on the D77 towards **Mazan**, then turn left onto the D150. Stop at the cemetery, where a row of some 60 Gallo-Roman sarcophagi are a reminder that you're pedaling along an ancient Roman road. Learn more about the *Comtadins'* culinary and farming routines at Mazan's museum of history and folklore. Leave Mazan on the D942 and continue towards Carpentras.

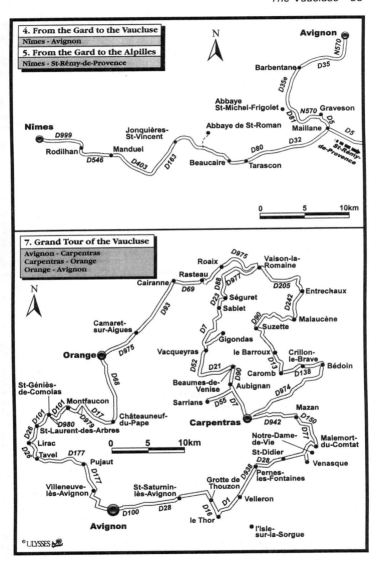

4. From the Gard to the Vaucluse
Nîmes - Avignon

5. From the Gard to the Alpilles
Nîmes - St-Rémy-de-Provence

N

Avignon

Barbentane
D35

D35e

N570 Graveson

Abbaye
St-Michel-Frigolet
D81

Abbaye de St-Roman Maillane D5

Nîmes
D999

Jonquières-
St-Vincent

Rodilhan Manduel
D546 D403 D163

Beaucaire Tarascon
D80 D32
St-Rémy-de-Provence

0   5   10km

7. Grand Tour of the Vaucluse
Avignon - Carpentras
Carpentras - Orange
Orange - Avignon

N

Roaix D975 Vaison-la-Romaine

Rasteau
Cairanne D69 D88 D977 D205 Entrechaux

D23 Séguret D242

Sablet

D93 D90 Malaucène
Suzette

Camaret-
sur-Aigues D7 Gigondas

Vacqueyras le Barroux Crillon-le-Brave

Orange D975 D52 D21 Caromb D3 Bédoin
D90 D138

Beaumes-de- Aubignan
Venise D974

D68 Sarrians D55 D7

St-Géniès-
de-Comolas Mazan

Montfaucon D942 D150

D101 D17 Châteauneuf- Carpentras
D26 D980 D979 du-Pape D71

Lirac St-Laurent-des-Arbres Notre-Dame- Malemort-
de-Vie du-Comtat

D26 Tavel D177 St-Didier
D28 Venasque

Pujaut D938
Pernes-
les-Fontaines

Villeneuve- Grotte de
lès-Avignon St-Saturnin- Thouzon Velleron
lès-Avignon D1

D177 D100 D28 D16 l'Isle-
le Thor sur-la-Sorgue

Avignon

0   5   10km

© ULYSSES

Enter **Carpentras** and follow Avenue Clémenceau as far as the traffic circle. Keep going, following the signs for the tourist office on Avenue Jean-Jaurès. If it's Friday, all of Provence and the Comtat's treasures of agricultural produce can be found at Carpentras' big market. Before leaving town, pick up a pretty box of "Berlingots", a local confectionery.

PRACTICAL INFORMATION ON CARPENTRAS

Population
25,886 *Carpentrassiens*

Tourist office: 170 Allée Jean Jaurès, 84200 Carpentras, ☎ 04 90 63 00 78, ⇒ 04 90 60 41 02

Market
Fridays

Major events: "Offenbach and his times" international festival (July and August)

Specialties: Côte-du-Rhône wines, *Berlingots* (candies)

Maps
IGN no. 66 or 60

Leg from Carpentras to Orange (via the Route des Vins): 70 km

To get out of Carpentras, head north on Avenue Notre-Dame de Santè towards **Aubignan** and **Beaumes-de-Venise**. Make sure you leave town on the D7. Continue to Abignan. Take the D90 to Beaumes-de-Venise. The Provençal word *"Beaumes"* means "grottos", and "Venise" is probably a version of Venaissin. So what are residents called? *Balméens*, of course. For an apéritif, sample a glass of chilled muscat. This mellow fortified wine, produced locally, is one of France's best.

The Route des Vins continues along the D21 for Vacqueyras and Sarrians. Stay on the D21. At the D52 junction, turn right towards **Vacqueyras**. Take the D7 to **Gigondas**. This small village is worth the detour. It produces an excellent red wine, mainly of the *grenache* variety. Numerous cellars offer tastings. Leave your bike in the square and walk through the narrow streets, lined with small houses, to the Église Sainte-Catherine. With its view of the vineyard, the church is a charming place for a picnic.

The **Dentelles de Montmirail** mountains are home to a wide variety of vegetation and attract climbers, walkers, shutterbugs and other outdoor enthusiasts. Leave Gigondas by returning to the D7. Continue towards **Sablet**. Take the D23 for **Séguret**. From the road, you'll be drawn to this picturesque village perched on a hill overlooking the plain. It's worth a detour to see its quaint streets, 15th-century fountain, 14th-century belfry and lovely view of the Dentelles de Montmirail from the 12th-century church.

PRACTICAL INFORMATION ON VAISON-LA-ROMAINE

Population
5,864 *Vaisonnais*

Tourist office: Place du Chanoine-Chautel, 84110 Vaison-la-Romaine, ☎ 04 90 36 02 11, ⊶ 04 90 28 76 04

Bicycle shops
Lacombe, Av. Jules-Ferry, ☎ 04 90 36 03 29

Market
Tuesdays

Major events: Fête de la Saint-Jean (June 24); Festival de Vaison (July)

Specialties: Côte-du-Rhône wines

Map
IGN no. 60

Get back on your bike and continue towards Vaison-la-Romaine on the D88 and then the D977. **Vaison-la-Romaine** is a highlight on this tour of ancient cities. Ruins in the lower part of town suggest it was one of the richest cities in all of Gaul, while medieval architecture fills a large section of upper town. Between the two, there's lots of history and a very steep slope! After your visit, go back to the Roman bridge (but don't cross it) and follow Quai Paul-Gontard and Avenue Jules-Ferry. Leave Vaison-la-Romaine by heading for Orange and Bollène. Make sure you depart the city on the D975. Proceed to **Roaix**.

Stay on the D975 as far as **Rasteau**. Perched on a hill, this village is also known for its muscat wine. You can learn more about the local wine industry at the Musée du Vigneron. Then head for **Cairanne** on the D69. At the D93, continue along the Aigues towards **Camaret-sur-Aigues**. Then take the D975 for Orange. Follow the signs for the Théâtre Antique and the tourist office.

Leg from Carpentras to Orange (via Bédoin): 85 km

Leave Carpentras by following the signs for Sault. At the intersection, take the D974 for Mont Ventoux and follow it as far as **Bédoin**. With its plane trees and market, this small village is very Provençal. It plays host to many cyclists who come to climb Mont Ventoux, an expedition that requires a lot of preparation, a bicycle that's in good condition, provisions, warm clothes (for when you reach the summit) and, above all, good weather.

Leave Bédoin on the D138, heading for **Crillon-le-Brave**. Climb up to the village. Louis de Berton de Crillon was Henri IV's companion-in-arms. This ancient fief is now a picturesque tourist town that's worth visiting. It's perched on a hill with a magnificent view of Ventoux. To leave Crillon-le-Brave, start on the main street with the city hall (*mairie*) on your left and the Hostellerie on your right and go down to the bottom of the village. Turn left and continue on to **Caromb**. This region is known for its Côtes-de-Ventoux wines.

Leave Caromb on the D13, heading towards Malaucène. Keep going until the D938 junction. Turn right onto the D938, still going towards Malaucène, and continue to the D78. Turn left onto the D78 and climb to **Barroux**, dominated by a fine Renaissance château. Follow the signs and the D90a for **La Roque Alric**, **Lafare** and **Suzette**. Turn right onto the V3 and go as far as Suzette. Get back onto the D90 heading towards Malaucène. This magnificent road rises to the Col de la Chaîne, then snakes down for four kilometres to **Malaucène**. Surrounded by large plane trees, this village is typically Provençal, with old houses, fountains, washhouses and old belfries. Check out the machicolated façade on its church, built for Pope Clément V, Avignon's first pope.

Leave Malaucène by taking the D242 towards the hamlet of **Veaux**. Pedal to the intersection with the **Entrechaux** road and turn left towards Entrechaux. Turn right after the bridge and follow the "Côte-de-Venteux" road into the village. Stay on the Route des Vins to get out of Entrechaux. Take the road on the left to cross the Ouvèze, then left again onto the D205 towards **Saint-Marcellin-les-Vaison**. Continue on the D151 until you rejoin the D975 to enter **Vaison-la-Romaines.**

Head for the Pont Romain (a Roman bridge that's more than 2,000 years old!) and follow the signs for the tourist office. It's time for a rest. Lock your bike and explore the city, founded in the year 20 B.C. Roads and pedestrian walkways lead through neighbourhoods of Roman, medieval and modern architecture. History and antiquity enthusiasts will need at least two hours for the tour.

To reach Orange, follow the directions of the preceding leg (Carpentras to Orange via the Route des Vins) from Vaison-la-Romaine.

PRACTICAL INFORMATION ON ORANGE

Population
27,502 *Orangeois*

 Tourist office: 5 Cours Aristide-Briand, 84140 Orange, ☎ 04 90 34 70 88, ✆ 04 90 34 99 62 (in summer, an office is open across from the Théâtre Antique)

 Bicycle shops
Cycles Lurion, 48 Cours A. Briand, ☎ 04 90 34 08 77
M.T.S. 84, 571 Boul. Daladier, ☎ 04 90 34 94 92

 Market
Thursdays

 Major events: Festival de la Bande Dessinée (comics festival, May); Chorégies, with operas and symphony concerts (mid-July)

 Specialties: Hare, thrush, truffles, Mont Ventoux mushrooms

 Map
IGN no. 60

Leg from Orange to Avignon: 50 km

Once a Roman colony under Augustus, **Orange** still has a triumphal arch and the best-preserved theatre in the entire Roman Empire. Ask at the tourist office about guided tours of this incredible ancient theatre. Strolling the lively old quarter is very pleasant. Head south out of Orange along the Rue de Châteauneuf and take the D68 to leave the city. Go under the highway and proceed to **Châteauneuf-du-Pape** on the D68. Enter the centre of the village and follow the signs for the "Château".

You can climb to the castle ruins, once the popes' summer residence. The castle was almost entirely destroyed during the last war; only the façade and one wall remain. But go anyway, for the view. You'll look out over an ocean of vineyards and surrounding mountain ranges – the **Ventoux**, the **Dentelles de Montmirail** and the **Alpilles**.

PRACTICAL INFORMATION ON CHÂTEAUNEUF-DU-PAPE

Population
2,1000 *Castels-Papals*

? **Tourist office:** 84,230 Châteauneuf-du-Pape, ☎ 04 90 83 71 08

Market
Fridays

Major events: Fête de Véraison (August)

Specialties: Châteauneuf-du-Pape wines

Map
IGN no. 66

Numerous cellars in the village offer tastings. You must sample this strong, heady wine. Leave Châteauneuf-du-Pape on the D17, heading towards Caderousse. Follow this road to the D976 intersection. Turn left towards Roquemaure and cross the Rhône. Turn right as soon as you're off the bridge (don't go into Roquemaure), go under the highway and continue on the D101 for **Montfaucon**. Entering the village, the private Montfaucon castle is to your right.

Continue on the D101. Then take the D980 into **Saint-Geniès-de-Comolas**. Get back on the D101, cross the Route Nationale and go into **Saint-Laurent-des-Arbres**. Tour this charming medieval village, dominated by a feudal keep and a fortified church. Take the D26 out of Saint-Laurent-des-Arbres towards **Lirac** and Tavel. The road continues to roll through Côte-du-Rhône vineyards. The wines of Tavel and Lirac have their own vintages. Go into **Tavel**, worth a short visit to see its municipal washhouse. Built in 1878, it's still in use. Maybe you'll want to use it yourself!

Leave the village by heading towards Pujaut and Avignon. Ride under the highway. Proceed along the D177 to **Pujaut**. Keep going on the D177 to **Villeneuve-lès-Avignon**. The "city of cardinals" offers so much to see that you should plan to visit. Get information at the tourist office. The top of the Tour Philippe le Bel offers a magnificent view of Avignon; in fact that's why it was built. After your visit, cross the Rhône and enter Avignon.

PRACTICAL INFORMATION
ON VILLENEUVE-LÈS-AVIGNON

Population
9,535 *Villeneuvois*

Tourist office: 1 Place Charles-David, 30400 Villeneuve-lès-Avignon, ☎ 04 90 25 61 33, ✆ 04 90 25 91 55

Market
Thursdays

Major events: Fête de la Saint-Jean; Rencontres Internationales à la Chartreuse (July and August)

Map
IGN no. 66

BURGUNDY

The name "Burgundy" evokes an immediate image of fine dining and drinking, a glorious past and a solid tradition of *bons vivants*. Gourmet cyclists need look no further. Part of the prestigious heritage of the Grand Dukes of *Occident*, Burgundy (*Bourgogne*) is world renowned for its delicious cuisine and great wines. Thanks to the Cistercian monks, Burgundy wines became famous. Today, the *grands crus* or great vintages that are the pride of the region continue to age in quiet, cool stone vaults in the villages and towns of the Côte d'Or. At harvest time, the rich fragrance of fermenting grapes permeates their streets, making for a "local scent".

THE CÔTE D'OR

The Burgundy region has four departments, including the Côte d'Or (literally, the golden hillside). One of the most beautiful vineyards in the world lies along its base. The tour snakes all the way along these hillsides, which are divided into two sections – the **Côte-de-Nuits** and the **Côte-de-Beaune**. The name of every village is familiar; road signs bearing their names are shaped like wine labels.

Dijon, the capital of Burgundy, boasts an enchanting protected heritage neighbourhood where churches, houses dating from the

Middle Ages and *hôtels particuliers* stand harmoniously among structures with wood frames, old stones and glazed tiles. The **Hautes-Côtes-de-Nuits** are blanketed with vineyards, grain fields, pastureland and small forests. Cassis, which goes into that incomparable Burgundy liqueur, Crème de Cassis, is also grown here. Canon Kir (1876-1968), the mayor of Dijon, popularized this famous cream by blending cassis with *aligoté*, a Burgundy white wine. He welcomed his hosts with the resultant blend, a "Kir," a practice that has become a tradition.

One tour runs in a loop out of Dijon to the Côte-de-Nuits and the Ouche valley, via the Dijon mountain, where picturesque villages and hamlets are bathed in pure, clean air. The trip involves a good climb, but also offers a spectacular descent through a lovely natural area. Back in Dijon, another tour leads to **Beaune** via the Route des Vins. As soon as you're outside **Chenôve**, thousands of feet of Pinot Noir grapes extend as far as the eye can see. They rise in terraces from the **Route des Grands Crus**, which undulates between stone walls separating various estates with celebrated names like **Gevrey-Chambertin, Vougeot, Vosne-Romanée, Nuits-Saint-Georges**, etc. From the 10th to the 12th century, life in the Duchy of Burgundy was intensely religious. Thus, the main châteaux in the region were ecclesiastic, including **Gevrey-Chambertin**, built for the abbey of Cluny, and the **Clos de Vougeot**, erected by the Cistercian monks.

The route stretches through valleys and hills to the wine-growing towns of the **Côte-de-Beaune**, some of which produce white wine and others red wine. Narrow roads wind through enchanting scenery between the different estates, bearing such illustrious names as **Aloxe-Corton, Pernand-Vergelesse, Savigny-lès-Beaune, Pommard, Meursault, Puligny-Montrachet**, etc. For cyclists who are unaccustomed to climbs, an easier ride through the peaceful fields of the Saône plain is recommended.

Ever since the era of the Grand Dukes of *Occident*, **"Beaune"**, the capital of Burgundy, has had the same vocation – the care of Burgundy's fine wines. Tours of its imposing, opulent wine cellars wrap up with tastings. The incomparable Hôtel-Dieu de Beaune was taking in patients right up until 1971. Now a museum and star attraction, the facility is witness to a glorious Flemish past and is a masterpiece of Burgundy-Flemish architecture.

Two very pretty tours lead out of Beaune to the Hautes-Côtes. One takes you to the majestic **La Rochepot** and **Gamay** châteaux. The other leads along the magnificent limestone cliffs of Orches and Bouilland, passing **Bessey-en-Chaume**, the highest farm village on the entire Côte-de-Beaune. Both routes offer nature sites and splendid views of the landscape.

You'll be seduced by Burgundy's towns of stone houses, it prestigious wine-producing villages and the splendour of its ancient towns. This is one of the best regions in France for cycling, what with its history, varied scenery, small, quiet roads and gastronomy. See for yourself how the easy-going locals welcome their visitors!

---

8. Loop from Dijon to the Vallée de l'Ouche to Dijon

Total distance: 55 km
Number of legs: 1
Level of difficulty: 🚲 🚲
Diagram: p 81
Map: A6

The **Dijon** train station faces Avenue du Maréchal-Foch, which leads to the tourist office on Place Darcy. The avenue is one-way in the wrong direction from the station, so you have to walk your bike to the tourist office. From there, head along Rue de la Liberté to the centre of the old town. Ask for the map of the city that has suggested tours on it, and then embark on a self-guided tour of Dijon. Don't miss the Musée des Beaux-Arts (fine arts museum, which has tombs of Burgundy dukes) in the Palais des Ducs, or the Cathédrale Notre-Dame, with its curious rows of gargoyles. Nearby, look for the small carved owl on the buttress of a chapel. Take off your gloves, put your hand on it, close your eyes and make a wish... By the way, it's on the street that bears its name (*chouette*), where the French film *Cyrano* was filmed.

To get out of Dijon, start at the train station and head towards Beaune and Chenôve. Leave Dijon on the N74. Be careful, because traffic is heavy around the city. Stay to the right. After the Bourgogne canal, take the D122, the Route des Grand Crus. It starts in **Chenôve** (the Chenôve winery has nearly disappeared thanks to the encroaching Dijon suburbs). Stop at the **Marsannay** château for your first tasting. The town produces excellent red and white wines, along with a rosé, something unusual for Côte-de-Nuits.

PRACTICAL INFORMATION ON DIJON

Population
145,570 *Dijonnais*

? **Tourist office:** Place Darcy, 21000 Dijon, ☎ 03 80 44 11 44, ⌐ 03 80 42 18 83

Bicycle shops
Tillot R (SA), 11 Av. Jean-Jaurès, ☎ 03 80 41 53 11
Cycles Degeuerce, 4 Boul. de l'Université, ☎ 03 80 65 18 88

Market
Tuesdays, Fridays and Saturdays

Major events: Festival de Dijon, musical summer (June); Estivade (July and August); wine festival (August and September); international gastronomic fair (November).

Specialties: Mustard, gingerbread, Kir (apéritif), marbled ham

Access from Paris: by car A6, A38; by train TGV Lyon station to Dijon

Map
IGN no. 37

Proceed on the D122, the Route des Grands Crus, to the old town of **Gevrey-Chambertin**. The château (*guided visits of about 30 min starting at 10am, closed from noon to 2pm and Sunday morning; ☎ 03 80 34 36 13*) stands at the edge of the village. Follow the signs, to the right. The château, in the Romanesque-Burgundy architectural style, was built by descendants of the powerful seigneur of Vergy and given to the Cluny monks in the 13th century. It is open to visitors and you can also taste the estate's wines. Go down Rue de l'Église to get to the centre of the village.

After your visit, leave Gevrey-Chambertin by returning to Rue de l'Église, and then take the D31 towards Chamboeuf and Semezanges. This is a fairly difficult section of the route; the road climbs progressively for about five kilometres up a wooded hill and finally reaches a plateau covered with grain fields. Leave **Chamboeuf** on the D31. At the intersection, turn right onto the D3 and then take the D35 for Quemigny-Poisot and Pont-de-Pany. Get ready for a long, dizzying

8. Loop Dijon - Vallée de l'Ouche - Dijon
9. Loop Dijon to Beaune

N

D10e Plombières-lès-Dijon
Talant
Dijon
Velars-sur-Ouche
N74
D905
D996
Pont-de-Pany
D122
Chenôve
Marsannay-la-Côte
Ouges
D35
Chevigny
Urcy
Fixin
D996
Quemigny-Poisot
Chambœuf
D31
Saulon-la-Rue
D35
D31a
D31
Gevrey-Chambertin
Morey-St-Denis
D122
D25h
Vougeot
Gilly-lès-Cîteaux
Clos de Vougeot
D25 D109c
Vosne-Romanée
St-Bernard
Nuits-St-Georges
Marey-lès-Fussey
Chaux
D118b
Boncourt-le-Bois
Fussey
D8
Agencourt
Échevronne
D18
D109g
Quincey
Antilly
Pernand-Vergelesses
D35c
D20
Argilly
D18
Longvay
D20
Gigny
Beaune

0   3   6km

© ULYSSES

descent that offers a splendid panorama and numerous bends en route to **Pont-de-Pany** in the Ouche valley.

At the intersection, turn right onto the D905 for **Verlars-sur-Ouche** and Dijon. This part of the route is popular among Dijon cyclists. The road follows the Burgundy canal and, unfortunately, it also runs alongside the highway for a few kilometres. Next take the D10f for La Verrerie, **Plombières-lès-Dijon** and Dijon, where you can get onto the bicycle path. Take a few moments to explore the man-made shores of **Lac Kir**. Bike with caution as you head to the centre of Dijon.

Gevrey-Chambertin to Dijon via the plain (optional route): 40 km

I recommend less hardy cyclists take this route over the Saône plain.

Leave Gevrey-Chambertin via its vineyard and continue along the D122 through Morey-Saint-Denis to Clos de Vougeot. From the village of Vougeot, cross the Route Nationale and proceed on the D25 to Gilly-lès-Cîteaux. At the intersection, get onto the D25h for **Saint-Philibert** (don't cross the highway). At the Satenay pond and the D31, turn right for **Saulon-la-Rue**.

Proceed along the D996 to **Chevigny**. Then take the little road that goes under the highway and ends in **Ouges**. Proceed to Dijon on the D996.

---

9. Dijon to Beaune

Total distance:	65 km
Number of legs:	1
Level of difficulty:	🚲 🚲
Diagram:	p 81
Map:	A6, A7

To get out of Dijon, start at the train station and head for Beaune on the N75. Leave Dijon via the Boulevard Jean-Jaurès. Stay to the right and take the D122, the Route des Grand Crus. Follow the D122 to Fixin and Gevrey-Chambertin (see preceding route). If you're into Romanesque art, I suggest a small excursion to the upper part of the village of **Fixin**, in the hamlet of Fixey, to see the little Église Saint-Antoine, the oldest Romanesque church in all of Côte-d'Or. If you've already visited Gevrey-Chambertin, leave through its vineyard and proceed along the D122 through **Morey-Saint-Denis** to **Clos de Vougeot**. Follow the signs for the château.

The **Château du Clos de Vougeot** (*guided tours of about 30 min starting at 9am, closed from noon to 2pm;* ☎ *03 80 62 86 09*), property of the "Ordre de la Confrérie des Chevaliers du Tastevin", is considered to be among the most outstanding of Burgundy wineries. The buildings were constructed by the Cistercian monks to make wine. The château was added in 1551. Don't miss this magnificent estate.

To proceed, stay on the Route des Grands Crus, which leads to **Vosne-Romanée** and **Nuit-Saint-Georges**. The *côte* is named after the latter town, which stands at the edge of the Meuzin. With its Romanesque church, belfry, 17th-century clock tower, robust and well-rounded wines, this little capital is well worth a visit. Share the *joie-de-vivre* of the locals!

PRACTICAL INFORMATION ON NUITS-SAINT-GEORGES

Population
5,460 *Nuitons*

Tourist office: Rue Sonoys, 21700 Nuits-Saint-Georges, ☎ 03 80 61 22 47, ✉ 03 80 61 30 98

Bicycle shops
Cycles Tillot, 4 Place de la République, ☎ 03 80 61 41 48

Market
Fridays

Major events: Vente des Hospices de Nuits-Saint-Georges (sale, March); Fête du Vin Bourru (new wine festival, November).

Specialties: Crème de cassis, raspberry, mulberry and peach; Amour de Nuits cheese; wine

Map
IGN no. 37

Head out of Nuits-Saint-Georges towards Beaune, then take the Chaux road and the D8. Some cyclists will find the climb difficult. The road rises above the village of Nuits towards the **Hautes-Côtes de Beaune**. Ride to **Chaux**. Proceed on the D8 to **Marey-lès-Fussey** and **Fussey**. At the intersection, take the D18 towards Beaune. Proceed to **Echevronne** at the junction between the Hautes-Côtes de Beaune and the Hautes-Côtes de Nuits. The village church features a 12th-century chapel. Then glide down the pleasant descent to the picturesque village of **Pernand-Vergelesse**. This wine-growing village produces fine red wines and respected Burgundy whites.

Continue through the vineyard to Beaune on the D18. Go under the highway and ride cautiously to the centre of the city. The tourist office is on Place de la Halle across from the Hôtel-Dieu.

Vougeot to Beaune via the Saône plain (optional route): 35 km

This route is very flat and runs through a pleasant farming region. It also offers a beautiful lookout over the Côte-de-Beaune.

After visiting the château, return to the village of **Vougeot** and cross the Route Nationale. Proceed straight ahead on the D25 to **Gilly-lès-Cîteaux**. The Gilly-lès-Cîteaux château, once part of the Clos de Vougeot winery, is today a superb luxury hotel. Take the time to visit it.

Take the D109c to **Saint-Bernard**. Take the D116 to **Boncourt-le-Bois** and **Agencourt**. Leave Agencourt on the D8 and immediately take the D109g for **Quincey**. Proceed towards **Antilly** on the D35c. Then take the D20 to **Argilly, Longvay, Gigny** and Beaune. Enter Beaune on the D20 and follow the signs for downtown and the Porte Saint-Nicolas (gate).

---

10. Loop from Beaune to La Rochepot to Beaune

Total distance:	40 km
Number of legs:	1
Level of difficulty:	🚲 🚲
Diagram:	p 87
Map:	A7

PRACTICAL INFORMATION ON BEAUNE

Population
21,127 *Beaunois*

 Tourist office: Rue de l'Hôtel-Dieu, 21200 Beaune, ☎ 03 80 26 21 30, ↩ 03 80 26 21 39

 Bicycle shops
Beaune Cyles, 12 Rue du Faubourg Saint-Martin, ☎ 03 80 24 10 39
Cycles Tillot, 48 Pace Madeleine, ☎ 03 80 24 70 08
Grappin Frères, 16 Boul. Jules-Ferry, ☎ 03 80 22 20 07

 Market
Saturdays

 Major Events: Fêtes Internationales de la Vigne (international wine festival, September); Rencontres Cinématographiques (film festival, October); sale of Hospices de Beaune wine (November)

 Specialty: Wines

Map
IGN no. 37

Beaune, an ancient city encircled by ramparts, is the fiefdom of the major trading houses. In the vast underground city made up of wine cellars, premium wines are aged to perfection before being bottled. On the third Sunday in November, the famous auction of fine **Hospices de Beaune** wines unfolds according to tradition. Nearby, the former Hôtel des Ducs de Bourgogne houses the Musée du Vin.

The Saturday morning market is a divine opportunity to taste cheeses and other regional produce. Have you heard of Époisses? Nobody is indifferent to this strongly-scented cheese. Try it!

To get out of Beaune, take the ring road towards Chalon-sur-Saône. Don't go all the way out of the city; watch on the left for the white sign for Bligny-lès-Beaune via the D18 and Avenue de la Résistance (if you get to the Route de Pommard junction, you've gone too far). Leave Beaune and ride along the D18 to **Bligny-lès-Beaune**. Go through the village and stay on the D18 as far as the D23 junction. Turn right toward the Meursault hospital.

Cross the Route Nationale and enter **Meursault**. Go straight ahead to reach the centre of this charming little town, the Côte-d'Or's capital of white wines. The Église Saint-Nicolas, dating from the 14th century, dominates the town with its 57-metre stone spire. The Hôtel de Ville, with its roof of glazed tiles, is a former 14th-century fortified castle.

Wine lovers can taste some very fine vintages in the cool wine cellars at the Château de Meursault.

Leave Meursault on the D17e towards Auxey-Duresses. To the west of Meursault, the **Auxey-Duresses** vineyard produces fine red wines as well as elegant whites. Take the D973 to **La Rochepot**. Arriving at the village, the road climbs and the hill becomes steeper as it nears the château (*guided visits of about 45 min starting at 9:30am, closed from 11:30am to 2:30pm and Tuesdays; ☎03 80 21 71 37*). But it's worth the detour. The 13th-century fortified castle, renovated in the 19th century, stands at an altitude of 500 metres in a beautiful natural area. You can visit with or without a guide.

Take the same road back down to the bottom of the village and leave on the D33 (at the fountain) for Saint-Aubin. Get your camera ready! This road climbs above the town and offers a wonderful view of the Château de La Rochepot.

Then ride leisurely down to the small village of **Saint-Aubin**. Climb to its church. To avoid the Route Nationale, take the Route des Vignes, to the right of the church. At the fork (monument to the dead), veer left and ride to the hamlet of **Gamay**, in the middle of a vineyard. Its 10th- and 11th-century château is private, but worth a look. Return to the middle of the hamlet and follow the signs for **Blagny** (don't confuse it with Bligny). Despite its difficult slope (15% grade in some spots), this small road above Gamay is a must! It offers an unparalleled view over the **Puligny-Montrachet** vineyard and its neighbour, Meursault. At the intersection at the foot of the hill, turn left and ride through this "ocean of vineyards" to Meursault. If you want to visit the village of Puligny-Montrachet, turn right. Afterwards, come back along the same road.

Next climb to the centre of Meursault and take the D23 for **Monthélie**. Cross the D973 (nice view of the vineyard) and continue straight ahead towards Bligny and Nantoux. The route rises gently. Stay on the D23 to the D17 junction and turn right to **Pommard**, an adorable, flower-strewn village of old Romanesque houses nestled at the foot of the hills. World-renowned Pommard wine is one of the Côte's finest. Treat yourself to a tasting. Leaving Pommard, ride past the château

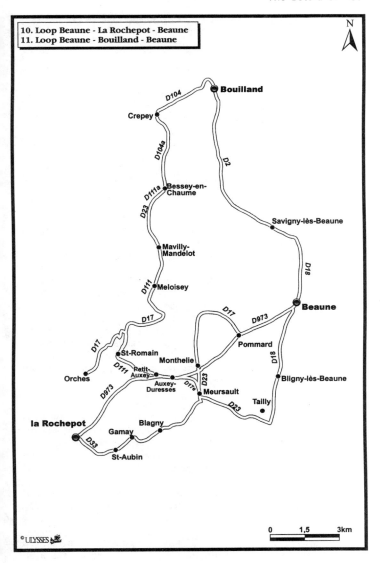

10. Loop Beaune - La Rochepot - Beaune
11. Loop Beaune - Bouilland - Beaune

and proceed to Beaune on the D973 or by the road to the left that runs through the vineyard.

---

11. Loop from Beaune to Bouilland to Beaune

Total distance: 50 km
Number of legs: 1
Level of difficulty: 🚲 🚲
Diagram: p 87
Map: A7

Leave Beaune on the ring road heading towards Chalon-sur-Saône on the N74. Keep right and continue on the D973 to Pommard. Keep going on the D973, across the Volnay, Monthélie and Auxey-Duresses vineyards.

In **Petit-Auxey**, take the D17e to **Saint-Romain**. The hill is difficult; go into low gear! The charming village of Saint-Romain sits at the base of an impressive limestone cliff that looks like a Greek amphitheatre. I recommend crossing the Saint-Romain cliff. The three-kilometre excursion offers one of the most beautiful views on the Côte-de-Beaune, encompassing the Meursault valley, the villages of Saint-Romain and Auxey-Duresses and the Saône valley. To get there, leave Saint-Romain and climb the hill to the first intersection. Turn left onto the D17 for Ivry-en-Montagne and Orches. On the left, take the road that continues to climb. Just before the small village of Orches, there's a great lookout that makes for an ideal rest stop. Next, make a short visit to **Orches**, which also offers a magnificent panorama, before turning around and heading back.

Go back to the intersection at the foot of the hill (it's a very pleasant descent) and head for Beaune on the D17. At the crossroads, take the hill for **Meloisey** on the D111. Continue climbing to **Mavilly-Mandelot**. Proceed on the D23 towards Bligny-sur-Oche. Finally! Ride slowly; after all, you're in the land of the *Helix pomatia*, better known as the *escargot de Bourgogne*, or the Burgundy snail.

Cross the D970 and take the D111a to the little farming village of **Bessey-en-Chaume**, isolated in the highlands where chickens and such are raised in the most natural conditions.

Continue towards Aubaine on the D104a. There's a good view as you enter **Crepey**. Leave the village via the D104. The road rises a bit more, then goes into a splendid descent through forests to **Bouilland**. Slow down, because there's a very tight turn as you get to the village. Replenish your water supply at the washhouse on the main square.

Take the D2 out of Bouilland and through the cool Rhoin valley to **Savigny-lès-Beaune**. The road is extremely pleasant, because it descends for 10 kilometres! Savigny-lès-Beaune is famous for its wine and its stately 17th- and 18th-century château that's home to four museums dedicated to wine, motorcycles, cars and aeronautics. Take the time, too, to tour the village.

Return to Beaune on the D18.

FRANCHE-COMTÉ

Franche-Comté, a delightful region in eastern France, is an exceptional summer-vacation destination. This little-known area blends plains and mountains, offering cyclists who like peaceful, open spaces an array of rich, unspoiled natural areas. Some 42% of its land is forested, it has about 5,000 kilometres of rivers and its limestone subsoil is dotted with pits and grottos. With all those places to provide cover from the noon-day sun, it's a perfect region to explore in summertime.

This crescendo-style route starts in Burgundy and goes through the Franche-Comté to the **Parc des Ballons des Vosges** just before Alsace. The route leads along a network of small, extraordinarily quiet roads, across plains and down into gullies and valleys, to the foot of the **Vosges**. The scenery en route is charming and varied. The route is dotted with small, hospitable villages that have fountains and washhouses, as well as fascinating cities like **Auxonne**, **Dole** and **Bescançon** offering fortifications, churches and old houses. The itinerary leads from river to river – the Saône, the Doubs, the Loue, the Cuisance and the Ognon, each among the prettiest in France.

The tour begins in **Beaune** on the Côte d'Or, a stop on the preceding Burgundy tour. As soon as you leave the city, you're pedaling across the Saône plains, blanketed in fields of wheat, barley, sunflowers and corn. Not entirely in Burgundy and yet not in the Franche-Comté either, this is an easy expedition through sun-drenched fields, forests, ponds, farms and pretty villages with red-brick and brownstone houses. Next, you come to the Rivière Saône, first in **Saint-Jean-de-Losne** and then in **Auxonne**, where the river shores seem tailor-made for a break and some idle observation of the boats going by and the swimmers nearby. Before leaving these historic cities, stroll around their old towns. They are important heritage sites. Bonaparte trained with an artillery regiment in Auxonne when he was 18. A statue and a small museum remember him.

The Doubs (pronounced "doo"), a tributary of the Saône, weaves its way through many twists, turns and gorges. But before following its meandering shoreline to Besançon, tour the scenic **Jura**, where a loop starts in Dole and leads first to **Arbois** on the shores of the Cuisance. This small town is famous partly thanks to Louis Pasteur, who grew up there, but mainly because of its exceptional "yellow wine", the pride of the region.

Next you go to **Salins-les-Bains**, which stretches along the Furieuse. Today, the brackish Salins-les-Bains waters are used for thermal-spring water cures, but the underground saltworks is still open to visitors. Claude-Nicolas Ledoux's Royal Saltworks were erected in **Arc-et-Senans** in the 18th century. This utopian project, never completed, is testimony to how daring architecture can be. The old saltworks, saved from ruin in the nick of time, are worth a look. It'll help you understand to what extent salt and wood have brought wealth and fortune to the Jura region. Dole stands over the Doubs, reflected in its waters. Louis Pasteur, the great scientist and benefactor of humanity, was born there in 1822. His father's house – his father tanned hides for a living – is now a museum.

After the trip into the Jura, the rolling route (with some surprises) follows the majestic Rivière Doubs, across alluvial plains and past limestone cliffs. The **Osselle grottos** near Besançon provide an opportunity for a more "in-depth" exploration of the region. Besançon, France's first "green town", nestles in a curve of the Doubs. A monument to the genius of Vauban, the Besançon citadel is a gem of military architecture. The hill leading to it is steep, and the view from the ramparts unforgettable.

It was in Besançon that I first witnessed the arrival of a leg of the Tour de France. It was a Sunday in July and I was just completing a segment of my trip. I arrived in the village a good hour ahead of the

Tour. The streets were closed to cars and thousands of people already stood behind barriers, eagerly awaiting the racers. So I arrived in Besançon pedaling along the streets between rows of spectators who applauded and shouted that I was the first arrival! Maybe you'll be lucky enough to come across the Tour de France as well.

We veer away from the Doubs at **Baume-les-Dames**, named after a Benedictine abbey reserved for the daughters of the nobility. The next leg of the trip features other, less well-known rivers, like the Ognon and the Savoureuse.

And what about the terrain? Well it becomes more challenging, especially as you approach Parc des Ballons des Vosges, which you can start to see near **Ronchamp**. Over centuries, erosion has carved the mountain range into rounded, balloon-like hills. Anyone can do this part of the tour, thanks to gear changes. Continue to the small plateau. Take time to catch your breath. The few hills shouldn't stop you from admiring the scenery, an endless tableau of green. The trip gets easier as you near Alsace, where the colours change as you pedal through flower-festooned villages of pastel houses. Details later!

On this route, you'll also discover regional specialties and produce. It is said of the Franche-Comté that it has more cheese factories than all the rest of France put together. The rigours of the Jura winter led to the creation of a marvelous recipe for a famous gruyere cheese with a subtle, unique aroma. There's one cheese, Cancoillotte, that you can only find here; purely a local tradition, it's served hot, like cheese fondue. This is also the land of Mont d'Or, Morbier, Bleu de Gex and the best known cheese in the world, La Vache qui Rit. Freshwater fish, including trout, perch and pike, is another local specialty that you'll find on every menu.

TOUR OF THE FRANCHE-COMTÉ

Total distance: 365 km
Number of legs: 5

12. The Saône Plain

Total distance: 75 km
Number of legs: 1
Level of difficulty: 🚲
Diagram: p 95
Maps: A7, A8

Leg from Beaune to Dole (via Auxonne): 75 km

To get out of Beaune, take the ring road and follow the signs for Dijon.
Turn onto the first street on the right, just before the exit for Dijon
towards Gigny. This is the Rue de Chorey. It becomes the Route de
Saint-Jean-de-Losne. Make sure you exit Beaune on the D20. Keep
going towards Gigny, Longvay, Argilly and Saint-Jean-de-Losne. At the
D996 junction, follow the signs for Auvillars and then get back on the
D20. Veer left at the fork and go into **Saint-Jean-de-Losne**.

Water is the main attraction in Saint-Jean-de-Losne, the oldest river
port in France. The Burgundy canal and the Saône both flow right
through the heart of town. The Église Saint-Jean-Baptiste across from
the bridge is worth a visit. It has a Burgundian roof, an asymmetrical
steeple and a Renaissance-style portal. Inside, the flagstone floor is
made up of tombstones, the organs date from the 18th century and
the votive offering of a boat is from the 19th century.

N.B.: If you want to shorten this segment by 20 kilometres, head
towards Dole from Saint-Jean-de-Losne. Cross the bridge to **Losne**.
Take the D24 for **Saint-Symphorien** and **Saint-Seine**. Continue on the
D31 and then the D6 to Dole.

To continue to Auxonne, take the D968 out of Saint-Jean-de-Losne
towards **Saint-Usage**. Then, at the edge of town, fork right on the D20
for Echenon and Auxonne. Stay on the D20. Cross the Saône and
enter **Auxonne**.

You can picnic beside the river at a spot immediately to the left after
the bridge (a tap lower down provides drinking water). Be sure to visit
the château and the fortifications, the artillery arsenal, the Musée de
Napoléon and the Église Notre-Dame (12th century to 14th century).
Auxonne also has a beach. Its July 14 sailing event is well known.

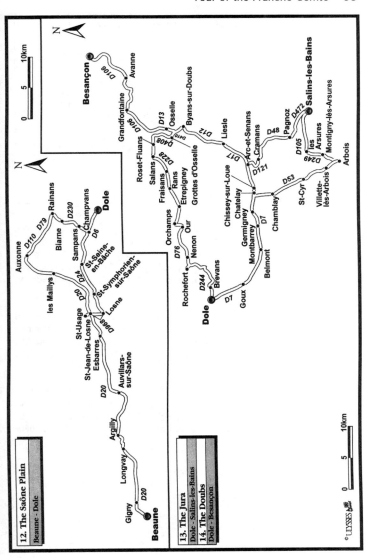

PRACTICAL INFORMATION ON AUXONNE

Population
7,868 *Auxonnais*

 Tourist office: 23, Place d'Armes, 21130 Auxonne, ☎ 03 80 37 34 46, ⊷ 03 80 31 02 34

Major events: Carnaval à Auxonne (May); nautical demonstrations (July 14)

Specialties: Market-gardening produce, onions, fish and *pôchuses* (fish stew)

Map
IGN no. 37

Take the N5 out of Auxonne towards Dole. Pedal for two kilometres and turn left onto the D110a for Dole, Sampans and Rainans. The winding road rises gradually through woods and meadows. Don't enter **Rainans**; just before the village, fork right to the C1 and cross a field of sunflowers to **Biarne**. At the intersection, turn right and proceed on the D230 to **Sampans**.

Continue on the D322 to **Campvans**. Go down to the right into the village and continue to Dole on the D6. You have to go over a small plateau to climb to Dole. Follow the signs for downtown and the tourist office. Be careful, because traffic is heavy and many of the streets are one-way.

The capital of ancient Franche-Comté, Dole boasts a rich architectural heritage that is reflected in its unusual hotels, ancient convents, Hôtel-Dieu (hospital) and the 16th-century Église Notre-Dame, with its 75-metre belfry that served as the old city's lighthouse. Get off your bike and explore the town on foot.

PRACTICAL INFORMATION ON DOLE

Population
28,000 *Dolois*

? **Tourist office:** 6 Place Grévy, 39100 Dole, ☎ 03 84 72 11 22, ⌨ 03 84 82 49 27

Bicycle shops
Cycles Moto Sport, 1 Rue du Gouvernement, ☎ 03 84 72 23 62
Cycles Bulle, 82 Rue des Arènes, ☎ 03 84 72 19 25

Market
Tuesdays, Thursdays and Saturdays

Major events: *"La Fabuleuse Histoire du Sel en Franche-Comté"* (multivision show on the history of salt in the region, July and August); Journées du Patrimoine (heritage celebration, September 14 and 15)

Specialties: Freshwater fish, Jura wines

Map
IGN no. 37

13. The Jura

Total distance: 100 km
Number of legs: 2
Level of difficulty: 🚲 🚲
Diagram: p 95
Map: A8

Loop through the Jura: 100 km

The tour of the Jura starts in Dole, leads to Salins-les-Bains and then returns to Dole via the Saline Royal (Royal Saltworks) of Arc-et-Senans. You can also go directly to Osselle from Arc-et-Senans and proceed to Besançon without returning to Dole.

From Dole, head for Genève, Poligny and Goux. Cross the bridge over the Doubs and proceed along the D405. Going up the hill as you leave town, watch on the left for the sign for Goux. Get onto the D7, which goes through the Chaux forest to **Goux, La Loye, Belmont, Montbarrey** and **Germigney**. On clear days, you can see the Jura plateaus from the road. Keep going as far as the D53 junction after Châtelay. Turn right and follow the D53 towards Chamblay. Continue, through fields of corn and sunflowers. Cross the little bridge and go on to **Chamblay**. Continue towards **Saint-Cyr** on the D53. The road winds through the Largançon forest. Take the D9 into Saint-Cyr. Follow the D9 to **Vadans** and Arbois. Immediately, on your left, get back onto the D53 towards Villette and Arbois. Peddle to **Villette-lès-Arbois**. The road goes through pretty woods and then opens up onto a view of the Arbois hills.

Cross the railway tracks and enter **Arbois**. The road climbs into the village. Head for the tourist office, immediately to your right as you enter on Rue Hôtel-de-Ville, to get information on the Rivière Cuisance, Pasteur's family home or the secrets of the famous yellow and straw wines.

PRACTICAL INFORMATION ON ARBOIS

Population
4,500 *Arboisiens*

 Tourist office: Rue de l'Hôtel-de-Ville, 39600 Arbois, ☎ 03 84 37 47 37, ⇌ 03 84 66 25 50

 Specialties: Arbois wines (white, rosé, red), straw wines and yellow wines

 Map
IGN no. 37

At the intersection, dominated by a fountain, take the Route des Vins out of Arbois towards Besançon. Head immediately towards **Montigny-lès-Arsures**. The road climbs steeply in the vineyard. At the fork, proceed on the D249, the Route des Vins. Pass the viewpoint indicator on your right. Continue towards **Les Arsures**, a pretty flower-bedecked village that offers a magnificent panorama. Pedal to the intersection of the D105. Fork right to **Marnoz** and keep going to **Salins-les-Bains**.

The little resort town stretches for a long way. Ride along its main street towards the "Salines" (saltworks) and the tourist office. Stop for a tour of the Église Saint-Anatole, one of the best examples in the Franche-Comté of 13th-century Gothic-Cistercian architecture.

PRACTICAL INFORMATION ON SALINS-LES-BAINS

Population
4,500 *Salinois*

 Tourist office: Place des Salines, 39110 Salins-Les-Bains, ☎ 03 84 73 01 34

 Map
IGN no. 37

Take the D472 towards Dole to get out of Salins-les-Bains. At the intersection, continue straight ahead towards Pagnoz and Poteric. Watch on the right for a street with no name or number. Turn right onto this street and proceed to **Pagnoz**. Continue on the D48 and then the D48e. After the railway track, head for **Cramans** on the D121. Cross the Loue and continue to **Saline Royale d'Arc-et-Senans** (*9am to noon and 2pm to 6pm; Saline Royale, Institut Claude-Nicolas Ledoux,* ☎ *03 81 54 45 45*).

At the entrance to the "Ville Nouvelle", you can see a copy of Claude Nicolas Ledoux's plan of the industrial town he set out to create. He was in charge of building the saltworks, from which the brackish water of the Salins was to be removed and heated by wood from the Chaux forest. Only half the planned town was erected. Today this important architectural model of a late 19th-century industrial town is housed in the Centre de Réflexion on the future.

Take the D7 for the return trip through attractive villages like Chissey-sur-Loue, Châtelay, Germigney, Montbarrey, Belmont, La Loye and Goux. Enter Dole on the D405.

If you don't want to return to Dole, leave Arc-et-Senans on the D17 for **Liesle**. Continue on the D12 to **Byans-sur-Doubs**. Take the D13 and then the D400 to reach the **Grottes d'Osselle** (30 kilometres) (*9am to 7pm in summer;* ☎ *03 81 63 62 90*). After visiting the grottos, follow the directions for the next leg: from Dole to Besançon.

---

14. The Doubs

Total distance: 130 km
Number of legs: 2
Level of difficulty: 🚲 🚲
Diagrams: pp 95, 103
Maps: A8, A9

Leg from Dole to Besançon: 65 km

Leaving Dole, take the D973 for Besançon and then take a little road
to the right for Brevans. In the village, get onto the Rue du Château-
d'eau and cross the bridges over the canal and the Doubs. Follow the
D244 to **Falletans**. Then take the road that climbs towards Rochefort.
Before the village, turn right on the D76 to **Nenon, Eclans, Our,
Etrepiney, Rans** and **Fraisans**. Take the D228 to **Salans** and **Roset-
Fluans**. At the church, take the D408 on the left to **Fluans** and the
Grottes d'Osselle.

The Osselle grotto chambers, discovered in the 13th century, served
as a priests' refuge and chapel during the French Revolution. Its
chambers are in different shapes and offer a large variety of naturally
coloured crystallization. A stone bridge built in 1751 allows visitors to
cross an underground river. As in any grotto, the air is cold (13° C),
especially for a cyclist in shorts. So cover up. Lock your bike in the
parking lot and go to the reception to find out about tour schedules.

Continue towards Besançon on the D400 and then the D13. Continue
on the D106 for **Grandfontaine** and ride down into the village as far as
the Rue de Besançon. Then take the D106 for **Avanne** and Besançon.
Enter Besançon on the D106. Be very careful, this is a big city! Take
the bicycle path that leads downtown. Cross the de la République
bridge (you'll have to walk your bike) to get to the tourist office, which
you absolutely must visit. It is very well-organized and offers a wealth
of indispensable information on the city and all of the Franche-Comté.

Leg from Besançon to Rougemont: 65 km

In **Besançon**, don't miss the **Citadelle de Vauban**, whose ramparts and
spectacular panorama of the city and Doubs valley make it a major
tourist attraction. To climb up to it, take a deep breath and start up the
street behind the Cathédrale Saint-Jean. The hill is a real challenge!
Take a break at the amazing astronomical clock, with 21 mechanisms

PRACTICAL INFORMATION ON BESANÇON

Population
120,000 *Bisontins*

Tourist office: Place de la 1re Armée-Française, 2500 Besançon, ☎ 03 81 80 92 55, ☏ 03 81 80 58 30

Bicycle shops
Cycles Gitane, 100 Rue Dole, ☎ 03 81 52 70 18
Véloland, 4 Rue Chalet, ☎ 03 81 53 51 54
Chauvez, 76 Rue Vesoul, ☎ 03 81 50 45 86

Market
Tuesdays, Fridays and Saturdays

Major events: Foire Comtoise (county fair, May); Festival de Jazz (late June and early July); Festival International de Musique – contest of young orchestra leaders (September)

Specialties: Trout with yellow wine, pike with Jura wine, Cancoillotte (soft, ripened cheese), pâté *en croûte*

Access from Paris: A6, A36, E60; by train TGV, Gare de Lyon to Besançon.

Map
IGN no. 38

and 60 faces marking hours, days, months, moons, tides and movements of the planets. There's lots to see inside the citadel walls, so count on a least an hour-long visit.

You absolutely must spend some time in the old section of town, crisscrossed with narrow streets and crowded with old houses; Victor Hugo and the Lumière brothers were born there. The Musée des Beaux-Arts houses works by the biggest names in paintings. Finally, to give your feet a break, consider a cruise of the Doubs, complete with commentary.

The route from Besançon to Baume-les-Dames zigzags along both sides of the Doubs. Pay attention to road signs because you don't want to end up on the Route Nationale. This portion of the tour runs alongside the river and offers pretty views (boats going through locks).

Note that there are few hotels in Rougemont proper. To find out about lodging in the Rougemont area, ask at the tourist office in Besançon or Baume-les-Dames. You'll probably have to stay in a neighbouring village, so it's important to plan ahead for this part of the tour.

Leave Besançon on the N57 for Lausanne (the river is on your left and the citadel on your right). Make sure you exit Besançon through the Porte Taillée, built during the Roman era. Right after the gate, turn left off of the Route Nationale (use caution) towards for Lamalate. Be careful! This small road is easy to miss. Take the D411 along the Doubs to **Chalèze**.

Then take the D323 to **Arcier, Corcelle** and **Vaire-Arcier**. In the village, take the Rue de l'Église and follow the signs for Besançon. Cross the bridge and proceed on the D266 on the other side of the Doubs to **Deluz** and **Laissey**. Take the D277 towards Baume-les-Dames. In **Ougney,** cross the Doubs again and continue on the D277 to **Esnans** and Beaume-les-Dames. The road runs alongside the river and canal. Cross the bridge into **Baume-les-Dames**.

Nestled amid five hills, this small peaceful village begs to be explored on foot. Legend holds that the young Saint Odile, patron saint of Alsace, took refuge in the Baume-les-Nonnes abbey and there recovered her sight. In the 13th century, the town's wealth derived from the abbey. Nowadays, it operates several small industries, including the famous (among smokers) Ropp pipes. Sample the "Petit Dormois", the local cheese. The tour now leaves the Doubs, so take the opportunity to enjoy a last picnic on the riverbank.

PRACTICAL INFORMATION ON BAUME-LES-DAMES

Population
5,800 *Baumois*

? **Tourist office:** 25110 Baume-les-Dames BP 101, ☎ 03 81 84 27 98

✕ **Specialty:** Petit Dormois cheese

Map
IGN no. 38

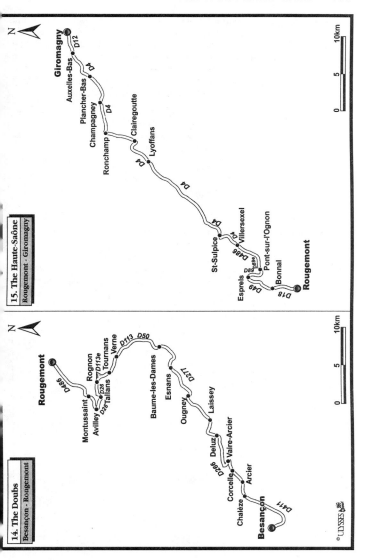

15. The Haute-Saône
Rougemont - Giromagny

Giromagny
D12
Auxelles-Bas
D4
Plancher-Bas
Champagney
D4
Claingoutte
Ronchamp
D4
Lyoffans
D4
D4
D4
Villersexel
St-Sulpice
D9
Pont-sur-l'Ognon
D486
D89
Esprels
D9
Bonnal
D18
Rougemont

N 0 5 10km

14. The Doubs
Besançon - Rougemont

Rougemont
D9
Montussaint
Rognon
D113e
Avilley
D26
Tournans
Tallans
Verne
D113 D50
Baume-les-Dames
Esnans
D271
Ougney
Laissey
D683
Deluz
Vaire-Arcier
Corcelle
Arcier
Chalèze
D411
Besançon

N 0 5 10km

© ULYSSES

Take the D50 out of Baume-les-Dames towards Rougemont, Clerval and Autechaux. Stay on the D50 for about five kilometres. Be careful, because traffic is heavy and the hill fairly steep. Get off the D50 and turn left towards **Verne** and the D113. Continue to **Tournans** and take the D113a towards **Rognon** and **Avilley**. At the bottom of the wonderful descent, take the D26 to Avilley. Then take the D486 towards **Montussaint** and Rougemont. Enter Rougemont.

---

15. The Haute-Saône

Total distance:	60 km
Number of legs:	1
Level of difficulty:	🚲 🚲 🚲
Diagram:	p 103
Maps:	A9, A10

Leg from Rougemont to Giromagny: 60 km

Rougemont, a pretty little town in the Ognon valley, has a long history. Julius Caesar battled there against the German Ariovistus. Nowadays, visitors can view a good selection of heritage sites, including the Couvent des Cordelliers, a convent, and the 15th-century Maison

---

PRACTICAL INFORMATION ON ROUGEMONT

Population
1,279 *Rubrimontains*

? **Tourist office:** Mairie, 25680 Rougemont, ☎ 03 81 86 90 06, ⋇ 03 81 86 95 72

Market
Fridays

Major events: Saint-Jean fireworks (June 23); Fête du Parc (July)

Specialties: *Rocher Rubrimontrain* (almond meringue), *Jésus en brioche* (pastry), ham *à la crème*

Map
IGN no. 30

Philibert de Molans. Be careful! The climb to the convent is steep, and the descent just as bad. Better to go on foot. The Maison d'Autrefois depicts the life of peasants of long ago, while the Château de Vorget (18th century) is next to the Porte du Moulin (gate).

Take the D18 out of Rougemont towards Bonnal. Enjoy the pleasant descent into the **Vallée de Bonnal**, a recreation area on the Ognon. It has a big campground and offers canoeing and kayaking. Then head towards Lure and Villersexel on the D89e as far as **Esprel**. Next, take the D89 to **Pont-sur-Ognon**. At the village's old washhouse, turn left towards Villersexel via the D89e. At the D486 junction, follow the signs for Villersexel and enter the village. **Villersexel** is a good example of a small Franche-Comté village spread around its castle. Take the D486 out of the village towards Lure. Keep to the right to head towards **Saint-Sulpice** and the D4. Follow the D4 to **Lyoffans**, where the Ballons des Vosges become visible. Go through the village towards Héricout, then turn left and proceed to Ronchamp on the D4. You'll have to make a final effort, because this section of the route is a long rise. Cross the bridge and enter **Ronchamp**.

There will be more architecture students than cyclists on the Ronchamp hill because the abrupt one-kilometre climb is a real thigh-buster and the Chapelle Notre-Dame-du-Haut is one of the· best examples of French architect Le Corbusier's design concepts. To get there, climb the D264, across from the church on the square. You won't be disappointed!

To get out of Ronchamp, take the N19 for one kilometre, following the signs for Belfort. Then take the D4 to **Champagney** and Giromagny. The road goes through more verdant landscapes and includes some good climbs. You're following the Route des Village Fleuris, literally the flowering villages routes. Stay on it as far as **Plancher-Bas**. The road number changes in **Auxelles-Bas**, becoming the D12. Proceed on the D12 to **Giromagny**. Follow the signs for the tourist office on Rue du Parc-du-Paradis-des-Loups.

You're now in the **Parc Naturel Régional Ballons des Vosges**. Giromagny, like other communities in the park, draws hiking enthusiasts; kilometres of roads and trails are marked for walking, horseback riding and mountain-biking.

From Giromagny, you can climb up to the **Ballon d'Alsace** pass. There are superb vistas all along the way. The altitude is 1,178 metres and the distance to cover, 16.5 kilometres.

Before leaving this lovely region, be sure to sample some of the regional specialties and produce, like crayfish, Munster cheese, bilberry pie, Vosges candy, mineral waters, etc.

PRACTICAL INFORMATION ON GIROMAGNY

Population
3,794 *Giromagniens*

Tourist office: Parc du Paradis-des-Loups, 90200 Giromagny, ☎ 03 84 29 09 00

Market
Saturdays

Major events: Feu de la Saint-Jean (fireworks and dancing, July 13); Fête de la Montagne au Ballon d'Alsace (mountain festival, August).

Specialties: *Épaule du Ballon* (stuffed lamb shoulder), trout with almonds, deep-fried carp, bilberry pie, *Belflore* (local pastry), farmer's cheese

Map
IGN no. 31

ALSACE

The Alsace wine route, called the **Route des Vins d'Alsace**, extends along a 120-kilometre stretch of the Rhine, a dream landscape set on the first versants of the Vosges mountain range. It is one on the most charming country routes in France. The tour that follows explores gorgeous vinicultural villages of brightly coloured, half-timbered houses, with flower-filled lanes, delightful signs, Renaissance fountains, Romanesque churches of yellow and red sandstone, splendid town halls — in short, museum-villages nestled into sun-drenched hillsides of ripening grapes. Here, another world opens up to the cyclist who appreciates the picturesque and the traditional. However, to discover these treasures, you must necessarily climb hills and share the road with cars.

The tour here outlined need not necessarily be taken as such. The order of the legs can be easily changed. Take your time; let yourself be charmed by the beauty and atmosphere of the villages, so attractive with vintners' signs adorning houses where tasting-cellars await. Alsace is steeped in vinic folklore. Certainly it is in autumn that the golden-hued landscape is most captivating, livened by the activity of harvesters, tractors, and visitors.

Alsace has not been spared by war; it has changed nationality five times since Louis XIV. The Middle Ages were a particularly prestigious period of Alsatian history. The inhabitants of this romantic land carved their prosperity into stone, wood, and iron. The church, an important consumer of wine, encouraged viniculture. Due to the proximity of the Rhine, Alsatian wines were easily exported. These remained the most sought-after vintages of the Holy Roman Empire until the 17th century. Alsatian vineyards today produce luminous white wines, fruity and aromatic, each designated according to the type of grape from which it is pressed.

The Route des Vins is the soul of Alsace. Before discovering its treasures, the tour begins at **Giromagny** and takes you through the **Parc des Ballons des Vosges**. Hang on to your handlebars because the road is quite demanding. From **Masevaux**, the Joffre road climbs steadily into the mountains in a succession of curves, reaching the **Col du Hundsrück** at 748 metres. Now keep a firm hold on your brakes, because the road descends in a series of S-turns through woods, opening up before you on the Vallée de la Thur, at **Thann**.

Alsatians value their lore. Like many other villages, Masevaux and Thann are steeped in poetic legend. *Thann* signifies "fir" in German. A chapel was erected in a fir grove, the site of a miracle. The Gothic collegiate church of Saint-Thiébaut, built on this same site, is the most ornate in Alsace. Its portal is adorned by more than 450 figures. Its bell tower is of interlacing stonework, its pews of sculpted oak, and its stained glass work dates back to the 15th century.

Thann is the departure point of Alsace's Route des Vins, or wine route, a magnificent road, winding and hilly. Although Alsace is the smallest region of France, it has the third highest population density. Opportunities to rest and resupply are plenty. In every village and town, you will find a fountain, a café and cascades of white, red, and pink geraniums. From village to village the landscape unfolds before you, full of colour and overflowing with flowers. Even in the vineyards almost every row of grapes is headed by a rosebush, for practical as well as aesthetic purposes. The rosebushes assist in the early detection of parasites.

The Route des Vins offers many sightseeing opportunities. Among the most famous are the weather station of **Trois Épis** (altitude: 650 m), where the Virgin is said to have appeared brandishing three ears of corn, and the sacred mountain of the Alsatians, **Mont Sainte-Odile** (altitude: 764 m).

If you are an art lover, set aside extra time for the stop in **Colmar**. The city proclaims itself the best-preserved in Alsace. It is the birthplace of Bartholdi, celebrated sculptor of *Petit Vigneron de Colmar* and the world-famous Statue of Liberty. The Petite Venise (little Venice) quarter will charm you with its array of boats moored under balconies.

Riquewihr appears in the middle of the tour. Viniculture has remained the base of the city's activity for five centuries. The town constitutes an ensemble of 15th- to 18th-century houses unique in the world. From the **Château de Kintzheim**, and its Volerie des Aigles (eagle eyrie), a beautiful road takes you to the **Forteresse du Haut-Kœnigsbourg** (altitude: 757 m). Of the Romanesque period, and built in the tradition of imperial castles, the fortress boasts imposing red sandstone walls.

Alsace is wine country to be sure, but the region is also an important producer of beer and sauerkraut. The last portion of the route leading to Strasbourg crosses agricultural fields of cabbage, onion, and hops.

Strasbourg, a European capital and a large, animated city surrounding the arms of the Ill, is reached by bicycle path. It took four centuries to erect the Cathédrale Notre-Dame, the tallest cathedral in France. Its spire towers above a pedestrian quarter surrounded by beautiful buildings like the Cerf pharmacy (1268) and the famous Kammerzell house (1467 and 1589). Strasbourg is very picturesque, with its Quartier de la Petite France and its covered bridges.

Thanks in part to its wines, Alsace is one of the most epicurean regions of France: sauerkraut, delicatessen (the classic Alsatian plate), *Bæckœffe* (baker's oven) composed of three meats and potatoes, onion pie, *tarte flambée* (thin bread pastry garnished with cream, bacon, and onions), Munster (flavourful cheese), fruit pies, *Kougelhopf* (sugar-dusted brioche), and Bretzel in a double knot shape that is the perfect complement to beer and Alsace's famous foie gras (goose liver pâté), invented in Strasbourg in 1780.

This tour outlines a network of very busy, smaller roads dotted with sumptuous villages, local museums, and *winstub*, where the best vintages are served up in pitchers in a simple and convivial atmosphere. Village traditions are maintained with vigour and are deservingly perpetuated by many celebrations infused with the joviality and singing intonations of the Alsatian accent. Let loose your appetites!

16. THE ALSACE TOUR

Total distance: 195 km
Number of legs: 4
Level of difficulty: 🚲 🚲 🚲
Diagrams: pp 113, 117
Maps: A10 to A12

Leg from Giromagny to Thann: 30 km

Leave **Giromagny** (see p 106 for practical information on Giromagny) by taking the D12 toward **Rougegoutte** and Mulhouse. Follow this road to **Etueffont**. Then take the D2 to **Rougemont-le-Château** (long ascent and descent). Continue on the D2 toward Masevaux. The road rises, and, on the right, you can see the Rougemont golf course. Enter **Masevaux** by the D110. Continue straight toward the fountain in the square.

From Giromagny, an alternative route is to climb to the col of the **Ballon d'Alsace**. All along this road there are superb views. The distance to the pass is 16.5 km and the altitude there is 1,178 m. You may choose this route to get to Masevaux and connect with the **Route des Vins d'Alsace** there. Including the climb to the pass, the distance from Giromagny to Masevaux is 40 km.

Masevaux is a small commercial town and the principal municipality of the canton of La Doller. Its origins go back to the 12th century. According to legend, the Comte Mason, the count who was the nephew of Atticus and the father of Sainte Odile, constructed a castle on the hill of Schlossberg and founded an abbey when he was struck by the tragic death of his son. Masevaux was established around the abbey and the castle. Its fountains and older buildings attest to the town's opulent past.

Be sure that your brakes are in good condition before undertaking the ascent on the Joffre road to the Col du Hundsrück (Hundsrück pass). This scenic road was built by the army during World War I to ensure communication between the valleys of La Doller and La Thur. During the winter of 1944-1945, it reassumed its military role, being the only access route to Thann.

From the fountain, follow the directions for the D14b, the Joffre road, toward Houppach, Bourbach-le-Haut, and the Col de Hundsrück

(altitude: 748 m). The road climbs and winds to the hamlet of
Houppach, then slowly descends to **Bourbach-le-Haut**. Continue your
ascent to the **Col du Hundsrück** via the D14b. There is a park here for
picnicking, or you can get something to eat at the inn. Your well-
deserved descent begins in a beautiful forest. Glimpses of the **Vallée
de la Thur** are visible through openings in the woods. Enter **Thann** via
the N66. Use the bicycle path.

More and more Alsatian villages are developing into small cities; be
vigilant for traffic is heavy. Cities have reserved lanes for cyclists: use
them. Despite the traffic, this is the region of France in which I
encountered the largest number of bicycle travellers.

PRACTICAL INFORMATION ON THANN

Population
7,800 *Thannois*

Tourist office: 6 Place Joffre, 68800 Thann, ☎ 03 89 37 96 20,
⇰ 03 89 37 04 58

Bicycle shops
Kippelen Cycles, ☎ 03 89 37 52 01

Market
Saturday

Major events: Fête de la Crémation des 3 Sapins (celebration of the
cremation of the three firs, June 30); Journées Musicales (music days,
August)

Specialties: river fish, Alsatian wines, mineral water

Access from Paris: A4-E25-N66; by train: Gare de l'Est Basel line,
Mulhouse stop, transfer for Thann

Map
IGN no. 31

Leg from Thann to Turckheim: 60 km

During the months of July and August, town criers wearing the
Hapsburg colours march through Thann announcing current events.

Leave Thann via the D35 toward Vieux-Thann and Cernay. Follow the bicycle path to enter **Cernay.**

Leave Cernay on the D5 toward **Uffholtz, Vieil Armand,** and **Soultz,** following the Route des Vins toward Guebwiller. From Soultz, continue on the D430 to **Guebwiller.** Ride to the Eglise Notre-Dame at the town entrance. You may continue straight on Avenue de la République to the tourist office in the town centre. Stretched along the Lauch, Guebwiller was prosperous in the 19th century thanks to a thriving textile industry. The town's three churches are Romanesque (10th century), Gothic (14th century), and neoclassical (18th century).

Return to the Eglise Notre-Dame and take the street just in front of it toward Colmar via the Route des Vins. At the traffic light, continue in the direction of Colmar. At the traffic circle, take the D5 toward **Orschwihr** via the Route des Vins.

Continue on the D5 to **Soultzmatt.** This road offers a pleasant descent and a panoramic view of surrounding vineyards. To visit the charming town of **Rouffach,** turn right. Its Place de la République is bordered by Renaissance buildings and the old Tour des Sorcières (witches' tower). Take note of the Gothic Église Notre-Dame and the lovely oriel-windowed houses.

After your visit to Rouffach, return to the square, and follow the D18b. Ride through Soultzmatt (mineral water source) to the mountain (about 1.5 km). Soultzmatt is situated at the foot of the most elevated *Grand Cru* (vinery plantation) on the Route des Vins, which we now momentarily leave for an excursion through the woods. The forests of the Vosges mountain range, of various arboreal species, are an important resource for local people. Chestnut trees, for example, provide the vineyardists with vine-props and perches. *(Parc Naturel Régional des Ballons des Vosges, Maison du Parc, 1 Cour de l'Abbaye, 68140 Munster, ☎ 03 89 77 90 20, ≈ 03 89 77 90 30).*

Take the D18bis in the direction of **Osenbach** and Munster. Continue on the D40III toward Munster, Soultzbach, and **Wintzfelden.** The road rises into the forest. Proceed on the D40. At the intersection, take the D1v, which descends to **Gueberschwihr.** With a magnificent view of the vineyards, villages, and plains along the Rhine, the road approaches Husseren-les-Châteaux. You will appreciate the calm and cool as you cycle through the woods of Westhalten. The road climbs for approximately eight kilometres, but then it descends for five kilometres! As well as bypassing the busy Route Nationale between

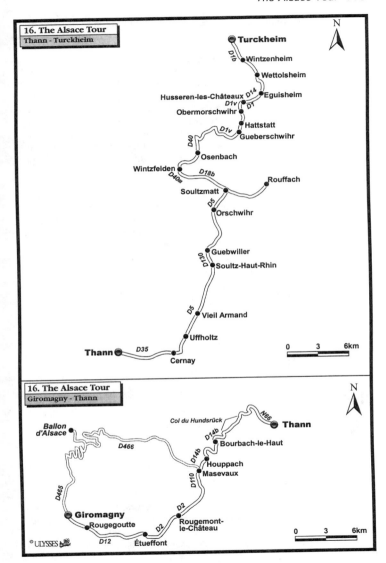

16. The Alsace Tour
Thann - Turckheim

N

Turckheim
D1b
Wintzenheim
Wettolsheim
Husseren-les-Châteaux   D14   Eguisheim
D1v   D1
Obermorschwihr
Hattstatt
D1v
D40   Gueberschwihr
Osenbach
Wintzfelden   D18b
D40m   Rouffach
Soultzmatt
D5
Orschwihr

Guebwiller
D130   Soultz-Haut-Rhin

D5   Vieil Armand

Uffholtz
Thann   D35
Cernay

0   3   6km

16. The Alsace Tour
Giromagny - Thann

N

Ballon d'Alsace
Col du Hundsrück   N66   **Thann**
D466   D14b
Bourbach-le-Haut
D14b
Houppach
D110   Masevaux
D465
Giromagny
Rougegoutte   D2
Rougemont-le-Château
D2
© ULYSSES   D12   Étueffont

0   3   6km

Rouffach and Gueberschwir, the D1v provides a magnificent view as it leaves the forest.

Continue on the D1v, the Route des Vins, toward **Hattstatt**, Obermorschwihr, and Husseren-les-Châteaux. At the crossroad turn left onto the D1, which climbs through vineyards to **Obermorschwihr** and **Husseren-les-Châteaux**. Keep travelling on the D1 to the D14 (the highest point of the Route des Vins). Just before it, on the left, is the turnoff for the forest road of the "five castles". Follow the D14 as it descends to **Eguisheim**. This little vinicultural village, enclosed in its ramparts, has preserved vestiges of a feudal castle. A Renaissance fountain pays homage to the most famous count of Eguisheim, Pope Leo IX.

Next take the D1bis to **Wettolsheim**, cycle through the village, and continue on toward **Wintzenheim**. While riding in the village, use the bicycle path. At the first traffic light, turn right toward **Turckheim**. Follow the "blue bicycles": they lead directly to old Turckheim. Inside Turckheim's medieval gates a traditional night watchman sings through his rounds every night at ten o'clock. You may join him; he leaves from the Corps de Garde.

PRACTICAL INFORMATION ON TURCKHEIM

Population
3,600 *Turckheimiens*

Tourist office: Corps de Garde, 68230 Turckheim, ☎ 03 89 27 38 44, ⇥ 03 89 80 83 22

Bicycle shops
Grosshenny Cycles, 84 Grand' rue, ☎ 03 89 27 06 36

Major events: Fête au Pays du Brand (early August); Fête du Vin (wine festival, late July)

Map
IGN no. 31

From Turckheim you can make a pleasant excursion to the weather station, **Trois Épis**, crouched in a fir grove on a plateau above Turckheim (altitude: 650 m). From this height the view is imposing. If you enjoy hiking, there are several marked trails here of about an hour's duration.

Leave plenty of time for your stay in **Colmar**, a typical Alsatian town of narrow streets and half-timbered houses. Colmar is home to a famous museum, the Musée d'Unterlinden (one of the most prestigious in France), which houses the Alsatian masterpiece: *Issenheim Altarpiece*, painted by Mathias Grünewald. Equally worth seeing are the Maison des Têtes, the Maison Pfister, the Maison Adolph, and the Musée Bartholdi, birthplace of the famous sculptor (Statue of Liberty, *Lion de Belfort*). The old Quartier des Tanneurs (tanners' quarter) opens onto Petite Venise (little Venice) mirrored by the waters of the Lauch.

PRACTICAL INFORMATION ON COLMAR

Population
65,000 *Colmariens*

Tourist office: 4 Rue des Unterliden, 68000 Colmar, ☎ 03 89 20 68 92, ☏ 03 89 41 34 13

Bicycle shops
La Cyclothèque, 31 Route d'Ingersheim, ☎ 03 89 79 14 18
Cycles Geiswiller, 6 Boul du Champ de Mars, ☎ 03 89 41 30 59
Cycles Meyer, 6 Rue du Pont Rouge, ☎ 03 89 27 41 13

Market
Thursday and Saturday

Major events: International music festival (July), Regional wine fair (week of August 15)

Speciality: Alsatian wines

Access from Paris: A4-E25; by train: Gare de l'Est-Strasbourg-Colmar

Map
IGN no. 31

Leg from Turckheim to Barr: 65 km

Leave Turckheim by riding to the end of the parking lot and taking the D10v toward **Niedermorchwihr**. The road rises steeply. Enjoy the wonderful view. Continue on the D11ll to **Ingersheim**. Proceed on the D10. At the traffic circle, go toward Riquewihr and Ribeauvillé. A short

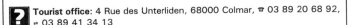

distance past **Bennwihr** and **Mittelwihr**, look for the D3, which takes you to the gates of Riquewihr. Leave your bicycle outside; the town's tortuous streets of old paving stones are overrun in the high season.

The old city of **Riquewihr**, a veritable open-air museum, has successfully preserved its medieval character. Grande Rue rises a gentle slope from the town hall (at the lower gate), crosses the town, and opens on Le Dolder, the high gate of the inner enclosure. Here you will discover the belfry, the city emblem; the Tour des Voleurs (thieves' tower) with its torture chamber; the Château des Ducs de Wurtemberg, today converted into the Musée d'Histoire des "PTT" (postal service) d'Alsace; and sumptuous bourgeois houses dating from 1494 to 1686. The Association des Commerçants (merchants' association) has a guided tour every day at 5:30pm. Don't miss it!

PRACTICAL INFORMATION ON RIQUEWIHR

Population
1,050 *Riquewihriens*

? **Tourist office:** 2 Rue de la 1re Armée, 68340 Riquewihr, ☎ 03 89 47 80 80, ⟿ 03 89 47 88 96

Major Events: *Feu de la Saint-Jean* (June); *Fête du Vin* (wine festival, September 14-15)

Specialties: Sauerkraut, Riesling

Map
IGN no. 31

The vineyards that surround the town produce the whole gamut of Alsatian vintages, notably Riesling, the king of wines. At Hugel, you can see the "Caterine": the oldest wine cask in the world still in use, dating from 1775. The harvests generally occur at the beginning of October. If you would like to stay in Riquewihr during this period, be sure to reserve a room.

Leave Riquewihr by one of its gates and follow the D3ll and the D1b to **Ribeauvillé**. This little town, resplendent with old towers and ancient fountains, is famous for its large vineyards. On the first Sunday in September, at the Fête des Ménétriers (festival of fiddlers), a village fountain flows with wine.

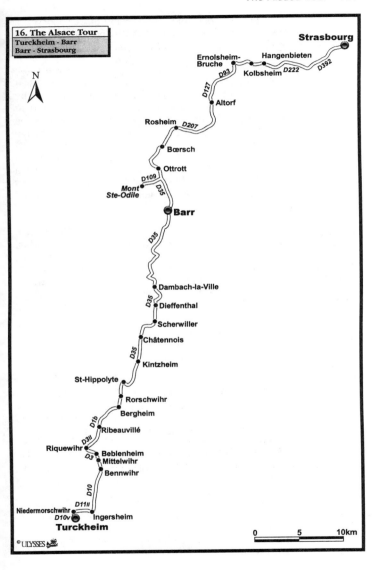

16. The Alsace Tour
Turckheim - Barr
Barr - Strasbourg

N

Strasbourg

Ernolsheim-Bruche
Hangenbieten
Kolbsheim
D93
D222
D392
D127
Altorf
Rosheim *D207*
Bœrsch
Ottrott
D109
Mont Ste-Odile
D35
Barr
D35
Dambach-la-Ville
D35
Dieffenthal
Scherwiller
Châtennois
D35
Kintzheim
St-Hippolyte
Rorschwihr
Bergheim
D1b
Ribeauvillé
D3II
Riquewihr
Beblenheim
D3
Mittelwihr
Bennwihr
D10
Niedermorschwihr
D11II
D10v
Ingersheim
Turckheim

0   5   10km

© ULYSSES

Leave Ribeauvillé by the D1bis, following the Route des Vins as it climbs toward **Bergheim, Rorschwihr,** and **Saint-Hippolyte.** Proceed on the Route des Vins in the direction of **Châtenois.**

To reach the **Château Fort du Haut-Kœnigsbourg** *(information,* ☎ *03 88 82 50 60),* you must take the road from **Kieintzeim,** the most accessible route. The eight-kilometre distance may be broken up by several stops. On a visit to the Volerie des Aigles, the eagle eyrie at the medieval castle of Kieintzeim, for example, you can watch large birds of prey flying free. Further up the road there is a forest enclave of about 300 wild Barbary apes. Finally, at the Château du Haut-Kœnigsbourg, you may visit a vast fortress which, incinerated in the 12th century, was rebuilt at the beginning of this century. With a guide you can cross the drawbridge and walk through castle rooms housing a collection of furniture and armaments from the 15th and 17th centuries.

Back in Kieintzeim, take the D35 toward **Scherwiller** and **Dieffenthal,** and enter **Dambach-la-ville** through its magnificent medieval gates. Cross the village, and exit through the other gates of its rampart, following the signs to Barr. The Romanesque and Gothic Chapelle Saint-Sébastien is in the heart of the vinery, on the left. Enter **Barr** via the D35. Located at the foot of Mont Sainte-Odile, this little industrial town is the lower-Rhine capital of Alsatian wine. A wine fair is held here around the 14th of July.

Leg from Barr to Strasbourg: 40 km

Odile, patron saint of Alsace, founded a convent perched on a butte of red sandstone in the 7th century. Her mortal remains reside in a half-Romanesque, half-Gothic chapel. Mont Sainte-Odile is the sacred mountain of the Alsatians and its enormous monastery attracts large crowds. Note that this bicycle excursion is very difficult.

Exit Barr by the D35 in the direction of Rosheim and Strasbourg. The road rises for about two kilometres. Keep riding on the D35 to **Ottrott** (its castles are very important remnants of the 12th and 13th centuries), **Boersch,** and Rosheim.

PRACTICAL INFORMATION ON BARR

Population
4,836 *Barrois*

Tourist office: place de l'Hôtel de Ville, 67140 Barr, ☎ 03 88 08 66 65, ⇥ 03 88 08 57 27

Bicycle shops
Cycle Motsch, 41 Grand'Rue, ☎ 03 88 08 95 20

Market
Saturday

Major events: Feu de la Saint-Jean (July 22); Fête du Vin et des Escargots (festival of wine and escargot, around July 14); Fête des Vendanges (harvest festival, early October)

Specialties: foie gras (goose-liver pâté), spice bread, leather tannery, the great wines of Kirchberg

Map
IGN no. 31

Enter **Rosheim**. The oak well at the Place de la Mairie dates from 1605. The Maison Païenne, the pagan house, is the oldest building in Alsace. The Église Saint-Pierre et Saint-Paul is a typical monument of Alsatian Romanesque architecture. Take the time to visit it before you cross the village and leave Rosheim. Just past the gateway turn right onto the D207 in the direction of **Bischoffsheim**. **Krautergersheim**, the largest producer of cabbage and sauerkraut in Alsace, is five kilometres down the D207. You may be overwhelmed by the odour as you approach the town. At any rate, there is cabbage as far as the eye can see...

From the D207, take the D127 on the left toward **Griesheim** and **Altorf**. Continue on the D127 in the direction of Dachstein. Immediately after the level crossing, turn right toward **Ernolshein**, **Kolbershein**, and **Hangenbieten**, following the D93. This beautiful road through farmland and fields of grain, crosses the Bruche several times. Continue toward **Strasbourg** on the D222. Enter the city via the D392. Use the bicycle path. Pass under the parapet, and follow the signs for downtown and the tourist office at Place de la Cathédrale.

PRACTICAL INFORMATION ON STRASBOURG

Population
252,300 *Strasbourgeois*

Tourist office: Place de la Cathédrale, 67000 Strasbourg, ☎ 03 88 52 28 28, ☎ 03 88 52 28 29

Market
Tuesday through Saturday

Major events: music festival (June); jazz festival (July)

Specialties: Alsatian wines, foie gras, sausage, sauerkraut, onion pie, *tarte flambée*, beer

Access from Paris: A4-E25; by train: Gare de l'Est to Strasbourg

Map
IGN no. 12

For an overview of 20 centuries of Alsatian history you can attend the sound and light show presented at Cathédrale Notre-Dame. This building of red Vosges sandstone is without a doubt the most marvellous monument in Strasbourg. Its exceptional astronomical clock strikes every day at half past noon. Ask at the tourist office about the guided walking tour of the city. You may end your stay in Strasbourg with a river trip, a pleasant way to explore the city's old buildings reflected in the branches of the Ill.

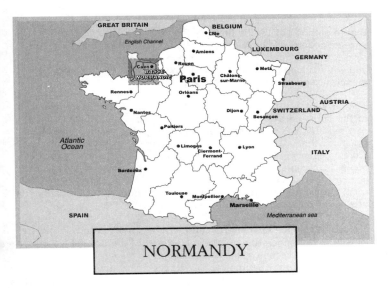

NORMANDY

For a breath of fresh air, head north to the departments of **Calvados** and **La Manche** (the French name of the English Channel), in Basse-Normandie. Between land and sea, these are two of the most invigorating tours you could take. You are invited to travel this bucolic corner of the world: Normandy is a truly rural region of France and agriculture is its main activity. At the pace of a bicycle tour, you will discover rustic Norman villages in a pastoral setting.

During the course of this tour, you will have occasion to sample exquisite Norman cuisine: soft camembert and pont-l'évêque cheeses, fresh oysters or mussels in rich cream sauce, leg of salt-meadow mutton or Vallée D'Auge chicken. All may be sprinkled with aromatic cider, or cut with Calvados, in the *trou normand* style... So many delicious foods justify the trip of themselves!

The hundred or so kilometres that make up these two tours explore a Normandy different from that of the Allied landings of 1944: one that is Romanesque, Viking, English and French. From the shore to the back country, beautiful surprises appear around every bend in the road: imposing flamboyant cathedrals, sumptuous manor houses, refined castles, elegant abbeys, villas, perfumed gardens and fine-sand beaches.

Before setting out on the first leg of the tour, a loop that leads you into the countryside of **Auge**, you land in **Ouistreham**, a large seaside resort. On the other side of the Estuaire de l'Orne, **Cabourg** seduces you with its long beach, chic casino, and the prestigious Grand Hôtel, immortalised by author Marcel Proust.

The back country, amid apple orchards (symbolic fruit!), is the realm of the purebred. Around sturdy, half-timbered manor houses, mares and stallions are raised for breeding, riding, and racing. Villages in Auge are announced by the stone bell towers of their little churches. From a distance, Saint-Pierre-sur-Dives is signalled by the three spires of its 11th-century monastic church. A large market is held in the heart of this village every Monday at the Halles de Saint-Pierre. The framing of the market building, which dates from the 13th century, was assembled with 290,000 chestnut dowel pins!

The tour leads next to **Thury-Harcourt**, in a region of rolling hills known as Suisse Normande (the most elevated part of the Bocage Norman, in the southern section of the department of La Manche). The moment arrives to confront some uphill grades! The tour, now more challenging, traverses a peaceful, lush oasis in the Orne valley. Through rich prairie pastures, the result of elevated levels of rainfall, the route quietly retraces the little roads of Bessin... is not the dairy cow the symbol of Normandy?

Bayeux, in the heart of Bessin, is an ideal departure point for a trek in the footsteps of a noted duke of Normandy, William the Conqueror. The Tapisserie de Bayeux records an important page of his history: *The Conquest of England in 1066* (a large page — the tapestry measures 70 metres by 55 metres!). Unique in the world, the tapestry formerly adorned the Cathédrale Notre-Dame de Bayeux.

The tour toward the Côte de Nacre and the beaches of the Allied landings (since D-Day, renamed Sword, Juno, Utah, Gold, and Omaha) begins at Bayeux, the first liberated city in World War II. This emotional journey, along high cliffs charged with historical significance, may represent, to some, a sort of pilgrimage. The Battle of Normandy was marked by 77 days of combat between June 6th and August 22nd, 1944. In visits to the numerous sites, cemeteries, and museums dedicated to the liberating soldiers you will be reminded of the terrible violence of the war and the toll, in loss of life, it took.

The tour leaves the **Côte de Nacre** for the rural interior. **Parc Régional des Marais du Cotentin** allows you to discover, over the course of one leg of the tour, a very special landscape. While riding through polder and marshland, you come across peaceful hamlets of clay, thatched-roof houses.

A few kilometres inland from the La Manche coast, you come upon the Bocage Norman, land of prairies and small, shadowy woods. So close to the sea, the salty air is carried inland by westerly wind and fog. Charming seaside resorts with beautiful, sandy beaches alternate along the route with pleasant little towns, perched on rock, full of art and history. To conquer them, you must first attack their hill sides!

The sky caresses **Coutances**, dominated by its elegant Gothic cathedral. The climb is challenging, but your reward is at hand in the charming alleys of the town's old quarter, or, in the evening, under soft light amid the 47,000 plants of its splendid garden. A few pedal pushes from Coutances, you can visit the romantic Château de Gratot.

The tour leads next to the seaside and the very picturesque little village of **Regnéville**. All evidence indicates that the town was a very important port. Vestiges of a medieval castle, old, granite houses, and a beautiful 13th-century church attest to the town's past importance.

From atop its promontory, **Granville**, with its old fortified city, juts proudly into the sea. In the 18th and 19th centuries, *grand'pêche* (the eel fishery on the Grands Banks of Newfoundland) and oyster fishing contributed to the prosperity of the town. Since time immemorial, the fishing industry has been omnipresent here; the village carnival, born of the *grand'pêche* 150 years ago, remains one of the most popular in France. Leave your mount, many activities await you here. If time allows, why not treat yourself to a boat trip on La Granvillaise, a traditional, 19th-century fishing sailboat?

Past Cap de Granville, to the south, **Baie du Mont-Saint-Michel** opens up before you. You can observe the highest tides in Europe here. During spring tides, called *vives-eaux*, there is an almost 15-metre difference between high and low seas! Acquire a tide calendar at the tourist office. The tour hugs the coast all the way to **Avranches**, at the mouth of the Sée. Herds of salt-meadow sheep graze in pastures, adding a picturesque element to the striking panorama of Mont-Saint-Michel. As you approach the hill, the sights draws you in; you will not be able to take your eyes off it!

17. GRAND TOUR OF CALVADOS

Total distance: 240 km
Number of legs: 4
Level of difficulty: 🚲 🚲
Diagram: p 125
Map: A13

Leg from Bayeux to Ouistreham: 60 km

The Bayeux train station is located south of the city. To reach the tourist office from Place de la Gare, ride toward downtown on Boulevard Sadi-Carnot. Once in the centre of Bayeux, take Rue Larcher. The tourist office is at the Saint-Jean bridge, at the corner of Rue Saint-Jean.

PRACTICAL INFORMATION ON BAYEUX

Population
15,000 *Bayeusains*

Tourist office: Pont Saint-Jean, BP 343, 14403 Bayeux Cedex, ☎ 02 31 92 16 26, ⚐ 02 31 92 01 79

Bicycle shops
Roué, Boul. Winston Churchill, ☎ 02 31 92 27 75
Le Domesday, 20 Rue Larcher, ☎ 02 31 22 01 21

Market
Wednesday and Saturday

Major events: Marché Médiéval (medieval market, 1st weekend in July); Bal du 14 Juillet (14th of July ball)

Specialties: Sainte-Ève (pastry), porcelain, lace

Map
IGN no. 7

Bayeux, capital of Bessin, was the first city liberated by the Allies on June 7th, 1944, and fortunately it was completely spared by the war. Traditionally religious and middle-class, the town has preserved an old-fashioned atmosphere with timber-framed homes and manor houses

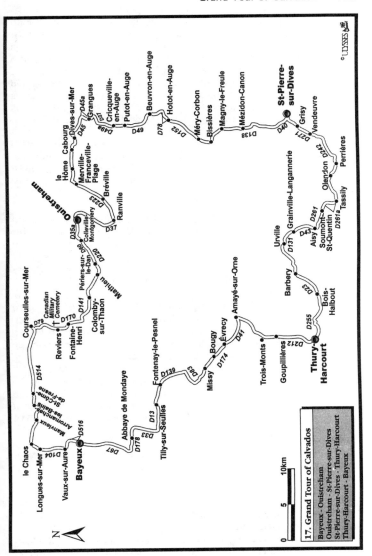

17. Grand Tour of Calvados

Bayeux - Ouistreham
Ouistreham - St-Pierre-sur-Dives
St-Pierre-sur-Dives - Thury-Harcourt
Thury-Harcourt - Bayeux

flanked by large stairwell towers. Bayeux is a city of human proportions; having no large commercial or industrial buildings, it remains linked to the rural world. Every Saturday a major market is held at Place Saint-Patrice. With the Aure flowing through the centre of the old quarter and its pedestrian malls, Bayeux is a welcoming city from which to begin your bicycle tour of Normandy. The immense and splendid Cathédrale Notre-Dame dominates the city and is unmistakable, its three spires serve as a useful landmark. Bayeux is also home to important museums that are well worth seeing.

To leave Bayeux, ride to Place Saint-Patrice. Pass Église Saint-Patrice and take the ring road towards Caen and Arromanches via the N13. Use the bicycle path. Pass the campground and then take the D516 toward Arromanches and Tracy-sur-Mer. Barely out of the city you will have the joy of riding through large, agricultural fields.

At the D513, turn left toward **Vaux-sur-Aure**. Cross the village, and continue on the D104 toward **Longues-sur-Mer**. At the traffic light, continue straight, following the signs for Batteries de Longues, where you may view the remains of a German artillery battery. It consists of well-preserved, reinforced-concrete shelters and is the only artillery station to have kept its long cannons. The visit is free.

Continue on the D104 to the high cliffs of the coast where the wind is strong and the view is superb. Sections of rock, sculpted by erosion, have detached themselves from the clay cliff to form what is called Le Chaos. A rather steep footpath leads down to the configuration. Be careful of falling and sliding rock on the descent!

You may proceed toward Cap Manvieux on the trail that runs along the cliffs. This dirt road, which is in fact part of a longer, marked excursion, is only passable in good weather, and, even then, it is best to use a mountain bike. At the end of the road, turn left onto the D514 toward **Manvieux** and ride to Tracy-sur-Mer.

In bad weather, opt for the D514 from the village of Longues-sur-Mer, by turning right at the stoplight, and ride on it all the way to **Tracy-sur-Mer**.

Continue toward Arromanches-les-Bains and Courseulles-sur-Mer on the D514. A pleasant descent offers a beautiful view of the village and the ocean. Enter **Arromanches** via the D87. This little seaside resort survived a remarkable ordeal. In 1944, an artificial port, prefabricated in England (Mulberry B), permitted up to 9,000 tons of material to be unloaded here per day for 100 days. Ships run aground at sea formed breakwaters, and hot-air blimps formed barricades, protecting the port from German air raids. The Musée du Débarquement, facing the relics of the port, provides powerful testimony to the incredible history of Port Winston, from its secret construction to the liberation of the coast.

As you leave the village, toward Courseulles-sur-Mer, do not miss the opportunity to visit the circular cinema, which "stretches" the history of Arromanches and the coast. *Le Prix de la Liberté*, a film about the Allied landings in Normandy, is projected on nine screens at once, creating a 360° image, not to mention 18 minutes of strong emotion!

A good climb on the D514 brings you to the top of the cliff that overhangs Port Winston (viewpoint indicator) and to the circular cinema. Proceed to the parking lot, leave your bicycle, and use the walkway to the cinema entrance.

After the film, return to the D514 and descend toward **Saint-Côme-de-Fresne**, where you may notice a few sheep grazing. Continue in the direction of **Courseulles-sur-Mer**. Skirt the port, following the signs for downtown and keeping left at the intersection.

Courseulles-sur-Mer, a seaside resort on the Côte de Nacre, is famous for its pleasure-boat harbour and its oysters. Here you may visit the Musée du Vieux Courseulles, the Musée des Médailles et Décorations, and the Maison de la Mer, among other sites. Don't leave without seeing the Mémorial du 1er Hussard, dedicated to Canadian soldiers, and the Croix de Lorraine, erected in memory of General de Gaulle, who returned to France June 14th, 1944.

To leave Courseulles-sur-Mer, proceed in the direction of Caen, keeping right. Pass the cemetery and take the D79 toward Reviers and Douvres. At the traffic circle, take the D170, toward Reviers and Château de Fontaine-Henri. The tour follows the Route des Moulins, litterally the mill route, a quiet, pretty little road through fields of grain.

At the intersection with the D35, turn right to visit the Canadian Military Cemetery (2,048 graves). Return to **Reviers** and continue on the D170. The undulating road snakes through a little wood along the Mue. At the little town of **Fontaine-Henri**, follow the signs to the castle. This elegant, high-roofed, Renaissance château presents a richly sculpted façade. Indoors, its rooms house a collection of antique paintings and furnishings.

After the visit, descend to the old village by doubling back, and take the D141 in the direction of **Colomby-sur-Thaon**. The road circles behind the castle and rises to the middle of the forest. Continue on the D141 to **Mathieu**. At the traffic circle, exit onto the D220 toward Dives-sur-Mer, Blainville, and Colleville. At the next traffic circle, stay on the D220. Then turn right onto the D141 toward Colleville, Blainville, and Biéville. Take the D220 again, on the left, toward Périers-sur-le-Dan and Colleville, via Rue du 7 Juin 1944.

Enter **Périers-sur-le-Dan** on the D220. At the intersection, turn left to leave the village via the D220 toward Colleville and Montgomery. At the intersection, take the D60a. The coast begins to be visible at this point. Cycle through the village of Colleville.

Proceed on the D35a to **Ouistreham**. Pass the cemetery and continue straight. From in front of the church, follow the signs for "Car Ferry", and ride straight toward the harbour-station. Take Boulevard Maritime to the tourist office, at Jardin du Casino.

Leg from Ouistreham to Saint-Pierre-sur-Dives: 70 km

Ouistreham-Riva-Bella, a large resort on the Côte de Nacre at the mouth of the Orne, is endowed with a large pleasure-craft harbour. For sea-lovers, there is bird watching, land-sailing, sailing, deep-sea fishing and swimming. There are medicinal baths, cruises on the Canal de Caen, and a wide, three-kilometre-long beach, not to mention the old city and the museums. Park your bicycle, for there is enough here to distract you for quite a while.

The Musée du Mur de l'Atlantique, housed in the Grand Blockhaus, and the Musée no. 4 Commando, facing the casino, recount the dramatic disembarkment of commandos at Ouistreham, June 6th, 1944. Sixty percent of the city was destroyed, but, fortunately, Église Saint-Samson still stands watch over the town. Erected in the 11th century, the church acted simultaneously as sanctuary and lighthouse.

To leave Ouistreham, ride to the fish market at Place du Port. Cross the canal on the little bridge facing the market. On the other side of the canal, ride along the towing-road toward the Bassin de Plaisance.

PRACTICAL INFORMATION ON OUISTREHAM

Population
8,500 *Ouistrehamais*

 Tourist bureau: Jardin du Casino, 14150 Ouistreham-Riva-Bella, ☎ 02 31 97 18 63, ⇔ 02 31 96 87 33

Bicycle shop
Vérel, 77 Av. Foch, ☎ 02 31 97 19 04

Market
Tuesday and Saturday

Major events: Fête du Port (mid-July), theme festivals: cinema, song (mid-August)

Map
IGN no. 7

Hug the banks of the Orne for about five kilometres to a large intersection, then turn left onto the D514 in the direction of Merville, Franceville, and Cabourg. At the next traffic circle, take the road toward Ranville, cross the bridge over the Orne, and enter **Longueville**. Proceed in the direction of Ranville and Troarn on the D37. Enter **Ranville**, the first liberated village of France. At the foot of its Gothic Revival church stretches a commemorative British cemetery.

At the crossroad, make a left onto the D223, and ride to **Bréville**. An important German bastion, this city was liberated June 13th, 1944. Continue toward Merville-Franceville. This quiet road reaches a plateau; horses, cows, and sheep graze peacefully in the meadow. Enter **Franceville**.

Continue straight on the D223 and at the crossroad take the D514 toward Cabourg. Enter Hôme and then **Cabourg**. Pass the golf course and the campground and from the intersection follow the signs to the beach, the casino, and the Grand Hôtel.

Cabourg is a renowned, elegant seaside resort of magnificent villas. Try to imagine yourself at the turn of the century, during the period when author Marcel Proust spent summers at the Grand Hôtel: refined ambience, high society, bathing in the sea... The beach-side promenade, adorned with blue and white striped tents, bears his name today.

Leave Cabourg for **Dives-sur-Mer**. Cross the little bridge over the Dives and follow the signs to the centre of town and the 12th-century church. In 1066, at a time when Dives was a major sea port, William the Conqueror embarked from here on the expedition that would result in conquest of England. The sea's importance has diminished, but the town has preserved its historic quarter. Especially appealing are: the Église Notre-Dame, the 15th- and 16th-century markets (take the opportunity to stock up on provisions), and the Hostellerie de Guillaume le Conquérant, formerly a stopover for, among others, the Marquise de Sévigné and Alexandre Dumas (today it houses artisans' quarters).

To leave Dives, pass the Église Notre-Dame and at the intersection with the D45 head in the direction of Pont-L'Évêque. The road rises steeply, offering a nice panoramic view of the coast. Turn right onto the D45A toward **Grangues**. The road continues to climb, then descends in a series of zigzags to the Église de Grangues. Take note of its 15th-century bell-tower wall, and meanwhile take advantage of the Fontaine Saint-Roch for a refreshing drink.

Continue on the road just in front of the church, which climbs abruptly for one kilometre, and at the junction with the D27, turn right to follow the Route des Marais. At this altitude there is a lovely view of Cabourg and the coast.

Take the D49a toward **Cricqueville-en-Auge**, still following the Route des Marais. Let yourself glide down through the large curves. At the crossroad, continue along the Route des Marais toward Putot-en-Auge. At the junction with the D49b, continue straight, and then ride on the D49 and the Route des Marais toward Putot-en-Auge. Pass under the highway, and cross the Route Nationale. Next take the D49, the Route du Cidre, which climbs toward **Putot-en-Auge**. The town has preserved an old church and a manor that has been converted into a purebred farm. Ride to **Beuvron-en-Auge**. The flat road traverses a very nice landscape of marshes and half-timbered farmhouses in enclosed fields. You will fall for this charming "museum-village" in the middle of the marshes! The town square, known as the Place des Halles, is the ideal spot for a break and a bowl of farmer's cider.

Leave the village via the southbound D49. At the crossroad, take the D78 toward **Hotot-en-Auge** and then follow the D152 to **Méry-Corbon**. The view extends over the hills of Suisse Normande. Cross the village, and, in front of the church, turn onto the D152 toward Bissières. Keep right at the town hall, and leave the village on the D152. Cross the

N13, and continue toward Bissières and Mézidon-Canon. Along the Route des Cidres there are several tasting opportunities at farms that produce cider and Calvados.

Past the village of **Bissières**, take the D138 toward **Magny-le-Freule** and Mézidon-Canon. The Château du Canon, a historic, 18th-century monument, is surrounded by a wonderful park. A pleasant stroll through these sumptuous gardens is well worth the short delay.

To continue toward Saint-Pierre-sur-Dives, turn right at the Mézidon-Canon church. Ride along apple-tree-bordered Rue Principale. At the traffic circle, ride in the direction of Percy-en-Auge. Proceed on the D138, and then the D40, to enter **Saint-Pierre-sur-Dives**. Head for the centre of town. The tourist office is at the Musée de Techniques Fromagères, on Rue Saint-Benoît.

PRACTICAL INFORMATION ON SAINT-PIERRE-SUR-DIVES

Population
4,000 *Pétruviens*

Tourist office: 12 Rue Saint-Benoît, 14170 Saint-Pierre-sur-Dives, ☎ 02 31 20 97 90, ⊷ 02 31 20 36 02

Bicycle shop
Lebel, Boul. Collas, ☎ 02 31 20 01 07

Market
Monday

Major events: Terroir et Tradition (July and August, every Friday, 5pm to 8pm)

Specialties: sole, trout, tripe, cheese

Map
IGN no. 18

Leg from Saint-Pierre-sur-Dives to Thury-Harcourt: 50 km

The Benedictine monastery of Saint-Pierre-sur-Dives was founded in the 11th century. The aunt of William the Conqueror sponsored construction of the abbatial church, and it was solemnly consecrated in the presence of the King of England on May 1st, 1067. The Musée des Techniques Fromagères is located in the convent buildings of the old abbey. This is the place to visit to learn all there is to know about the making of Norman cheese...

The first part of the tour traverses large fields of rape and other cereal crops on lovely, quiet roads, punctuated by picturesque hamlets and grazing horses. Stock up on provisions before you leave.

To exit Saint-Pierre-sur-Dives, from the church ride in the direction of Caen. At the traffic circle, take the D40 toward Magny-la-Campagne. Pass under the viaduct, and turn left in the direction of Grisy and Vendeuvre. The road runs through a vast agricultural plain. Enter **Grisy**, a typical village of stone houses, on the D271. Take note of the beautiful Romanesque cross at the side of the road.

Proceed to the **Château de Vendeuvre**. This "castle-museum" (1750) is like a treasure chest, overflowing with gems and wonders. Automatons illustrate the daily life of an 18th-century aristocratic family; the park is landscaped with "surprise" water gardens; a collection of miniature furniture and silverware is exhibited in the Orangerie.

After the visit, continue on the D271 toward Pont and Falaise. Then take the D242, on the right, toward **Perrières** and **Olendon**. Proceed on the D242 toward **Tassily**. At the intersection with the D261a, proceed in the direction of Ouilly-le-Tesson. Follow the D261b to **Soumont-Saint-Quentin**.

The Musée de la Vie Rurale en Basse-Normandie allows you to relive the era of Normans two generations ago. Just past the museum, a footpath leads to Brèche au Diable, a registered natural tourist attraction. Count on an hour for the hike to the rocky overhang above the Gorges du Laizon, and the tomb of Marie Joly (1761-1798), a famous actress who committed suicide here.

Follow the wooded road that climbs to the village of Soumont and its beautiful and noble church, which dates from the end of the 12th century. Turn left onto the D91a toward Potigny and Grainville. At the second intersection, turn right toward Aisy (the sign is difficult to see). Climb, and take the little road on your left that runs parallel to the Route Nationale. At the factory, turn right onto the D43 (careful there is no sign).

At the intersection with the D658, ride in the direction of **Grainville-Langannerie**. Cross the village on the Rue Principale and at the second traffic circle take the D131 toward Urville. Pass the Polish cemetery and enter **Urville** on the D131. Ride to the bottom of the village. Continue on the D131, which climbs through a wood toward **Barbery**. At the intersection with the D23, proceed in the direction of Thury-Harcourt.

At **Bois-Halbout**, proceed via the D255. The road drops as you exit the village, to better climb toward Placy, at which point it offers a superb view of the hills of Suisse Normande. This is the beginning of switchback terrain: long descents into the valley, hairpin turns followed by steep climbs, all for about eight kilometres. This trek brings you to the centre of **Thury-Harcourt**. The tourist bureau is near the church, at Place Saint-Sauveur.

Leg from Thury-Harcourt to Bayeux: 60 km

In summer, Thury-Harcourt is very busy with rural tourism. This little town on the banks of the Orne is the departure point of several marked touring and hiking trails through Suisse Normande and the Orne valley. The current Duc d'Harcourt suggests a pleasant stroll through the 70-hectare park to admire the gardens of his castle, which unfortunately was lost to fire during the German evacuation of July, 1944.

PRACTICAL INFORMATION ON THURY-HARCOURT

Population
2,000 *Harcoutois*

? **Tourist office:** 2 Place Saint-Sauveur, 14220 Thury-Harcourt, ☎ 02 31 79 70 45

Bicycle shop
Laru, 9 Rue Raoul-Tesson, ☎ 02 31 79 05 59

Market
Tuesday

Map
IGN no. 7

Do some warm-up exercises, because the day promises to be challenging, from the minute you leave Thury-Harcourt. Ride to the Église Saint-Sauveur and proceed in the direction of Aunay-sur-Odon, passing the castle. Cross the bridge over the Orne and follow the D6 in the direction of Hom and Aulnay. Keep right on the D212 toward Hom and Goupillières. Cross the ramble of the river again, and continue on the D212, also known as the Route Touristique de la Vallée de l'Orne. The road rises for about one kilometre, then drops into the forest in a series of curves.

Climb to **Goupillières** on the D212, and continue along the Route Touristique de la Vallée de l'Orne. Steep rises and drops succeed each other. Enter **Trois-Monts**. Proceed through countryside to **Amayé-sur-Orne**. At the cenotaph, look carefully to the left for signs indicating the D41 toward Maizet and Évrecy. The road traverses a plateau of immense fields.

Descend to the village of **Évrecy**. Cross it in the direction of Aunay and watch on the right, just before the gendarmerie, for the D174 toward **Bougy** and **Missy**. Be sure to leave Évrecy on the D174. Traverse Missy, and ride in the direction of Cheux on the D83. Pass over the highway and at the traffic circle continue on the D83 toward Cheux. At the crossing, take the D139 toward Fontenay and Seulles. Pass the Commonwealth cemetery and enter **Fontenay**.

Proceed via the D139 toward Tilly-sur-Seulles. At the intersection with the D13, make a left, and ride cautiously to **Tilly-sur-Seulles**. Leave Tilly-sur-Seulles on the D13 in the direction of **Lingèvres**. The little Musée de la Bataille de Tilly is located in the 12th-century Chapelle Notre-Dame du Val. After the Lingèvres church, make a right onto the D331 toward Abbaye de Mondaye, and Bayeux, and then keep right for the D33. Along the road you can stop at cider-tasting cellars.

Next, take the D178 toward **Abbaye de Mondaye** and Juaye. The abbey bell-tower is visible. Skirt the wall and turn left to reach the reception area. The monastic church, in classical style, was reconstructed and decorated in the 18th century by Canon Restout of the Ordre des Prémontrés. You may also visit the farm-house and abbatial buildings which contain, among other attractions, a library of close to 40,000 volumes. A guided tour is available afternoons between two and six o'clock.

Proceed on the D178 toward Noron. At the intersection, continue toward Bayeux on the D67. The road climbs; do not be discouraged, you are almost there. As you approach the city, you will notice the three spires of the Cathédrale de Bayeux. Enter Bayeux.

---

18. TOUR OF LA MANCHE

Total distance: 230 km
Number of legs: 5
Level of difficulty: 🚲 🚲
Diagrams: pp 139, 141
Maps: A14, A15

Leg from Bayeux to Isigny-sur-Mer: 55 km

To leave Bayeux, proceed to Place Saint-Patrice via Rue des Bouchers and Rue du Marché. Fork to the right onto Rue du Docteur Michel, and travel in the direction of Port-en-Bessin and Huppain on the D6, riding carefully for about three kilometres. Turn left onto the D169 in the direction of Sully.

At **Sully**, follow the C1 toward **Maisons**. At the intersection with the D100, turn right toward **Commes** and then continue via the D6 to Port-en-Bessin. Follow the signs to the centre of town, Omaha Beach, and D-Day via the D514. This fishing port, tucked between two cliffs, is twinned with Saint-Pierre-et-Miquelon. If you are a morning person, you may arrive early enough to hear the auction. Although the fishery specialises in scallops, other catches like crustaceans, molluscs, rays, mullet and gurnet are also common. You can climb the cliffs to appreciate the beautiful view of the coast, access them by the footpath via Tour Vauban.

Cycle with care since charter buses run without interruption on the roads along the Plages du Débarquement (the beaches of the Allied landings). Skirt the port and, after the church, take the D514 on the right toward **Omaha Beach**. Continue toward **Sainte-Honorine-des-Pertes** and **Colleville-sur-Mer**. Be careful! Do not descend at the first sign indicating Omaha Beach because the grade is too steep. Instead, ride to the traffic circle at the American cemetery and follow the signs to the bicycle parking area.

Respectable attire is recommended for this visit. The immense American cemetery (70 hectares) occupies a remarkable site above Omaha Beach. The main aisle, in the shape of a cross, brings you to the middle of an impeccable lawn lined with 9,346 Latin crosses and stars of David. An observation deck, on the ocean side of the cemetery, overlooks the beaches and displays battle plans of the invasion along with a viewpoint indicator. Allot a full half-hour for the trip down the stairway to the beach and back.

After your visit, return to the traffic circle, and proceed in the direction of **Saint-Laurent-sur-Mer** and Grand Camp-Maisy on the D514. Follow the D517 to the Musée d'Omaha (military vehicles, armaments, costumed mannequins), and then continue toward **Vierville-sur-Mer**. The road hugs the coastline, and it is very windy! Proceed on the D514 toward Grand Camp-Maisy.

Pass a manor on the right, and continue to **Pointe du Hoc**. This historic, cliff-top site was bombed on June 6th, 1944. A little trail links the relics of the bunkers and a monument has been erected on the old gunnery station.

Proceed, always on the D514, toward **Grand Camp-Maisy**. The road climbs as it approaches this little seaside resort, fishing port, and pleasure-craft harbour. If you have a yen for a swim, here is a perfect opportunity. To leave the village, follow the signs for the oyster bed. Ride to the junction with the D199a and turn right toward **Géfosse** and **Fontenay**. Pass a farm, and take the D200, on the left, toward Osmanville and Isigny-sur-Mer.

At the intersection with the D124, ride in the direction of Isigny-sur-Mer and Carentan. Cycle cautiously as you enter Isigny-sur-Mer. The tourist office is situated on Rue Victor-Hugo.

Leg from Isigny-sur-Mer to Coutances: 55 km

Sixty percent of the town of **Isigny-sur-Mer**, on Baie de Veys, was destroyed by bombardment. Today, surrounded by green pastures, it is renowned for its butter and cream which bear a trademark of origin. At breakfast, ask for the best!

This stage of the tour crosses **Parc Régional des Marais du Cotentin**, an area of large prairies and peat-bogs. To avoid the worst of the automobile traffic, be sure to leave Isigny-sur-Mer on the D197a in the direction of Carentan. Ride for about two kilometres on the Route Nationale, then fork onto the D444 toward **Montmartin-en-Graignes**.

PRACTICAL INFORMATION ON ISIGNY-SUR-MER

Population
3,500 *Isignais*

Tourist office: 1 Rue Victor-Hugo, 14230 Isigny-sur-Mer, ☎ 02 31 21 46 00, ✉ 02 31 22 90 21

Bicycle shops
Denis, 20 Rue Delaunay, ☎ 02 31 22 06 10
Navarre, 24 Place de Gaulle, ☎ 02 31 22 01 75

Market
Wednesday and Saturday

Specialties: butter and cheese with the controlled Isigny label, caramel

Map
IGN no. 6

Cycle on the D44, through open countryside, to the intersection with the N174. Cross it and continue straight on the D444 (no sign). Pass a farm, **La Planque**, on your left. Do not take any side roads. At the fork, keep left toward Le Ménage. At the next fork, keep right for Saint-Nicolas. Pass another farm, Le Petit Hameau, and continue to the bridge.

Proceed on the D89 in the direction of Ganges. The countryside rises and falls, and offers a lovely panorama of the marshes. Enter **Graignes**, and cross the village. Continue via the D57 to **Tribehou**. A large hippodrome is located at the end of the village. The next section crosses a very scenic region of marshland.

Leave Tribehou on the D29 toward Saint-Georges-de-Bohon and Carentan. Ride to the D57 and turn left toward Auxais and Marchésieux. A short excursion of two kilometres (return) is possible to the Maison des Marais. Follow the signs from the intersection.

Situated in Marais Saint-Clair, the Maison des Marais was built in 1773 and inhabited until 1953. Its walls are made of a mixture of clay and straw, and its roof of thatch. The house is representative of and illustrates the history and development of the Marais du Cotentin, the marsh. You may take advantage of a stop at this charming site by picnicking and charging your batteries. The last section of the tour is more challenging, and you will have to climb some precipitous grades. Remember: the steeper the road, the better the view!

Return to the crossroad and continue on the D57 to **Feugères**. The landscape gradually changes from marshland to farmland. Proceed along the D57 toward **Le Mesnilbus**. Take note of the lovely little Romanesque church. At the intersection, continue riding toward **Monthuchon**. Proceed to **Coutances** via the D971. As you approach the city, the spires of its marvellous cathedral become visible. Hold on! The final climb is difficult all the way to the town centre. The tourist office is at Place Georges-Leclerc.

Leg from Coutances to Granville: 50 km

Towering over the countryside from the height of its promontory, **Coutances** is appealing. The cathedral is in the purest Norman Gothic style. The museum houses a rich collection of Norman ceramic

---

PRACTICAL INFORMATION ON COUTANCES

Population
9,715 *Coutançais*

? **Tourist office:** Place Georges-Leclerc, 50200 Coutances, ☎ 02 33 45 17 79, ⌨ 02 33 47 12 45

Bicycle shops
Lerouxel, 8 Boul. Alsace-Loraine, ☎ 02 33 45 18 52
Le Guillois, 12 Boul. Alsace-Loraine, ☎ 02 33 45 03 77

Market
Thursday

Major events: Festival de Jazz (Ascension Day); Festival Ciné-Monument (August)

Specialties: Coutances cheese, Cosedia (cake)

Map
IGN no. 16

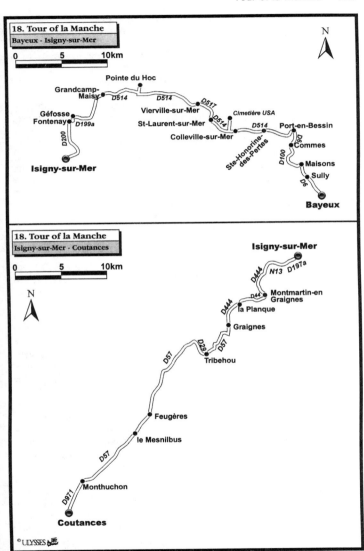

pieces, the oldest of which dates from the Renaissance. With its Renaissance church and its old houses, Quartier Saint-Pierre makes a pleasant stroll. The Jardin des Plantes, one of the most beautiful gardens in Basse-Normandie, is a required stop. It comprises more than 47,000 plants in French-style flower beds, English-style groves, Italian-style terraces... all illuminated on summer evenings.

To leave Coutances, return to the tourist office. Descend along the garden to the ring road and travel in the direction of Coutainville, Saint-Malo-de-la-Lande, and the Château de Gratot. Be sure to leave Coutances by way of Rue de Saint-Malo and the D44.

To visit the **Château de Gratot**, follow the signs from the traffic circle. This castle (14th to 18th century) belonged to the Argouges family for five centuries. Since 1968, its restoration has been taken up by a team of volunteers. Leave your bicycle at the parking lot. To access the courtyard, cross the little bridge over the water-filled moat.

After your visit of the castle, saddle your mount and return to the D44. At the intersection with the D57, make a left in the direction of Pont-de-la-Roque and Montmartin-sur-Mer. Continue via the D20 to **Pont-de-la-Roque**, and cross the bridge over the Sienne in the direction of Montmartin. At the fork, continue via the D49 toward **Regnéville-sur-Mer**.

The seaside resort of Regnéville-sur-Mer will charm you with its beach and its small pleasure-craft harbour. To learn the history of maritime activity on the coastline of La Manche (French name for the English Channel) and the process of lime production since ancient times, visit the Musée du Littoral et de la Chaux, at the end of the village. The visit takes about 60 minutes.

Leave Regnéville-sur-Mer via the D49 toward **Montmartin-sur-Mer**. Keep right and follow the coastline on the D156 toward Hauteville-sur-Mer. Salt-meadow sheep graze peacefully in pastures along the coast. Enter **Hauteville-sur-Mer**, and cross the village. If there is too much wind for cycling, you can always trade your bicycle for a land-sailer — the resort is renown for this sport.

Continue on the D20 toward **Annoville** and Bréhal. This section of coastline is a major area of early-vegetable cultivation; spring carrots, along with other crops, are grown here. Ride on the D20 for about five kilometres, then make a right onto the D442 toward Les Salines. Continue toward **Les Salines** via the D135, and then the D442 again.

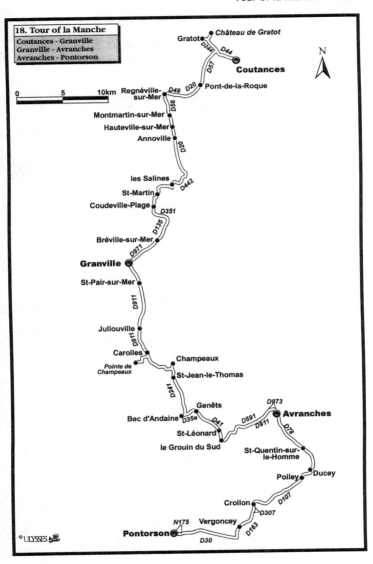

Be careful! This road is easily flooded and is impassable during high tides. Ask the locals about the condition of the road before setting out. Not far from shore a gathering of piles sprouting from the sea marks an oyster bed. The sight is unforgettable! At low tide, the D375e leads to a protected marsh area where sheep browse.

Proceed toward **Saint-Martin**, pass the campground, and turn right toward the village. Follow the signs for Granville, hugging the coast all the way to **Coudeville-Plage**. Continue toward Granville via the D351, and then the D135 toward **Bréville-sur-Mer** (careful for dead-ends toward the sea).

Be ready to confront some steep hills on the way to Granville. Leave Bréville-sur-Mer by taking the road that climbs to the junction with the D971. Ride prudently on the D971 for the five kilometres to Granville. Again you will be put to the test as you enter the city: Avenue de la Libération climbs abruptly to the old city on the summit. A map of Granville will be useful, as the city is difficult to get around in. The tourist office is in the lower city, on Boulevard Cours Jonville.

Leg from Granville to Avranches: 35 km

On Baie du Mont-Saint-Michel, **Granville** is a very animated seaside resort that is home to the Centre Régional de Nautisme (a nautical centre) and a pleasure-craft port. Christian Dior, the famous fashion designer, was born in Granville and designed a garden of cockscomb for the city in 1920. This magnificent public park is a lovely example of turn-of-the-century villa gardening. A nice spot from which to contemplate the ocean is Îles Chaussey. From the park, you can access the beach bordered by the sea-wall.

The visit of the city ends with its museums. The Musée du Vieux Granville presents a nice exhibit of old-time maritime life. For lovers of the unusual there are the Musée des Coquillages (a seashell museum), the Palais des Minéraux (a mineral exhibit), and Jardin des Papillons (a butterfly garden).

To leave Granville, take Boulevard des Amiraux-Granvillais toward the Centre de Nautisme. Follow Rue de la Crête toward Saint-Pair-sur-Mer. The road rises sharply along the coast. Leave Granville via the D911. There is a very beautiful view. Enter **Saint-Pair-sur-Mer**, and continue in the direction of **Jullouville** and **Carolles** on the D911. A five-kilometre beach links these two resorts. This stage of the tour is not

PRACTICAL INFORMATION ON GRANVILLE

Population
12,800 *Granvillais*

Tourist office: 4 Cours Jonville, 50400 Granville, ☎ 02 33 91 30 03, ✉ 02 33 91 30 19

Bicycle shops
Hall Moto Cycle, 40 Rue du Vieux-Moulin, ☎ 02 33 50 11 61
Lecoulant, Route de Coutances, ☎ 02 33 50 03 10

Market
Thursday

Major events: Fête de la Musique (June 21st); Grand Pardon de la Mer (July 28th)

Map
IGN no. 16

long, so you can take a stroll at Carolles-Plage. Count on about an hour for the stop.

Proceed in the direction of the Lude valley and Avranches. Be careful! You must at times attack steep uphill grades in busy traffic. A path leads to the cliffs of **Champeaux**, from which you may enjoy a gorgeous view of Mont-Saint-Michel. This section of road has been nicknamed "the most beautiful kilometre in France". Don't miss it!

Continue to **Saint-Jean-le-Thomas** in a wonderful, long descent along the ocean. Stay on the D241 toward the beach and Cale Saint-Michel (shipyard). Hug the coast. At the crossroad, follow the road to Dragey and Genêts to leave Saint-Jean-le-Thomas. Keep on in the direction of Genêts, and ride toward **Bec d'Andaine** on the D35e. The pleasant, fine-sand beach and dunes invite lounging. Enjoy the extraordinary view of Baie du Mont-Saint-Michel. In the Middle Ages, pilgrims, known as *miquelots*, crossed the sand flats at low tide on foot, as a short cut to the mountain. In summer, it is still possible to retrace this six-kilometre expedition with competent guides. Inform yourself at the Maison de la Baie, in the village of Genêts. You are advised not to explore these flats by yourself, as the bay can prove dangerous!

Proceed to the village of Genêts on the D35e, and then on the D911 toward Vains and Avranche. At **Genêts**, follow the signs for the

Maison de la Baie. This little town, nestled at the bottom of a bay, was once a supply port for the mountain. The port has since completely disappeared under the sand. The 11th-century granite church is worth seeing. Continue along the coastline, on the D35e toward Jullovance. At the large intersection, follow the shore toward **Saint-Léonard**, and leave Genêts via the C9.

Proceed via the D41 toward the coastal road, to the point at **Grouin-du-Sud**. From this lovely, airy road the view stretches over Mont-Saint-Michel and pastures dotted with flocks of salt-meadow sheep: a picture perfect scene! Continue on the D591 and then the D911 toward Avranches. Cross the bridge over the Sée, and enter Avranches via the D973. At the large traffic circle, keep on toward Avranches on the Route Nationale, which climbs to the centre of the town. The tourist office is on Rue du Général-de-Gaulle.

Leg from Avranches to Pontorson: 35 km

Avranches's past was as glorious as it was tumultuous. During the last war, the city was almost completely ravaged. Nonetheless it jealously preserves treasures from its grand monastic era. The Église Saint-Gervais encloses the celebrated Rélique de Saint-Aubert, bishop of Avranches in the 13th century and founder of Abbaye du Mont-Saint-Michel. The Bibliothèque du Fonds Ancien (library) and Musée

---

PRACTICAL INFORMATION ON AVRANCHES

Population
10,000 *Avranchinais*

? **Tourist bureau:** 2 Rue Général-de-Gaulle, 50300 Avranches, ☎ 02 33 58 00 22, ✆ 02 33 68 13 29

Market
Saturday

Major events: Fête de la Musique (June); Musique en Baie (July); Fête des 3 Quartiers (September)

Specialties: salt-meadow mutton, dairy products, early vegetables

Map
IGN no. 16

Municipal house a collection of manuscripts from the abbey, inherited from the monks of Mont-Saint-Michel (7th to 15th century).

Avranches also offers two magnificent viewpoints of the Mont: from the end of Jardin des Plantes and from the platform at the site of the old cathedral (demolished in 1796) where Henry II, Plantagenet King of England, made honourable amends after the confessed murder of his friend, Thomas Becket, Bishop of Canterbury.

To leave the city, continue straight from the tourist office to Rue de la Constitution in the direction of Mont-Saint-Michel. At the large traffic circle, Place Patton (officially decreed American territory), take the exit for Saint-Quentin-sur-le-Homme. Leave Avranches on the D78. The road comprises long climbs and descents. Ride to **Saint-Quentin-sur-le-Homme**. At the village, just past the church, turn onto the D78 toward Ducey.

Proceed to **Ducey**, located on the right bank of the Sélune. The castle, in the process of being restored, was built in 1624 by Gabriel II de Montgomery. At the N176, proceed in the direction of Saint-James and Avranches. Cross the bridge over the Sélune. Be careful! Immediately following the bridge, turn left toward **Poiley** via the D107. The road snakes through large horse farms. Continue to **Crollon**, and at the village church, continue straight toward Vergoncey via the D307. At the intersection, proceed on the D163 to **Vergoncey**.

Continue toward Pontorson on the D163. The road is rather hilly at this spot. Keep straight at the intersection with the D80, and, just past it, take the D30 to Pontorson. Enter via the N175 toward the centre of town; the tourist office is on Place de la Mairie.

Pontorson is a crossroads town between Normandy and Brittany, just 10 kilometres from Mont-Saint-Michel. Orson, a Norman chief, had a bridge constructed over the Rivière Couesnon in 1031, hence the name of the town. William the Conqueror narrowly escaped death crossing the dangerous waters of this river. The episode is illustrated on the famous Tapisserie de Bayeux (see p 157 for general information of Pontorson).

You can continue to Saint-Malo by following the Tour of Brittany, specifically the leg from Pontorson to Saint-Malo via Mont-Saint-Michel.

If you would like to take the TGV back to Paris, follow, in the opposite direction, the leg from Rennes to Pontorson of the Tour of Brittany; or take the train to Rennes, making sure to check your bicycle directly through to Paris.

BRITTANY

"*Bretagne, terre de vélo*" (Brittany, land of cycling)... the title may be simple, but it marks the start of a real adventure! It was here in this unaffected and mystical region that I spent my first cycling trip in France. In the following pages, you, my fellow bicycle-lovers, will find the itinerary for a grand tour of Brittany, which will take you through all four of the region's departments. Pedaling away along the thousand kilometres of roads in Armorica, land of the sea, inland to Argoat, land of the forest, you can explore the infinite variety of Brittany's rich heritage. What a trip! There's enough to keep you going for at least three lovely weeks of adventure. If you're short on time, you can do only one part of the grand tour — the north, the south or better yet, a little of each. The choice is yours!

The first part of the grand tour, "Haute-Bretagne", starts in **Rennes**, the regional capital. A city of art and history, graced with varied architecture, Rennes will strike modern-day visitors as a young, dynamic and lively place. With its 210,000 inhabitants, nearly a quarter of whom are students, its universities and its numerous schools, this Breton metropolis welcomes you and starts you off on your journey of discovery in this fabulous region.

Firmly in the saddle, you can thus set off on a tour that covers the magnificent seascapes of the Baie du Mont-Saint-Michel, the Côte d'Émeraude and the Côte de Goëlo. The **Château de Combourg**, where the memory of writer François René de Chateaubriand lives on, is a must for anyone who has read his *Mémoires d'outre-tombe*. This imposing feudal castle is separated from the old village by the *lac tranquille* and a stand of chestnut trees.

Next, the road winds through the countryside to the sea, to the salty bay where the sublime **Mont-Saint-Michel** looms up between the water and the sky. The closer you get, the harder it is to tear your eyes away from the monastery. It started out as a simple oratory in the 7th century, then became a major pilgrimage site in the Middle Ages, at which time it took on the name "Mont-Saint-Michel-au-péril-de-la-mer" (at the mercy of the sea). A marvel of medieval architecture built on three levels, it has been listed as a historic monument since 1874. The Baie du Mont-Saint-Michel boasts grandiose scenery that you will never tire of contemplating and photographing.

Riding along the Côte d'Émeraude toward Saint-Malo, you are likely to pass some land-sailers near **Cherrueix**. With its long, windswept strands, this part of the coast is perfect for this sport. Inhabitants of the charming little town of Cherrueix rely on fishing and farming for their livelihood. Take a little break at the bar, where you might have the chance to chat with one of the local fishermen over a bowl of cider.

When you reach **Saint-Malo**, park your bike; this city of privateers and master mariners beckons you to walk along streets echoing with the footsteps of Jacques Cartier (Canada), Robert Surcouf (the Indies) and Duguay-Trouin (Brazil). Once the domain of wealthy shipowners, the city has preserved its granite houses and *hôtels particuliers* (private mansions), with their pointed roofs. These are hemmed in by massive ramparts, forming a restored architectural heritage that is truly one of a kind!

From Saint-Malo, the tour leads up the steep shores of the Rance to **Dinan**, at the end of the estuary. The fortified city, perched 75 metres above the Rance, makes for an impressive sight. Some yachts and a few fishing boats are moored along the banks of the river below. Local production of woollen cloth and canvas enabled Dinan to prosper when the New World was first being colonized. It was this port that supplied Saint-Malo with sailcloth. Today, Dinan has many cafés and restaurants where you can relax, daydream and satisfy your appetite.

The tour continues along the northern shore of Brittany to magnificent natural sites where the wind blows harder than a cyclist might hope. Still, the scenery is absolutely extraordinary — pink sandstone cliffs and capes sheltering thousands of seabirds; an invigorating sea and powdery beaches and golden dunes that beckon you to kick back and relax. In addition to these wonders of nature, you'll discover the region's traditions, rural heritage and fishing villages with their pink-coloured houses and churches. To top it off, there are a few stately châteaux. Amidst the gorse and heather on the unspoiled moors of **Cap Fréhel**, you'll find Fort La Latte, an imposing pink fortress overlooking the sea from a height of about 60 metres.

At the evocatively named seaside resort of **Sables-d'Or-les-Pins** (literally "Golden Sands-the Pines"), which in my opinion is the loveliest beach on the entire tour, you'll start heading inland, your back to the wind coming off the sea. After a little pedaling, you'll enter the heart of Brittany, far from all the hustle and bustle along the coast. The villages are picturesque and some are clustered around their *enclos paroissial*, an enclosed, sacred space containing a church, a cemetery and a calvary (a sculptured depiction of the Crucifixion). This form of parochial art is peculiar to Brittany and flourished from 1550 to 1650, approximately. Your journey will be puctuated by roadside crosses, pilgrimage chapels in the middle of the countryside, and churches with iconographic stained-glass windows showing the Passion or the tree of Jesse — all part of the religious heritage of this region, which has been profoundly influenced by Christianity.

The tour leads through little towns steeped in history. In the 12th century, **Lamballe** was the capital of the duchy of Penthièvre, a branch of the Maison de Bretagne. Today, this little town is associated with its national stud farm, which houses as many as 400 horses: Breton post-horses, thoroughbreds, Connemaras. **Moncontour** was a large fortified town in the duchy of Penthièvre. It prospered in the mid-17th century by making and selling *berlingues* (linen and hemp cloth). Full of character, this little town is an enchanting place to regain your strength in this rolling countryside.

On the last leg of the tour of Haute-Bretagne you'll come to **Pontivy**, a bustling university and commercial town whose fairs and lively atmosphere are sure to charm you. An old Argoat city, it bears the stamp of the Dukes of Rohan, with its 15th century military-style château. Stretched along the left side of the Blavet, Pontivy has two adjoining neighbourhoods built in different eras. The old city, with its winding alleys, wooden houses and basilica (Notre-Dame-de-la-Joie), lies in the heart of the pedestrian zone, while Napoléonville is distinguished by its imperial architecture, grid pattern, large boulevards and squares.

The grand tour of Brittany continues into the heart of Argoat, a region of rivers and forests that have inspired many legends. Cyclists will pass through the magnificent **Forêt de Pont-Calleck** (beech, chestnut, sorb, yew, etc.) in the Scorff valley, a popular place to go fishing or simply enjoy a stroll. You'll have to exert yourself more in this region, which is very hilly between the Scorff and Ellé rivers. According to legend, the **Roches du Diable**, a pile of strangely shaped granite boulders on the Ellé river, belonged to the devil. Despite their name (literally, the Devil's Rocks), these rapids attract large numbers of kayakers.

Quimperlé, *"Cité des Trois Rivières"* (city of the three rivers), is a very pretty little town built at the confluence of the Ellé and Isole rivers, which come together to form the Laïta river.

The tour of the **Côte-sud** starts in Cornouaille, Brittany's "Midi" (South). **Quimper** stretches along the Odet. The cafés on its wharves offer the perfect vantage point from which to observe the comings and goings of the local residents while savouring the regional gastronomy. I'm not talking about *galettes de sarrasin* or *crêpes de froment* here, although a buckwheat crêpe washed down with a bowl of cider is still the traditional meal for festivities, and certainly makes vegetarian cyclists happy. I'm thinking more of *cotriade*, a sort of fish chowder; salt-meadow lamb stew; *andouille de Guéméné* (a kind of sausage) and of course, *homard à l'armoricaine* (lobster). Belon oysters are farmed on both the south coast (Belon) and the north coast (Cancale). Unfortunately for cyclists, the best time to eat them is from September to April. And have you ever tried *cervoise*, Asterix's beer, or *chouchen*, a mead once drunk by druids? How about *lambig*, a cider brandy?

Enough with the pleasures of the palate; let's give our eyes a treat now by moving on to other enchanting places. As the tour continues, you'll explore charming little ports, inlets and bays that shelter slumbering sailboats. It is worth taking the time to follow the roads all the way to the end. You'll discover a whole way of life here in Cornouaille, at **Sainte-Marine**, **Bénodet** and the **Pointe de Mousterlin**, with its unspoiled beach of big rocks and fine sand. This place is perfect for a picnic and offers a lovely view of the Îles de Glénan.

The tour continues along the coast to the seaside resort of **Beg-Meil**, with its sandy beaches lined with pines and lovely villas where Marcel Proust, Sarah Bernhardt and many other notables have stayed. **Forêt-Fouesnant** boasts the region's largest sailing harbour, which adds life to the picturesque town. Make sure not to leave without tasting the highly reputed and deliciously fragrant cider produced locally. A magnificent wooded area separates Forêt-Fouesnant from **Concarneau**, a big fishing port. Your gaze will then fall on the charming little walled city, the historic heart of Concarneau.

Pont-Aven, nestled in the Aven valley, owes its fame to Paul Gauguin and his friends, who stayed here in the late 19th century. Gauguin fans should schedule some time for a short excursion to the **Chapelle de Trémalo**, in the Bois d'Amour. The wooden Christ in the nave was the model for the artist's famous *Yellow Christ* (1889).

Still following the coast, the tour leads into Morbihan, the only department with a Breton name, to **Guidel-Plage**, located at the mouth of the Laïta. **Lorient** owes its existence to the East India Company, founded by Louis XIV. Spices, carpets, porcelain, silks, etc. made the town's fortune. Lorient was virtually destroyed by bombs during World War II. To this day, the local economy is still centred around the ports (commercial, naval, fishing and sailing). Lorient is the point of departure for the ferry to **Ile de Groix**.

Sainte-Anne-d'Auray is the most popular pilgrimage site in Brittany. Saint Anne, Mary's mother and the patron saint of Brittany, has been honoured here since the 6th century. She appeared to a pious labourer in 1624 and 1625. The cloister, listed as a historic monument, houses the treasury of Saint-Anne-d'Auray, where the pilgrims' votive offerings are kept. Among these countless objects is the yellow jersey worn by cyclist Jean Robic during the Tour de France!

Those fascinated by the unknown won't want to miss a visit to **Carnac**, "*le lieu où il y a des monticules de pierre*" ("the place where there are mounds of stone"), where you can explore an enigmatic region abounding in megaliths. For four kilometres between the **Golfe du Morbihan** and the Étel river, the ground is strewn with rough stones of varying sizes, arranged in lines, some upright and others lying down.

The gulf is actually a small inland sea dotted with little islands, which stretches into the hinterland in rivers. The tour follows its shores through **Arradon** to the **Baden-Armor** point, which faces due south.

The climate is hot; you'll see fig trees, oleanders, camelias and mimosas. It was in **Vannes**, which has emerged intact from the past, that the duchy of Brittany was officially united with France on August 13, 1532. Its old quarter, enclosed by sturdy ramparts, jealously guards the treasures of that era.

The winding road to **Muzillac** will make you sweat a bit; to get your mind off the strain, focus on the view of the Pen-mur pond, the domain of kingfishers and moorhens. As you near the Pays de la Loire, you'll see a gradual change in the surroundings. The tour keeps following the coast to **Piriac-sur-Mer**. Several 19th-century writers (Flaubert, Daudet and Zola) fell under the spell of this town, with its small-scale fishing port and lovely homes. If you'd like to cool off a bit, the pretty beach west of the village is easy to get to.

USEFUL ADDRESSES

Fédération française de cyclotourisme (bicycle-touring federation)
Ligue de Bretagne, La bouderie
35440 Dingé
☎ 02 99 45 00 86

ABRI-Maison de la Randonnée (Gîtes d'étape; dormitories)
9 Rue des Portes Mordelaises
35000 Rennes
☎ 02 99 31 59 44

Boat to Ile de Groix
Contact the MN company
☎ 02 97 64 77 64

Nicknamed the Breton Carcassonne, the medieval town of **Guérande**, surrounded by ramparts with four fortified entrances, dominates the salt marshes to which it owes its prosperity. Honoré de Balzac described it as "a magnificent jewel of feudalism". Before leaving this salty region, kick back and relax for a little while on the Côte d'Amour's famous eight-kilometre beach.

The **Parc Régional de la Grande Brière**, a unique, unspoiled stretch of land, protects an outstanding natural heritage. Nature lovers will want to explore the real Brière by boat, which is the best way to see the reeds, water lilies, common herons, bearded tits and other treasures of the silent marshes.

From **Nantes**, at the meeting point of three provinces, the tour continues along the longest river in France, into the Loire Valley.

THE GRAND TOUR OF BRITTANY

The grand tour of Brittany (1000 km, 17 legs, very difficult) includes the tour of Haute-Bretagne, the legs from Pontivy to Quimperlé and from Quimperlé to Quimper, as well as the tour of the Côte-sud. It is also possible to take a shorter tour of Brittany (800 km, 13 legs, very difficult) by going straight from Quimperlé to Pont-Scorff (see p 170).

---

19. Haute-Bretagne

Total distance: 355 km
Number of legs: 6
Level of difficulty: 🚲 🚲 🚲
Diagrams: pp 155, 163
Maps: A16 to A18

Leg from Rennes to Pontorson: 65 km

This tour covers the north coast of Brittany and the interior as far as Pontivy. You can return to Paris on the TGV, by way of Vannes.

The streets of Rennes are fairly busy, as are the roads for about 20 kilometres outside the city. If you want to avoid cycling in the traffic on the way out of town, take the train to **Pontorson**. Be sure to stop in Rennes, though, so that you can explore the city. Afterward — say, two days later — you can proceed to Pontorson. If you're starting in Paris, however, make sure to check your bike directly through to Pontorson, and not to Rennes; that way, you won't have to wait for it, and more important, you won't have to put it back on the train and pay the transportation cost again.

Rennes enjoyed three centuries of prosperity during the Roman era. Later, fortifications were built all around the town, which, with its half-timbered houses, took on a medieval look. In 1720, Rennes was ravaged by a fire that broke out in a carpenter's workshop. It took about 12 years to rebuild the city. The neighbourhood around the Cathédrale Saint-Pierre survived the fire, however. Here, in a maze of little streets, lovely medieval houses nestle alongside *hôtels particuliers*

PRACTICAL INFORMATION ON RENNES

Population
210,000 *Rennais*

Tourist office: Pont de Nemours, 35000 Rennes, ☎ 02 99 79 01 98,
✆ 01 99 79 31 38

Bicycle shops: Guédard 13 Boul. Beaumont, ☎ 02 99 30 43 78
Dubourg, 15 Rue André-Rolault, ☎. 02 99 50 21 50

Market
Saturdays

Major events: Feu de la Saint-Jean (fireworks, June 24); Festival de la
Création Bretonne "Les tombées de la nuit" (early July)

Specialties: *Casse Rennaise* (tripe), sweets

Access from Paris: By road: A11, the Océane; by train: TGV, Gare
Montparnasse to Rennes

Map
IGN no. 16

dating from the 16th through the 18th centuries. The Porte Mordelaise
is all that remains of the ramparts.

You can also stroll around the wharves along the Vilaine (did you know
that there was a river flowing right through the middle of Rennes?).
The Vilaine is no longer visible, as it was canalized in the 19th century.
The Musée des Beaux-Arts et d'Archéologie, on the Quai Émile-Zola,
is full of treasures, including a large collection of 17th-century
paintings. On the ground floor, the Musée de Bretagne is a prelude to
your trip. The nearby Jardin du Thabor, four hectares of greenery right
in the middle of downtown Rennes, has formal gardens, landscape
gardens with greenhouses, rose gardens, sculptures, a romantic
bandstand and a lovely 19th-century stairway that serves as the
entrance to the garden on Rue de Paris.

To leave Rennes, take Avenue Jean-Janvier from the Place de la Gare.
Cross Pont Pasteur and ride along the wharves, following the big
boulevards toward Saint-Malo. At the major intersection (traffic light),
cross the bridge. Immediately after, turn right toward Saint-Grégoire

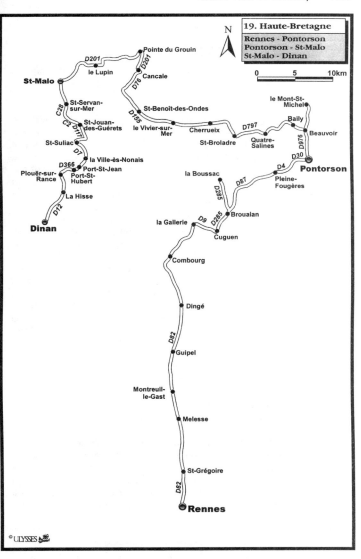

© ULYSSES

(D82). Ride alongside the cemetery walls. Use the bike lane. At the big traffic circle, stay on course for Saint-Grégoire. You'll be able to ride in the bike lane for three kilometres.

Ride into **Saint-Grégoire**, then continue on the D82 toward **Melesse, Montreuil-le-Gast** and Guipel. The road is hilly, and the traffic will probably be quite heavy for about 20 kilometres, so be extra careful!

The traffic eases up around **Guipel**. Cross the Canal d'Ille and the Rance, and continue to **Dingé**. The road climbs up through big tracts of farmland. Keep following the D82. There will be a long downhill stretch on the way into **Combourg**. Ride alongside the big pond and then into the town. The château still belongs to the descendents of the celebrated Breton writer François René de Chateaubriand. Visitors can tour the rooms where he lived as a young man and see his furniture and personal belongings. Open to the public every day but Tuesday.

Leave Combourg by following the signs for Fougères and Vitré. Keep your eyes peeled; on the left, a small sign nailed to the wall of a bar shows the way to Lourmais. Make sure to take the V17 out of Combourg. At the fork with the cross in the middle, keep right and ride straight ahead (don't take any of the perpendicular roads) to **Lourmais**. On the way out of town, you'll come to an intersection in front of a field. Turn left to continue toward the little town of Galerie (no sign). At the D9, turn right toward Mon Idée; a few metres farther, you'll see a marker reading D9 on the side of the road. Proceed to the cute little village of **Cuguen**.

The road climbs to the centre of the village. Head for Pleine-Fougères on the D83, then turn left toward **Broualan**. Stop for a bit and enjoy a stroll in this charming town. Make sure to take a look at the calvary in the square, which is carved with inscriptions in Gothic letters. The 15th-century church is also noteworthy.

Next, take the D87 toward La Boussac and Dol-de-Bretagne, then continue toward Dol-de-Bretagne on the D285. After a long downhill stretch, you'll reach **La Boussac**. At the intersection on the way out of the village, turn right on the D87 (no sign). About 20 metres farther, at the crossroads, head for the Ferme Pierre-Blanche by following the sign with the green logo on it. The road leads up into the hills, offering a pretty panoramic view.

Keep following the D87, which runs across a big highway. Continue straight ahead toward **Saint-Broladre**. At the D4, head for Pleine-

Fougères. Take the D4 and the D30 to Pontorson. Ride into the centre of town, to the tourist office on Place de la Mairie.

Leg from Pontorson to Saint-Malo (via Mont-Saint-Michel): 70 km

Pontorson is a crossroad town on the border of Normandy and Brittany. Orson, a Norman leader, had a bridge built over the Rivière Couesnon in 1031, hence the name of the town (*pont* is the French word for bridge). The church was built at the request of William the Conqueror, after he had been rescued from the treacherous waters of the river.

PRACTICAL INFORMATION ON PONTORSON

Population
3,400 *Pontorsonnais*

Tourist office: Place de la Mairie, 50170 Pontorson, ☎ 02 33 60 20 65

Market
Wednesdays

Specialties: Traditional omelets, *prés-salés* (salt meadow lamb), *saumon de la Baie* (salmon), seafood

Map
IGN no. 16

Head out of Pontorson on the D19, toward Mont-Saint-Michel and Beauvoir. Ride past the youth hostel (*auberge de jeunesse*). At the traffic circle, take the D976 toward **Mont-Saint-Michel**. As you leave Beauvoir, you'll catch your first glimpse of the bell tower of the abbey church, itself the centrepiece of Mont-Saint-Michel. According to legend, a huge tidal wave cut off Mont Tombe from the continent. Access to the island is gained by 1,800-metre dike, which was built in 1877 and always remains above water.

Take a quick look at the parking lot; I find it hard to stop myself from telling you about the million or so visitors that flock here every year. Mont-Saint-Michel is one of the most popular attractions in France!

Ride up to the entrance, then lock your bike somewhere right out in the open. Wear a pair of good walking shoes, as the only street in the little town climbs steeply up the side of the hill all the way to the abbey. Visitors to the abbey must be accompanied by a guide, and the tour lasts about an hour. If you want to explore the entire site (the Grande-Rue, abbey, museums and ramparts), which takes about three hours, you'll have to cut short this leg of the tour, by sleeping at Cancale, for example (50 kilometres instead of 70 kilometres).

After touring Mont-Saint-Michel, head back toward **Beauvoir**. Follow the signs for the *polder panorama* and the Rive du Couesnon. This tiny, unnumbered road runs past farms and truck gardens. The view of the hill, the shore and the salt-water meadows is magnificent. Continue straight ahead, toward Dely, Lahaie and Foucault. Just past the farmhouse, you'll find yourself opposite a dead-end. Turn left. At the intersection, take a right toward **Quatre-Salines**. Follow the signs for Quatre-Salines and Saint-Malo. At the D797, head for **La Poultière** and Saint-Malo. The road is narrow and hilly, and the traffic fairly heavy.

Stay on the D979 to **Saint-Broladre**. At the village, take the coastal route toward Cancale and Saint-Malo. After about 10 km, you'll see a little road leading right, toward the sea. Follow it until it forks, then head right, in the direction of l'Angle (look for the little green logo). This small road runs along the shore, passing through a patchwork of farmland (carrots, potatoes, lettuce, etc.) on its way to the village of **Cherrueix**.

Ride out of Cherrueix and head for **Vivier-sur-Mer** on the D155. A ride aboard *La Sirène-de-la-Baie*, an amphibious boat, is a chance to drink in the beauty of the bay's scenery at a slower pace, while savouring locally bred mussels. On the main street of the village, furthermore, there are counters where you can purchase mussels and oysters.

Next, you'll catch your first glimpse of the Pointe de Cancale. Stay on the D155 to **Saint-Benoît-des-Ondes**, then pick up the D76 and continue following the coast in the direction of Saint-Malo. The wind blows hard here! On your way into **Cancale**, take the panoramic route on the right, which is studded with scenic viewpoints looking out onto the port and the Pointe du Hoc. Ride into Cancale by way of the Port de la Houle. Cancale has long been renowned for its flat oysters, which used to be served at the king's table twice a week! At low tide, you can see the oyster beds in the bay.

Head out of Cancale on the D201, in the direction of Pointe du Grouin and Saint-Malo (Route Touristique). Ride straight ahead to **Pointe du Grouin**. You can leave your bike in the parking lot near the semaphore and take a stroll along the footpath. It is very windy here, so cover up well. Seabirds from the Ile de Landes can be observed here.

Keep following the D201 along the coast toward Paramé and Saint-Malo. The panorama is magnificent. The windswept road runs downhill in lovely curves. There are footpaths leading to beautiful sandy beaches. The road overlooks the sea again along the cliffs. Be careful! The little trails heading down to the beaches end at campgrounds. You'll have to climb back up these steep slopes to continue along the main road.

Upon arriving at **Le Lupin**, you'll be able to drink in a lovely view of the peninsula and the pretty sailboats anchored in the cove. The road runs past a former *malouinière* (bourgeois country house).

The Manoir Jacques-Cartier is located in the Rothéneuf neighbourhood, at the edge of Saint-Malo. First, go to Place du Canada, in the centre of Rothéneuf, then take Rue David-MacDonald-Stewart. A restored *malouinière*, this museum focuses on the daily life and voyages of the man who "discovered" Canada. Guided tours every day during summer.

To visit Saint-Malo, go back to Boulevard de Rothéneuf (D201) and head for *centre-ville intra-muros*. Ride along the boulevards and the dyke. During the spring tides, you might get splashed by the sea! Proceed to the port and the Porte Saint-Vincent. The tourist office will be on your left.

Leg from Saint-Malo to Dinan: 35 km

The walled city of **Saint-Malo** was faithfully reconstructed after being bombed in 1944. Thanks to a signposted tour (starting at Place Chateaubriand), visitors can be sure not to miss a thing when exploring the local streets. The fascinating rampart walk is a classic; the view is even more magical at sunrise or sunset. Take the stairs at the Porte Saint-Vincent. At low tide, you can visit Ilot Grand-Bé, where you'll find the tomb of writer François René de Chateaubriand and the Fort National, built by Vauban in the 17th century to reinforce Saint-Malo's defences.

PRACTICAL INFORMATION ON SAINT-MALO

Population
50,000 *Malouins*

 Tourist office: Port des Yachts, 35400 Saint-Malo, ☎ 02 99 56 64 48, ⇒ 02 99 40 93 13

 Bicycle shop: M'road, 2 Place de la Grande Hermine, ☎ 02 99 40 13 15
Cycle Le Bourg, 76 Rue de la Marne, Saint-Servan, ☎ 02 99 81 74 13
Cycle Diazo, 47 Quay Dugay-Trouin, ☎ 02 99 40 31 63

 Market
Every day but Sunday

 Specialties: *Patate de Saint-Malo* (marzipan), *Craquelins*

 Major events: Saint-Malo Folklore du Monde (early July); Fête du Clos Poulet (mid-July); Festival de Musique Sacrée (mid-July to mid-August)

 Map
IGN no. 16

If you wish to visit **Dinard**, an elegant seaside resort with a retro charm, you are better off taking a boat from the port of Saint-Malo. That way, you'll enjoy another superb view of the old pirate city and avoid the dangerous (for cyclists) ride over the bridge to Dinard.

To leave Saint-Malo, go to the port and the tourist office. Cross the bridge and follow the bike path. At the big traffic circle in front of the train station, follow the signs for *toutes directions* and **Saint-Servan-sur-Mer**, then those for the Barrage de la Rance (dam), Dinard and Bellevue. At the other circle, stay on course for the Barrage de la Rance, La Lorette and La Madeleine. Take an immediate right, and continue toward the dam and Dinard. Ride past the sign for La Goëletterie. Take the D201 out of Saint-Malo, ride under the viaduct and head for La Passagère. Right after, take the C28 toward the Château du Bos and La Passagère, then continue straight ahead to **Saint-Jouan-des-Guérets** and take the C2 into the village. Proceed to Saint-Suliac on the D117, which affords a pretty view of the Rance. Ride into **Saint-Suliac**. Take the main street, which leads down to the port. On the way back, stop at the 18th-century church. Take the D7 out of town, in the direction of Châteauneuf. Keep an eye out for the Dent de Gargantua (Gargantua's tooth), a menhir on the right. At the fork, head right toward **Ville-ès-Nonais**. The road leads uphill, offering a panoramic view.

Next, take the D366 toward Port-Saint-Jean and Ploüer-sur-Rance. Ride over the N176 and into **Port-Saint-Jean**. Cross the suspension bridge over the Rance. After a good uphill stretch, you'll reach the village of **Port-Saint-Hubert**. Continue to **Ploüer-sur-Rance** on the D366.

Turn left on the D12, in the direction of La Hise and Dinan. Skirt round the village church and ride down to the D12. Let yourself coast all the way down the nice, long slope. Don't take any of the perpendicular roads. Continue straight ahead to **La Hisse**. The road to Dinan has a few demanding uphill stretches. Steel yourself for the last kilometre — the hill leading up to the centre of town is a real challenge! Follow the signs for the tourist office, located on Rue de l'Horloge.

Leg from Dinan to Sables-d'Or-les-Pins: 60 km

The stunning medieval town of **Dinan** is sure to enchant you. It boasts a rich and well-preserved architectural heritage, including a large number of half-timbered houses (80). The ramparts, with their 14 towers and four monumental doors, are the oldest and largest in Brittany. Take the time to walk around them. The château of the Dukes of Brittany and its 14th-century keep now house the Musée d'Art et d'Histoire du Pays de Dinan. There is a great deal to see in Dinan; treat yourself to a guided walking tour (about 90 min). If you happen to be in town on Thursday morning, don't miss the big market on Place des Champs and Place du Guesclin.

The tourist office on the beach at the little seaside resort of Sables-d'Or-les-Pins is only open during summer. The town does have several hotels, however. These are listed in the accommodations guide for the Côtes d'Armor, available at the tourist office in Dinan. During summer, it is wise to make reservations.

Head out of downtown Dinan by following the boulevards toward the train station (*gare*). In front of the town hall and the post office, follow the signs for *"toute directions"*, Saint-Malo, Dinard and the *gare*, then

PRACTICAL INFORMATION ON DINAN

Population
13,000 *Dinannais*

? **Tourist office:** 6 Rue de l'Horloge - BP 261, 22105 Dinan Cedex, ☎ 02 96 39 75 40, ⌦ 02 96 39 01 64

Bicycle shop: Cycle Scardin, 30 Rue Carnot, ☎ 02 96 39 21 94

Market
Thursdays

Specialties: *Corbelets* (chocolate), *Gavottes* (thin crêpes)

Major events: Rencontres Internationales de Harpe Celtique (Celtic harp concerts; July); Fête des Remparts (biennial, in September)

Map
IGN no. 16

head for Quévert. Ride through the area around the train station and across the railroad tracks. At the traffic circle, take the D68 toward Quévert. A long uphill stretch awaits you at the edge of town. Ride to **Quévert**, a little town where you will be greeted by scores of flowers. The Courtil des Senteurs (garden of scents; *courtil* means garden in old French) contains over 5,000 aromatic plants and a pool of aquatic plants. Make sure to take a few good whiffs on your way through! Follow the C4 out of the village toward **Languenan**. At the fork, turn left (no sign), and take the D26 straight ahead to the town of Languenan, six kilometres away.

Continue on the D26, toward **Plessix-Balisson** and Saint-Jacut-de-la-Mer. The road is hilly and winds its way through big fields and herds of cows. Ride past the pretty little Romanesque church. At the circle, stay on course for Saint-Jacut. The village is visible off in the distance. **Saint-Jacut-de-la-Mer** lies on a peninsula. For many years, the residents of this seaside resort and fishing village depended largely on mackerel for their livelihood. The Grande-Rue will take you to the abbey beach. Leave your bike in the parking lot and take the stairs down to the beach. The peninsula is fringed by a number of other beaches as well.

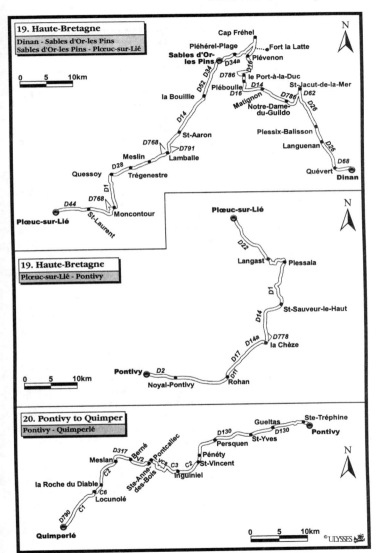

Take the D62 out of Saint-Jacut, toward Marignon and Notre-Dame-du-Guildé, then continue in the direction of Marignon on the D768. Enter **Le Guildo**. Cross the river and ride into **Notre-Dame-du-Guildo**.

Keep heading for Matignon. This is a long, arduous uphill stretch. At the circle, take the road leading to **Saint-Pôtan**, then take an immediate right onto an unnamed street (there is a road sign reading *"interdiction aux véhicules de plus de 3.5 tonnes"*). Follow this little road through the fields to **Matignon**.

Ride into the centre of the village, then head for Montbran on the D14. Watch out for the steep slope. At the crossroads, take the D16 toward Pléboulle and Cap Fréhel.

Ride up to **Pléboulle**. Continue toward Fréhel on the D16. At the D786, head for **Port-à-la-Duc**. Nestled in the curve of the Baie de la Fresnaye this village offers a lovely view of the surrounding cliffs. Be careful: there is a steep little climb leading into a curve in the D786. Continue on the D16 toward **Plévenon** and Cap Fréhel. The road winds its way along the left shore of the bay, affording a magnificent panoramic view the entire way.

A small road on the right leads to **Fort La Latte**. On the guided tour (approx. 45 min) of this outstanding historic site, you'll see the drawbridge, the guardroom, a set of private rooms, the chapel, the keep and the ramparts. This magnificent excursion to Fort La Latte covers a total distance of six kilometres.

Continue straight ahead to Cap Fréhel and the lighthouse. You can hear the cry of seagulls struggling in the wind. This pink sandstone cape rises 70 metres out of the sea. A path has been cleared along the ledge so that visitors can observe the birds that come here from northern seas, such as shags, kittiwakes, common guillemots, razorbills and oyster catchers. When you get back on your bike, hang on to your handlebars, lower your head and plunge into the wind!

Keep following the coast, heading for Sables-d'Or-les-Pins on the D34a. On the downhill stretch, you'll spot some lovely sandy beaches. Ride into Pléhérel-Plage. Continue on the D34a to **Sables-d'Or-les-Pins**, whose magical beauty is sure to win your heart. With its two-kilometre stretch of golden sand, wooded dunes and pine forest, the beach at Sables-d'Or-les-Pins is definitely the most beautiful one on the entire tour.

PRACTICAL INFORMATION ON SABLES-D'OR-LES-PINS

? **Tourist office:** On the beach (mid-June to mid-September), 22240 Sables-d'Or-les-Pins, ☎ 02 96 41 51 97

Leg from Sables-d'Or-les-Pins to Plœuc-sur-Lié: 55 km

Before leaving, take the time to clean you bicycle chain and derailleur, as some sand might have got stuck in there over the past few days!

Take the D34 out of Sables-d'Or-les-Pins. Next, head for Lamballe on the D786, then take an immediate left onto the D52, toward La Bouillie. The road leads down into the middle of the woods. Ride into **La Bouillie**, a pretty village of pink sandstone. Continue in the direction of **Lamballe**. At the intersection, take the D14 toward **Saint-Aaron**. The road winds through a rich farming region where cows and sheep can be seen grazing. Continue as far as Lamballe on the D14, then take the D791 into Lamballe-centre. In case you're looking for one, there is a bicycle shop right at the edge of town.

The Musée du Vieux Lamballe et du Penthièvre and the Musée Mathurin Méheut (paintings of traditional Brittany), are housed in the Maison du Bourreau (late 14th and early 15th centuries), on Place du Martray. The tourist office is also in this house. Don't leave town without visiting Notre-Dame de Grande Puissance. The former chapel of the château, it became a fortified church and then, in 1435, a collegiate church. Finally, horse-lovers will be pleased to learn that a national stud farm is open to the public on Place du Champ-de-Foire. Founded in 1825, it is the second largest stud farm in France. You can tour the stables, which house up to 400 horses, as well as the rest of the property.

To leave Lamballe, pick up the D768 at the town hall and head for Moncontour and Loudéac. The road climbs steeply at the edge of town. Next, turn right on the D28, toward Meslin and Quessoy. Take this small, hilly road to **Meslin**, then continue toward Quessoy, drinking in the vast panorama before you. At the town of **Trégenestre**, ride to the church to stay on course for Quessoy (D28). The town of **Quessoy** is home to three manors: the 18th-century Manoir de la Fontaine Saint-Père, the 17th-century Manoir de la Planche and the 18th-century Château La Houssaye.

Ride out of Quessoy to the D1, then continue in the direction of **Moncontour**. After a big, zigzagging downhill stretch, you'll find yourself at the foot of the ramparts of the medieval town. A park has been laid out so that people can relax and have picnics here. Follow the signs for *centre-ville*. It's a strenuous ride up.

Leave your bike on Place de la Carrière and stroll along the town's charming, shady little streets lined with half-timbered houses and private mansions adorned with wrought-iron balconies. Pick up the little guide of Moncontour and area at the tourist office (open July and August in the Maison de la Chouannerie et de la Révolution) or the town hall. Don't leave Montcontour without taking a look at the 16th-century stained-glass windows in the Église Saint-Mathurin. A market is held on the square on Monday mornings.

Take the D768 out of Moncontour, toward Plouguenast, then pick up the same road you came in on. As you leave the village, turn left (no sign). Ride up the D768 and through the Gare-de-Moncontour quarter. Take the D35 and then the D44 toward Plœuc-sur-Lié. Take the D44 into **Saint-Laurent** and then on to **Plœuc-sur-Lié**. Follow the signs for *centre-ville* and the *mairie* (town hall), on Place du Marché.

PRACTICAL INFORMATION ON PLŒUC-SUR-LIÉ

Population
3,000 *Plœucois*

? **Tourist office:** Town hall (*mairie*), Place Louis-Morel, 22150 Plœuc-sur-Lié, ☎ 02 96 42 10 33, ⁓ 02 96 42 86 83

Bicycle shop: Cycle Mazé, Rue de l'Église, ☎ 02 96 42 10 62

Market
Thursdays

Major events: Course Épique du 14 Juillet; Foire des Retrouvailles (1st Thursday in August)

Map
IGN no. 14

Leg from Plœuc-sur-Lié to Pontivy: 70 km

Plœuc-sur-Lié's Côte des Halles offers athletes a chance to go rock-climbing, hiking and hang-gliding or to fly a lightweight plane, and also organizes cross-country steeplechases. Information at the Plœuc-sur-Lié town hall.

Head out of Plœuc-sur-Lié from the Place du Marché and follow the D44 toward Moncontour, then take an immediate right onto the D22, in the direction of Plouguenast and Langast. There is a nice downhill stretch on the way out of the village. Take the D22 to the D768. Turn left and then immediately right to continue on the D22.

Ride into **Langast**. The rectangular Église Saint-Gal boasts the oldest stained-glass window in the region (1508), as well as magnificent Romanesque frescoes (9th century), which were recently restored. With its Merovingian herringbone masonry, this church, one of the three oldest in France, is definitely worth a visit. Continue toward **Plessala**, then pick up the D1 in the direction of Plémet.

The road winds its way through the fields. Cross the bridge over the Lié and follow the river to the edge of the Forêt de Loudéac. Pass the dam. At the fork, keep left to stay on the D1, in the direction of Plémet and La Chèze. After the town of **Saint-Sauveur**, continue toward La Chèze on the D14. The road is high up, affording a panoramic view.

Ride into **La Chèze** on the D778. Standing in the middle of the town are the ruins of a château built in the 12th century and destroyed in the 18th. At the nearby Musée Régional des Métiers, you can learn about the trades of yesteryear: clog-making, farriery, blacksmithing, slate-quarrying, cabinet-making, basketry, etc. You can have a picnic or simpy kick back and relax on the banks of the river, just opposite.

To leave the village, ride past the town hall, cross the bridge again and continue on the D14a toward Rohan. This road is very hilly and winds through a vast stretch of countryside to **Rohan**, at the edge of the department of Morbihan. Take the bridge over the river and follow the signs for Pontivy (D11).

The little village of Rohan, a vacation spot on the Oust, was the capital of the viscounty of Rohan for nearly five centuries. The château is no longer standing, but the Église Notre-Dame de Bonne Encontre, erected on behalf of Jean II de Rohan in 1510, bears witness to the town's prestigious past. A public garden and a small sailing harbour on the canal connecting Nantes to Brest add to the pleasure of visiting Rohan.

Take the D2 out of Rohan, toward Pontivy. Be careful: the traffic is likely to be a nuisance. The town hall of **Noyal-Pontivy** is a granite manor formerly owned by the Rohans. The church has an elegant 15th-century bell tower. Continue toward Pontivy on the D2. Follow the signs for *centre-ville*. Turn right to get to the château and the tourist office.

To return to Paris, you can take the train to Vannes and then the TGV to Paris-Montparnasse.

---

20. Pontivy to Quimper

Total distance:	120 km
Number of legs:	3
Level of difficulty:	🚲 🚲 🚲
Diagrams:	pp 163, 171
Maps:	A19, A20

Leg from Pontivy to Quimperlé: 65 km

You'll have to ride uphill for six kilometres as soon as you leave town, so warm up and do some stretches before you set out. Also, make sure to bring along plenty of water, as there are few large villages on this leg of the tour. Starting in the heart of the medieval village, take Rue du Pont out of Pontivy. Turn left on Quai Presbourg, then ride along the Blavet to the Pont du Quartier. Cross the river and turn left on Rue du 2e Chasseur a Cheval, toward Persquen and Saint-Tréphine (D130).

Stop at the **Chapelle Sainte-Tréphine**. The saint's life is depicted in nine 18th-century paintings inside. The legend of Sainte-Tréphine will remind you a lot of the story of Bluebeard. The old village still has a rural character, with its farms and bread ovens. Continue riding uphill. Take the D130 toward Persquen. This quiet, hilly road winds its way through small patches of woodland. Ride through the hamlet of Penvern, which has an 18th-century château.

Head for Inguiniel on the D130 without turning onto any of the intersecting roads. The road continues snaking over wooded hills that

PRACTICAL INFORMATION ON PONTIVY

Population
14,500 *Pontivyans*

? **Tourist office:** 61 Rue du Général-de-Gaulle, 56300 Pontivy, ☎ 02 97 25 04 10, ⌨ 02 97 27 87 09

Bicycle shops: Cycle du Blavet, 5 Rue Albert-de-Mun, ☎ 02 97 25 36 38 Lamouric, 39 Quai Arcole, ☎ 02 97 25 03 46

Market
Mondays

Specialties: *Pavés noirs du Château* (chocolate creams)

Major event: Festival de musique (June to August)

Map
IGN no. 15

have been left in an almost completely natural state. Take the C7 into **Pénéty**. The chapel, erected in 1600, contains ex-votos in the naive style. Go inside and take a look at them.

Continue in the same direction. Follow the signs for **Saint-Vincent** and **Kershého**. Take the C2 to **Inguiniel** and ride into the village. In front of the church, take the C3 toward Kernascléden. Be careful! Head left on the VC9, toward Pont-Calleck (there's a big white sign for an inn). Proceed straight ahead.

At the intersection, cross the D178 and continue toward Pont-Calleck. Take the bridge over the Scorff, then turn right. If you want to go to the inn, turn left, then backtrack to the bridge to continue. The road runs along the river through the Pont-Calleck forest. This is a perfect place for a picnic.

The road veers away from the river and starts to climb. At the fork, in front of an old chapel, head for Berné on the V2. Keep riding through the forest to the **Sainte-Anne-des-Bois** crossroads. You can go take a look at the Château de Pont-Calleck, which is now an orphanage owned by Dominican nuns. Movie-buffs might be interested to know that this château belonged to the Marquis de Pont-Calleck, whose sad story is partially recounted in Bertrand Tavernier's film *Que la fête commence*.

At the D110, turn right and ride a few metres to the gates of the château. This estate is private property, so you can only visit the garden. Go back to the intersection and take the V2 toward Berné. At the Croix Verte, keep left toward Berné (VC2) and proceed straight ahead. Cross the main road to continue toward Berné.

Follow the D109 into **Berné**. While you're there, take the opportunity to stock up on food. Ride in front of the church, and head for **Meslan** on the D317. Go through the village. The church still has lovely 16th-century woodwork. Head for Plouay on the D769, then take an immediate right on the C2, toward Locunolé and the Roches du Diable. Be careful crossing the Route Nationale. There is a parking lot right near the **Roches du Diable**.

The road continues through the woods. Follow the C6 toward the town of Locunolé. Take the bridge over the river. Ride up to the little plateau if you aren't already there; it's time for today's little climb. Ride into **Locunolé**, then proceed to Quimperlé on the C1. Be careful on the way down! At the D790, head for Quimperlé. Watch out: the traffic really moves here! Ride into **Quimperlé** and follow the signs for *centre-ville* and the tourist office.

Those who'd like to shorten the grand tour of Brittany can take the direct route (the D62 and then the D26) from Quimperlé to **Pont-Scorff**, a distance of 17 kilometres. When you get to Pont-Scorff, follow the directions for Auray (Leg from Lorient to Auray). The trip from Rennes to Nantes via Pont-Scorff covers a total distance of 800 kilometres.

Leg from Quimperlé to Quimper: 55 km

Quimperlé is made up of two sections. First, there's the upper town on the Colline Saint-Michel, with its park, lovely views of the surroundings and Gothic-style Église Notre-Dame-de-l'Assomption; to get there, take the pedestrian street, another steep commercial artery. Then there's the lower town, the historic quarter, with its narrow medieval streets, wharves, lovely houses and Romanesque, circular Église Sainte-Croix.

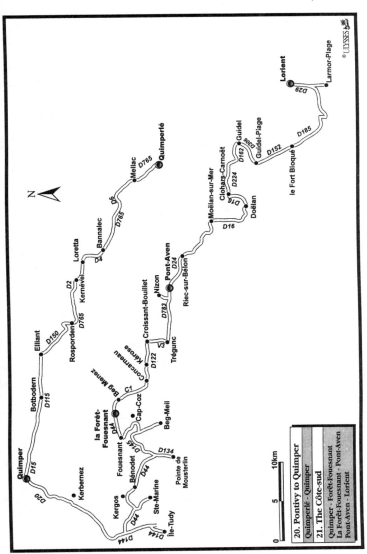

© ULYSSES

20. Pontivy to Quimper
Quimperlé - Quimper

21. The Côte-sud
Quimper - Forêt-Fouesnant
La Forêt-Fouesnant - Pont-Aven
Pont-Aven - Lorient

PRACTICAL INFORMATION ON QUIMPERLÉ

Population
11,400 *Quimperlois*

? **Tourist office:** Le Bourgneuf, 29300 Quimperlé, ☎ 02 98 96 04 32,
⇀ 02 98 96 16 12

Bicycle shop: Cycle Nicolas, 5 Rue de la Tour d'Auvergne,
☎ 02 98 96 05 18

Market
Fridays

Specialties: *Andouille de Baye* (sausage), *Chouchen* (fermented honey)

Major event: Festival de musique (mid-July)

Map
IGN no. 15

To leave Quimperlé, head for the tourist office, then cross the bridge.
Follow the D765 toward Bannalec. You'll have to ride uphill for about
2.5 km. Next, turn right on the road to **Mellac**. In the village, in front
of the church, follow the sign for Saint-Thurien. At the D6, turn left to
get back to the D765. Turn right and ride to Bannalec (no sign), then
take the D4 toward Scaër.

Keep an eye out on the left for the road to the Chapelle Saint-Mathieu.
Ride into **Loretta**. The little road is full of twists and turns. At the D2,
head for Kernével. Ride into **Kernével**, then continue toward
Rosporden. Take the D765 into **Rosporden**. Ride past the little pond,
follow the sign for the *gare* (train station) and Quimper, then head for
Elliant (D150). Go around the traffic circle and stay on course for
Elliant.

Ride into **Elliant** and head for Quimper on the D115. Cross the river.
You have to ride up a sizable hill to get out of town. At the top, the
road leads through some fields, where you'll see a few herds of cows
grazing. After, you'll come to a few long stretches up- and downhill.
As you near Quimper, the traffic will get heavier, so watch out!

PRACTICAL INFORMATION ON QUIMPER

Population
60,000 *Quimperois*

Tourist office: Place de la Résistance, 29000 Quimper, ☎ 02 98 53 04 05, ✆ 02 98 53 31 33

Bicycle shop: Cycles Lennez, 13 Rue A.-Briand, ☎ 02 98 90 14 81
Torch V.T.T., 58 Rue Providence, ☎ 02 98 53 84 41

Market
Wednesdays, Saturdays and Sundays

Specialties: *Torchettes* (cookies), *crêpes dentelles* (thin crêpes)

Major events: Festival de Cornouaille (late July); Semaine musicale (August)

Access from Paris: By road: A11 Rennes, CD765; by train: TGV, Gare Montparnasse to Quimper

Map
IGN no. 13

Take the D15 into **Quimper**. Be careful! At the circle, make sure to follow the sign for Quimper-centre, then follow the signs for the tourist office, located on Place de la Résistance, in front of some big parking lots.

21. The Côte-sud

Total distance: 525 km
Number of Legs: 8
Level of difficulty: 🚲 🚲
Diagrams: pp 171, 181, 185
Maps: A20 to A23

Leg from Quimper to the Forêt-Fouesnant: 65 km

Quimper still boasts a 13th-century cathedral, whose tall spires dominate the town. It took three centuries to build the Cathédrale Saint-Corentin, one of the oldest Gothic cathedrals in Brittany. The spires were financed by the parishioners, who each donated "one cent per year for five years". Rue Kéreon is another of the city's architectural jewels.

The Musée des Beaux-Arts houses a collection of old paintings (from the Flemish, Italian, Dutch and French schools), a large collection of 19th-century paintings with Breton and symbolist themes, and a number of major works from the Pont-Aven school. This museum is definitely worth the trip. If you wish, you can take a walking tour, during which a qualified guide will acquaint you with the town's neighbourhoods, cathedral and history. To find out the schedule, stop by the tourist office, open every day but Sunday.

Cross Pont Max-Jacob, opposite the tourist office, and take the Quai de l'Odet out of Quimper, toward Pont-l'Abbé. The road narrows. After two kilometres, you'll reach a large traffic circle. Go almost all the way around it, then veer off onto the D20, the château route. Ride in the bike lane.

Take the D20 left toward Plomelin (château route) then continue straight ahead. Keep an eye out for the road leading to the **Château de Kerbernez**, on the left. This estate belonged to Quimper native Alexandre Massé, an industrialist and inventor of the four-holed button. The château is now a horticulture school.

The road runs across the countryside over a series of hills, offering lovely views of the Odet. At the intersection, head for Bénodet and Ile-Tudy on the D144. At the traffic circle, take the D44 toward Ile-Tudy, riding in the bike lane. Follow the signs for the beach (*plage*). **Ile-Tudy** is a charming fishing village on a peninsula with a sailing harbour. For a long time in the past, the local men used to leave this cluster of white houses for months every year and head out to sea to go sardine fishing. A ferry crosses at Loctudy on the hour from Monday to Friday, and at less frequent intervals on Saturday and Sunday.

To continue, take the D144 out of Ile-Tudy and ride in the bike lane. Turn right on the street leading to the Chapelle Notre-Dame de la Clarté and Menez. At the fork, keep right. At the D44, turn right toward Saint-Marine and Bénodet (no sign). Ride in the bike lane.

Take the time to go to **Sainte-Marine**, a three-kilometre excursion that is truly worth your while; a fishing port, sailboats moored at the landing stages, a 16th-century chapel, a pink château and little cafés all add to the pleasure of visiting this town. Get back on the D44 and take the bridge across the Odet. Ride on the sidewalk. Make sure that your camera has film in it; the view is magnificent! The picturesque scenery of the Odet valley has inspired poets and painters alike.

Keep following the bike lane on the other side of the bridge. At the intersection, head for Bénodet, Fouesnant and Concarneau. If you are interested in châteaux, take the D34 toward Quimper, and turn left at the first road, which leads to the **Château de Kergos**. Winston Churchill once stayed in this 16th-century manor, supposedly to paint some watercolours.

Take the D34 into Bénodet. Go around the traffic circle, and stay on course for Fouesnant (D44). At the next circle, head for the **Pointe de Mousterlin** on the D134. At the crossroads, continue toward the point. After your visit, get back on the D134, ride to the fork and continue straight ahead toward Beg-Meil and Fouesnant on the D145. At the D45, keep heading for Beg-Meil and Cap-Coz. Use the bike lane, and ride to **Beg-Meil**, a seaside resort that gets very lively during summer.

Take the D45 out of Beg-Meil, toward Fouesnant and Cap-Coz. Use the bike lane. Turn right on the road leading to **Cap-Coz**. Ride into the port. On the Baie de la Forêt, which is dotted with boats, the view is magnificent. Leave the port and head for the centre of town. At the end of a good uphill stretch, you'll reach Fouesnant, perched 60 metres above the sea. Take the D44 toward Forêt-Fouesnant. After a nice ride downhill, you'll arrive at the village. The tourist office is located on Rue du Vieux-Port.

Leg from Forêt-Fouesnant to Pont-Aven: 30 km

Just opposite the tourist office in **Forêt-Fouesnant**, you'll see a 16th-century calvary and the flamboyant Gothic-style Église Notre-Dame. At the end of the street, facing due south, the Kerleven beach is a full-kilometre wide at low tide. Port-la-Forêt is the largest sailing port in the southern part of Finistère, and the activity here lends the town a lively atmosphere.

To leave Forêt-Fouesnant, ride to the church and follow the Route du Cranic to the circle. Follow the sign for Concarneau. The road leads along the coast, climbing sharply. Use the bike lane. Ride as far as **Beg Menez**, then continue toward Concarneau on the C1. Watch out: The downhill stretch is very steep! The road winds through a wooded conservation area, with several considerable climbs. In **Concarneau**,

PRACTICAL INFORMATION ON FORÊT-FOUESNANT

Population
2,400 *Forestois*

? **Tourist Office:** 2 Rue du Vieux-Port, 29 940 Forêt-Fouesnant, ☎ 02 98 56 94 09, ⊷ 02 98 51 42 07

Market
Sundays

Specialties: *Campagne aux pommes* (pâté sold at Barillec's), cider

Major events: Feu de la Saint-Jean; Soirées folkloriques (summer)

Map
IGN no. 13

there is a long downhill stretch leading to the shore, offering a magnificent view. Follow the road along the coast to the walls of the old city.

Rue Vauban is narrow and always packed during summer; you'll have an easier time touring the old city without your bicycle. Lock it up somewhere out in the open. Concarneau is the most important tuna fishing port in France; numerous other fish and shellfish are also unloaded here year round. At the beginning of the century, some artists organized a charity fair to help the fishermen who fell on hard times after the schools of sardines disappeared. Since then, the Fête des Filets Bleus, held on the second to last Sunday in August, has been a Concarneau tradition.

To get out of town, stand with your back to the tourist office and turn right on Rue Quai Carnot, the market street. At the circle, follow the D322a (*autres directions*), which will take you out of the port zone. Cross the bridge and head for Trégunc and Quimperlé, then turn left on the D22 (Route de Kérose), toward Melgven. At the fork, in the town of Lanriec, keep right, following the signs for the expressway and the D122. Ride into **Croissant-Bouillet**, then veer right on the V3, toward Trégunc. Keep an eye out for the Kérangallou menhir (7.2 metres high) on the left. On your way into **Trégunc**, on the road to the train station, follow the sign for Pont-Aven.

Continue toward Pont-Aven on the D783. Don't forget to stop in **Nizon**, to the left of the road, about three kilometres before Pont-Aven. The church's calvary, placed here to ward off the plague, was the model for Paul Gauguin's *Christ vert* (*Green Christ*) or *Calvaire breton*, executed in 1889. The restored church contains many naive wooden statues. Proceed to Pont-Aven on the D783, and follow the signs for downtown.

Leg from Pont-Aven to Lorient: 60 km

Pont-Aven is abounding in art galleries and attracts painters and other artists. For some, a trip to this "hallowed" place is like a pilgrimage. At the tourist office, you can pick up a small brochure about these painters called the *"Route des Peintres en Cornouaille"*. The Fête des Fleurs d'Ajoncs livens up the atmosphere here in early August. Make sure not to leave this little town without sampling one of the famous local *galettes de Pont-Aven* (butter cookies).

For part of this leg of the trip, you'll have to ride on roads where the traffic is a little heavier. Be careful. Take the bridge out of Pont-Aven and follow the D783 toward Quimperlé and Riec-sur-Bélon. The road climbs steeply on its way into **Riec-sur-Bélon**. Pick up the D24 in the direction of **Moëlan-sur-Mer**, and ride along the Belon river. **Belon**'s famous flat oysters, which have a very distinctive hazelnut flavour, are bred in the brackish waters along the river.

Continue toward Lorient on the D24. On your way out of Moëlan-sur-Mer, on the right, you can admire the lovely 16th-century Chapelle Saint-Philibert-et-Saint-Roch, with its calvary and fountain. It was dedicated to these two saints in order to protect the faithful from leprosy and the plague. On the left, you'll find a covered aisle and rows of menhirs.

At the circle, stay on course for Lorient, then take an immediate right onto the D16, in the direction of **Doëlan** (*rive droite*/right bank). Ride through the little fishing port and the charming village. At the second stop sign, turn left toward the bridge. Follow the signs for Doëlan (*rive gauche*/left bank). Cross the bridge and follow the sign for *"toutes directions"*. Stay on the D16 as far as **Clohars-Carnoët**. At the traffic circle, take the D24 toward Quimperlé. Immediately after, at the fork, head for Lorient and Guidel on the D224. After a long downhill stretch, take the Pont de Saint-Maurice across the Laïta (lovely view), riding on the sidewalk. At the other end of the bridge, you will enter the department of Morbihan. Proceed to **Guidel** on the D224.

Take the D306 out of Guidel, toward **Guidel-Plage**. This vacation spot has a pretty, powdery beach and some dunes. If you feel like taking a swim, here's your chance. Continue along the coastal road, which offers a magnificent view of the beaches and the little inlets. Ride toward **Fort Bloqué**. This beach, which faces due west, is renowned among windsurfers and surfers. Continue in the direction of Lorient (D152). Keep following the coast toward **Larmor-Plage** on the (D185). This large seaside resort, which boasts an immense beach, a water sports centre and a 12th-century church just steps from the sea, is known for its two big *pardons* (religious festivals; June 24 and July 2), a tradition that is still very much alive in Larmor.

Proceed to Lorient on the D29. Use the bike lane. Cross the bridge and head for Lorient-centre and the *"zone portuaire"*. Take the N465 into town. Ride past the fishing port, staying in the bike lane. Follow the signs for the tourist office, located at the port, on the Quai de Rohan.

PRACTICAL INFORMATION ON LORIENT

Population
59,300 *Lorientais*

Tourist office: Maison de la Mer, Quai de Rohan, 56100 Lorient, ☎ 02 97 21 07 84, ⇒ 02 97 21 99 44

 Bicycle shop: Évasion Sarl, 55 Rue Monistrol, ☎ 02 97 83 47 71

 Market
Saturdays

 Major events: Festival les Océanes (mid-July); Festival interceltique (early August)

Map
IGN no. 15

From Lorient, you can go on an excursion to **Ile de Groix**. To do so, go the harbour station, on Boulevard Auguste-Pierre, near the sailing port. The crossing takes 45 minutes, and you can easily tour the island by bicycle in a day. Still, plan on spending two days here so that you can relax for a while on the island's gorgeous beaches, which lie at the foot of tall cliffs, and take in its other beautiful sights.

Leg from Lorient to Auray: 65 km

During the Second World War, **Lorient** was reduced to ruins. Place Alsace-Lorraine is the centre of the new city. The French navy, the Royale, is the region's number-one employer. Rue de l'Assemblée-Nationale, a pedestrian shopping street, leads to Rue du Port, which is paved like a giant chessboard.

To leave Lorient, take Boulevard Cours de Chazelle to the train station. Head toward the banks of the Rivière Scorff on Boulevard Laënnec, then follow Boulevard du Scorff under the Pont Saint-Christophe. Take the bike lane (narrow) along the boulevard and the Scorff. Ride into **Kerdual** on the C5. Already, just a short bike ride from the centre of Lorient, you'll find yourself in a beautiful rural area. Ride over the highway.

Ride up the hill toward **Kergévant**. Follow the sign for Pont-Scorff. At the intersection, continue straight ahead. Ride past the entrance to the zoo. At the junction with the D6, keep heading for Pont-Scorff. Ride into **Pont-Scorff**.

On the square, you'll see the Rohan-Guémené house (1511), now the headquarters of the town council.

Take the D26 out of Pont-Scorff, in the direction of Hennebont and Caudan. Cross the bridge and take an immediate right off the D26, toward Caudan. The road runs over a series of hills on its way through a lush valley. Ride into **Caudan** and turn right on Rue Jean-Moulin. At the intersection, continue straight ahead on the Alée-des-Pins. At the light, turn left toward Plouay. Ride up into the village of Caudan, toward the church. Head for Trescouet Poteau Rouge on Rue du 10 Mai. Take the C13 out of the village and ride toward the **Trescouet Poteau Rouge**, then proceed to Hennebont on the D769.

Hennebont, located in the Blavet Valley, owes its name to a strategically located bridge on that river ("Hen Pont" means "old bridge"). Take a little break in this pleasant town, which was hard hit by the 1944-45 shelling. You can still see vestiges of the ramparts of a castle (1250) that used to stand on the right bank of the river. Access to the walled city is gained through the Porte Broërec, flanked by two massive towers that were once used as prisons and now house the town museum. Take the stairs on the left up to the rampart walk, where you can enjoy a lovely view.

The old Cistercian monastery, set on 25 hectares of land, has been used as a national stud farm since 1857. The stables (Breton stallions and work horses) are open to the public from July to September.

To leave Hennebont, ride past the Basilique Notre-Dame-du-Paradis (15th century) and follow the sign reading *"toutes directions"*. At the traffic circle, head for Brandérion. Follow the D765 out of town, then take an immediate right on the D164, toward Nostang.

This part of the tour, puctuated by old towns and chapels, leads along roads that snake through big fields. Ride into **Nostang**, located north of the Étel river. Continue toward Landévant on the D33. Take a look at the Chapelle de Locmaria, which dates from the 12th century, as well as the elegant 16th-century Chapelle de Légevin, built entirely of granite. Proceed to **Landévant**. On your way into the village, veer right, ride past the church and follow the sign for Landaul and Sainte-Anne-d'Auray (D33). Ride across the main road (D765) toward **Pluvigner**, then turn immediately in the direction of Landaul and Locmaria. Admire the Chapelle de Locmaria-er-Hoët, which was a stopping place for Sainte-Anne-d'Auray pilgrims.

Coast downhill and ride into **Landaul**. Take the D19 toward **Tréavac**. There will be a 17th-century fountain and a chapel adorned with a Renaissance sculpture on the left. Take the time to stroll through the picturesque town of Brech, then get back on your bike and take the D19 to Sainte-Anne-d'Auray.

After passing all those chapels, a stop in **Sainte-Anne-d'Auray** is a must in order to learn more about this region, which has been so profoundly influenced by Christianity. Believers from all over Europe flock to the big religious festival (*pardon*) on July 25 and 26. On the occasion of Pope John-Paul II's visit to Sainte-Anne-d'Auray, 1996 was decreed the "year of religious heritage" in Brittany.

To leave Saint-Anne-d'Auray, head toward Auray via the Chartreuse. Ride past the World War I memorial and the Belgian cemetery. Take the D120 out of the village, toward the Champ des Martyrs and the Vallée de Tréauray. The road leads downhill, then alongside the Kerzo marshes. A large lane leads to the Champ des Martyrs, where a chapel

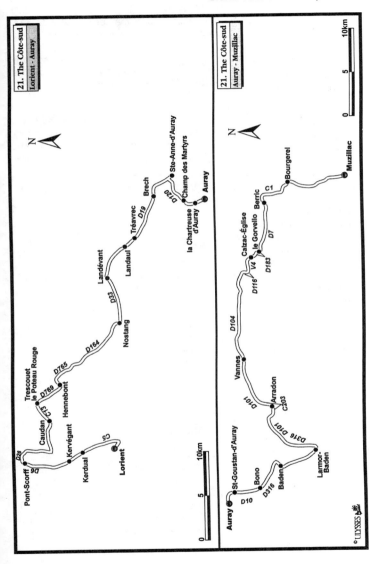

21. The Côte-sud
Lorient - Auray

N

Ste-Anne-d'Auray
Champ des Martyrs
Brech
Tréavrec
Landaul
Landévant
Nostang
le Poteau Rouge
Trescouet
Hennebont
Caudan
Pont-Scorff
Kervégant
Kerdual
Lorient
la Chartreuse d'Auray
Auray

D110
D19
D33
D164
D765
D769
C13
D26
9a
C5

10km
5
0

21. The Côte-sud
Auray - Muzillac

N

Bourgerel
Muzillac
Berric
C1
le Gorvello
Calzac-Église
V4
D7
D183
D116
D104
Vannes
Arradon
C203
D101
D316
Larmor-Baden
Baden
Bono
St-Goustan-d'Auray
Auray
D10
D316

10km
5
0

© ULYSSES

designed like a Greek temple was erected in memory of 952 émigré and *chouan* (anti-revolutionary peasants) prisoners executed in 1795.

Continue towards **Auray**. To see the Chartreuse and the mausoleum of the émigré and *chouan* martyrs, ride straight ahead across the D768. Follow the signs for *centre-ville*. The tourist office is located on Rue du Lait.

I recommend making a day-trip to **Carnac**, "the place where there are mounds of stones", so that you can explore a region full of mysterious menhirs and dolmens — the Saint-Michel tumulus, the Kerlescan, Kermario and Ménec menhirs, and finally the Petit-Ménec area.

PRACTICAL INFORMATION ON AURAY

Population
10,000 *Alréens*

Tourist office: 20 Rue du Lait, 56400 Auray, ☎ 02 97 24 09 75, ⊷ 02 97 50 80 75

Bicycle shop: Espace Loisirs, 108 Avenue Général-de-Gaulle, ☎ 02 97 56 29 87

Market
Mondays

Major events: Festival International d'Auray (July), Pardon de Sainte-Anne-d'Auray (religious festival: July 25 and 26)

Map
IGN no. 15

Leg from Auray to Muzillac: 65 km

The port of **Saint-Goustan d'Auray** was bustling with commercial activity under Napoleon III and up until the advent of the railway. Nowadays, Auray's charm lies in its sailing harbour, 17th-century stone bridge and old Quartier Saint-Goustan, at the foot of the town. Immerse yourself in history by strolling along the steep streets lined with houses with corbelled balconies, then wind up your visit by relaxing in the splendid Renaissance- and baroque-style Église Saint-Guildas, on the right bank.

Head out of Auray, toward Vannes and Bono, then take an immediate right on the street leading down to the Quartier Saint-Goustan. Cross the stone bridge and follow the signs for Bono and *"toutes directions"*, then keep right toward **Bono** (D101). Ride past Bono's tiny port, then continue toward Arradon and Baden on the D101. Ride straight ahead to the exit for Larmor-Baden and **Baden**. Be careful! If you take a right turn before this exit, you'll find yourself in a labyrinth of roads running through housing developments.

Pick up the D316 and proceed to Larmor-Baden. Continue straight ahead to the village, toward Vannes. The little town, set right in the middle of the Golfe du Morbihan, offers launch cruises through the numerous islands in the gulf. Prehistory buffs won't want to miss a visit to **Ile de Gravinis**, renowned for its huge and well-preserved cairn (burial mound). Larmor-Baden is the only point of departure for the island. Reservations are recommended, since only 20 people at a time can visit the island. Information: ☎ 02 97 42 63 44.

At the fork, take the D101 toward Arradon. Continue to the C203, then on to the town of Arradon, a residential suburb of Vannes. Ride out of Arradon, toward Vannes. At the D101, head for **Vannes**, using the bike lane. Follow the signs for *centre-ville* and the port.

Be extra-careful on your way in and out of town! If you try to bypass Vannes, you'll find yourself stuck in a network of highways and express lanes.

You can relax a bit at one of the outdoor cafés and restaurants on Place Gambetta, which lies in front of the sailing port, facing due south. If you don't have much time to spend at the former fortified city of the duchies of Brittany, at least take a quick look at the pedestrian area around the Cathédrale Saint-Pierre. Saturday is market day in Vannes.

To leave town, start at the port and ride toward the ramparts on Rues Francis-Deckeren and Maréchal-Leclerc, heading for Nantes. At the traffic light on Place Bir Hakeim, take Avenue de Verdun toward the Zone du Prat. Ride past the Navy (Marine) building. At the next traffic light, turn right on Rue Alain-Gerbault and head for the Prat industrial zone. The road follows the railroad tracks. At the traffic circle, take Rue Édouard-Michelin, then head out of Vannes on the D104. Ride over the Route Nationale and continue straight ahead.

After about five kilometres, you'll be back in the peaceful countryside. Head for Theix on the D116, take an immediate left toward **Calzac-Église** (V4), then pick up the D183 in the direction of **Le Gorvello**. This cute little village abounding in flowers has several listed houses. Once a major pilgrimage site, the Église Saint-Jean-Baptiste was modified in the 16th century. The town is worth a close look. Proceed toward **Berric** on the D7. The Château de Trémohar, built in the 16th and 17th centuries, is not open to the public.

Head out of the village in the direction of Questembert. Turn right toward Noyal-Muzillac on the C1. The road runs through a stretch of wooded countryside. A little river wends its way gently across the landscape, where a few sheep can be seen grazing peacefully. At the crossroads, continue toward Muzillac. Ride into the centre of the village. The tourist office is located on Place de l'Hôtel-de-Ville.

PRACTICAL INFORMATION ON MUZILLAC

Population
4,000 *Muzillacais*

? **Tourist office:** Place de l'Hôtel-de-Ville, 56190 Muzillac, ☎ 02 97 41 53 04, ⁊ 02 97 41 65 42

🚲 **Bicycle shop:** Cycles Flohic, 25 Avenue Général-de-Gaulle, ☎ 02 97 41 66 40

Market
Fridays

Specialty: Seafood

Map
IGN no. 15

Leg from Muzillac to Guérande: 70 km

Nature lovers come to **Muzillac** for its park, laid out around the Pen Mur pond. There is a mill that makes paper out of linen and cotton, using traditional methods, making for a highly instructive visit in a lovely setting. Muzillac livens up on Friday mornings, when the weekly market is held.

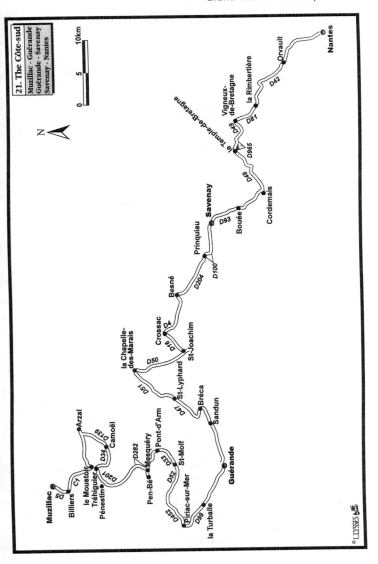

21. The Côte-sud
Muzillac - Guérande
Guérande - Savenay
Savenay - Nantes

0 5 10km

N

Head out of Muzillac toward Billiers and Roche-Bernard. Take the bike lane as far as **Billiers**. Set between the marshes and the sea, this little town welcomes both fishing boats and pleasure craft. At the old Cistercian abbey, there is a chapel containing the tombs of John I, Duke of Brittany; his wife Isabeau de Castille and Jeanne d'Angleterre.

Take the C1 out of the village, toward Arzal. Follow the road leading to the **Le Moustoir** point. Opposite, you'll see the village of Tréhiguier. Continue on this little road to **Arzal**. At the circle, in front of the church, take the D139 toward the Arzal dam (*barrage*). Head for the sailing harbour (it's fun to watch the boats go through the locks). Cross the Pont de la Vilaine and proceed to **Camoël** on the D139 and the D34.

Continue out of Camoël on the D34, then take a right on the coastal road to Tréhiguier. Ride into the port of **Tréhiguier**, and proceed to **Penestin**. Mussel breeding is the region's major activity. The Mine d'Or beach lies nestled at the foot of some red-ochre cliffs. Don't forget to make the detour.

Keep following the coast to **Pen-Bé** (D201 and D282). Ride around the Pen-Bé point, and return to **Mesquéry** in order to continue to Pont-d'Armes. There are some marshes on the right. The road ends at a row of trees. Turn right (no sign). Ride into **Pont-d'Armes**. Continue straight ahead through the salt marshes toward **Saint-Molf**, named after an Irish saint, then head for Piriac-sur-Mer and Turballe. At the fork, follow the D52. Keep following the coast, and take the D452 along the shore to **Piriac-sur-Mer**. Treat yourself to a touch of the exotic in this village, whose white-washed houses will remind you of Greece.

Follow the shore out of Piriac, toward Guérande and **La Turballe**, a large fishing port. Take the D99 to **Guérande**. The tourist office is located at the Porte Saint-Michel.

I suggest taking a day-trip to explore the Côte d'Amour and its famous eight-kilometre beach (Baule-les-Pins). Here's an interesting itinerary: take the D774 from Guérande to **Saillé**, a marsh town that is not to be missed. After touring the salt marshes, proceed to the charming port of **Croisic**, then follow the D45 along the coast to **Baule-les-Pins** and **Pornichet**. You can then head back to Guérande through the hinterland, via **Brais**, **Saint-André** and **Belle Étoile**. This excursion covers a distance of about 60 kilometres.

Leg from Guérande to Savenay: 65 km

A walk around **Guérande**'s ramparts offers a chance to take in a general view of the narrow streets lined with grey stone houses decorated with old signs. Balzac drew inspiration from this charming walled town when writing *Un drame au bord de l'eau*.

PRACTICAL INFORMATION ON GUÉRANDE

Population
12,000 *Guérandais*

Tourist office: 5 Place du Marché-au-Bois, 44350 Guérande, ☎ 02 40 24 96 71, ✆ 02 40 62 04 24

Bicycle shop: Cycles Belgrand, 7 Faubourg Saint-Michel, ☎ 02 40 24 91 44

Market
Saturdays

Specialties: Sea salt, eel, duck

Map
IGN no. 24

Head out of Guérande in the direction of Saint-Lyphard and Saint-André-des-Eaux. At the circle, follow the sign for the **Sandun** pond (*étang*). At the crossroads, stay on course for the Sandun pond and Kergourdin. Ride over the little bridge and continue toward the pond and Bréca. The road leads through a wooded area, then to the marshes, where you'll find some horses who will gladly take part in a photo session.

Ride to **Bréca**. Along the way, you'll pass a number of small thatched cottages typical of the Brière region.

At this point, you might wish to visit the **Parc Régional de la Grande Brière**, a watery stretch of land inhabited by marsh birds. You can explore the park by riding along its canals in a small boat, accompanied by a guide.

Keep following the little road to **Saint-Lyphard**. In the village, the church's bell tower offers those with the energy to climb 135 steps the chance to drink in a splendid panoramic view of Brière. Turn right on the D47. At the circle, take the D51 toward Chapelle-des-Marais. At the other intersection, stay on course for Chapelle-des-Marais and Pontchâteau (D33). The tourist office occupies the Maison du Sabotier (a *sabotier* is a person who makes clogs, an old Breton trade), on the way into town. On the staircase of the town hall, you can see a fossilized tree (*morta*) that was removed from the marshes in 1969.

Take the D50 out of Chapelle-des-Marais, toward Saint-Joachim. Ride through the Parc Régional de la Grande Brière then into the town of Saint-Joachim, a group of seven islands in the heart of the marshes.

Head for **Crossac** and Pontchâteau on the D16. At the intersection, pick up the D4 in the direction of Donges. You'll pass a dolmen on the way out of Crossac. Take a left on the D204 and ride to the village of **Besné**.

Continue on the D204 toward Prinquiau and Savenay. Ride past the old mill. At the village of **Prinquiau**, head for Donges and Saint-Nazaire (D100). Ride over the highway, then take an immediate left on the road parallel to it. You'll be following the railroad tracks. Go through the little tunnel, then head for Savenay right after. Pass the train station, keeping an eye out for the sign for *centre-ville*, on the left. You'll have to ride up a sizable hill; it's been a while, hasn't it?

Leg from Savenay to Nantes: 45 km

The little town of Savenay, in the centre of a farming region, is perched 100 metres above the Loire Valley. There is no tourist office here.

Head out of town, past the covered markets, and ride down the street. Take the D17 toward Saint-Étienne. Keep your eyes peeled for the exit for **Boué** and **Cordemais** (D93) on the right.

Ride out of Cordemais and head for Temple-de-Bretagne on the D49. Ride up the big hill. The road leads through a verdant stretch of countryside, where a few horses can be seen grazing peacefully. Ride into **Temple-de-Bretagne** (the headquarters of the Knights Templar in the 12th-century) and head for Vigneaux-de-Bretagne on the D965, then the D49 immediately after. Ride to **Vigneaux-de-Bretagne**. The Château du Buron belonged to the Marquise de Sévigné in the 17th century. Take the D81 toward Sautron, then turn left on the little road indicated by a white sign listing all the villages.

Ride through the fields to the D42, then turn right in the direction of Nantes and Orvault. Pass through **Orvault**, a residential suburb of Nantes. At the circle, stay on course for Nantes. Ride into Orvault-Granval and head for **Nantes**, *centre-ville*. Go past the big garden and up the big hill, then continue straight ahead for *centre-ville* and the tourist office, on Place du Commerce.

PRACTICAL INFORMATION ON NANTES

Population
245,000 *Nantais*

Tourist office: Place du Commerce, 44000 Nantes, ☎ 02 40 47 04 51, ⁓ 02 40 89 11 99

Bicycle shops: Seguin, 38 Rue des Allouettes, ☎ 02 40 46 56 32
Cycles Alkar, Boulevard Ernest Dalby, ☎ 02 40 49 34 24

Market
Wednesdays, Saturdays and Sundays

Major events: Printemps des Arts (late May), Festival International d'Été (early July), Rendez-vous de l'Erdre (early September)

Specialties: Fish, wine (Muscadet, gros-plant, pineau), LU Petit-Beurre cookies, *gâteau nantais au rhum* (rum cake), *berlingots* (candies)

Access from Paris: By road: A11, the Océane; by train: TGV, Gare Montparnasse to Nantes

Map
IGN no. 24

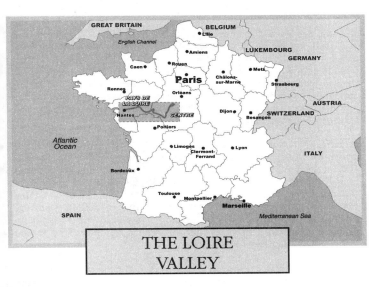

THE LOIRE VALLEY

History, literature, architecture, gastronomy and wine all come together in the Loire Valley, the discoveries to be made when exploring the shores of this majestic river and its numerous tributaries are thus endless.

This tour starts at **Nantes** and leads up the Loire, crossing Anjou and ending in Touraine, in the heart of the area known as Val de Loire. The river flows past large, fortified towns steeped in history, old villages abounding in flowers, cave dwellings, rolling fields, market gardens, fruit farms, forests and centuries-old vineyards.

The sweetness of life (and of cycling) prevails in these areas, which produce a wide variety of wines; the vineyards lie on the versants of the valleys. Muscadet, a dry, young, white wine, typifies the sunny quality of the Loire Valley wines. The Anjou and Touraine regions produce a vast range of white wines — some dry, others mellow — as well as light rosés and reds with violet and raspberry bouquets. After a day of exertion, you're sure to enjoy sampling all these light wines, or for that matter the more full-bodied reds of Chinon and the *crémants* of Saumur, made according to traditional methods.

This tour thus starts in the Pays de la Loire region, in Nantes, a city of art and history, and the former capital of Brittany (Bretagne). The

Château des Ducs is an imposing Gothic and Renaissance building. The city prospered during the colonial era, thanks to the shipping industry. Jules Verne came into the world in a house on Ile Feydeau, in what used to be the heart of Nantes. As an adolescent, he had a passion for the sea, and was greatly influenced by the Quai de la Fosse and its big schooners, as well as by the wife of a sailor lost at sea, who taught him to read. The Jules Verne museum will plunge you into the *Voyages Extraordinaires* of this Nantais writer.

In terms of topography, the **Anjou** region definitely requires the most effort, but you will be immensely rewarded by the charming scenery and magnificent views of the Loire. This part of the country inspired poet Joachim du Bellay, a member of the Pléiade: *"Heureux qui comme Ulysses a fait un beau voyage..."* ("Happy is he who, like Ulysses, has taken a lovely trip..."). One of the Counts of Anjou, Geoffroy Foulques, liked to wear a sprig of broom (a shrub with little yellow flowers; *genêt* in French) on his hat, hence the nickname of the Angevin line of counts, Plantagenêt.

The town of **Angers**, the start of the next leg of the tour, is watered by the Maine. Its fortress, erected in the 13th century, has truncated towers featuring even bands of dark shale, sandstone and granite. This majestic citadel, which encloses an area of 20,000 square metres, and is flanked by 17 large towers, is a splendid example of military architecture. Farther to the south, the **Château de Brissac** stands in a magnificent park near the Rivière Aubance, in an area renowned for its syrupy, golden wines. This château was rebuilt between two big, round, 14th-century towers when it first came into the Comte de Brissac's possession. His descendants still live here; the present owner is the 12th Duc de Brissac.

Between Angers and Montsoreau, the river is lined with houses made of pale tufa stone. In the village of **Cunault**, the Église Notre-Dame, a masterpiece of Romanesque art, boasts 223 beautifully carved capitals. You'll also find a number of cave dwellings along the cliffs near Saumur.

Mushrooms are cultivated in immense underground tunnels that were bored in order to extract tufa stone. Under the reign of Louis XIV, the old catacombs in Paris were used for that same purpose. From 1850 on, this crop became more and more popular, and began to be grown in the Loire Valley. The mushrooms continued to be known as *champignons de Paris*, however. Visiting a mushroom bed is a very unusual experience — and pleasantly refreshing on a hot day. In addition to the traditional *champignons de Paris*, you'll find wood-blewits, oyster mushrooms (yellow, pink and common) and shiitakes.

Saumur lies stretched amidst its vineyards on the south bank of the Loire. The château of the Dukes of Anjou, overlooking the town, is sure to catch your eye with its elegant, bright white architecture. A city of equestrians and the horse capital of France, Saumur owes its renown to its École de Cavalerie (Cavalry School), founded in the early 19th century, under the Restoration. The school trained several generations of officers before closing in 1969.

From Louis XI to Francis I, the kings of France were very fond of the Loire Valley, known for its Renaissance châteaux, through which it is still possible to piece together many pages of history. Francis I prized the large forests nearby, where he could go hunting. Several châteaux were built during his reign. The Loire Valley is a classic European destination for bicycle touring. During summer, the region welcomes a huge number of cyclists, and at the entrance of each château, your hosts have taken care to provide a space where you can leave your bike.

Touraine, a rich farming region also known as the "garden of France", was annexed to the kingdom in 1259. At the meeting point of Anjou, Poitou and Touraine, the **Château de Montsoreau**, made famous by Alexandre Dumas's *La Dame de Montsoreau*, represents two eras; it is half-fortress, half-residence, with a splendid Renaissance-style main staircase. The extraordinary epic of Joan of Arc began in 1429 at the **Château de Chinon**, when, convinced that she was on a divine mission, the young woman applied to the Dauphin, Charles VII, for an audience. *"Je suis envoyée par Dieu pour bouter les Anglais hors de France"* ("I have been sent by God to drive the English out of France"), she claimed, and the Dauphin ended up entrusting her with that very task. Chinon was the capital of England in the 12th century; the château was the favourite residence of the Plantagenet kings. In the 15th century, Chinon became the capital of France, and was also the birthplace of writer François Rabelais, "father" of Gargantua.

Charles Perrault surely drew inspiration from the remarkable architecture, tall, white silhouette and magnificent site of the **Château d'Ussé** for his fairy tale *Sleeping Beauty*. The Duchess Anne, who had succeeded to the crown of Brittany at the age of 11, celebrated her wedding to Charles VII at the **Château de Langeais**. Through this union, the duchy of Brittany became part of the French realm. Erected in the 15th century by order of Louis XI, the château is a powerful, severe-looking structure.

The Renaissance-style **Château de Villandry** is completely different. It is famous for its gardens, which have been patiently restored so that they now appear just as they did in the 16th century. These gardens, unique in Europe, comprise an ornamental vegetable garden, an ornamental flower garden and, above, a "water garden". An absolute must for gardening buffs!

At the edge of Touraine, the **Citadelle de Loches**, has seen numerous wars and held many prisoners. It stands on a promontory in the **Vallée de l'Indre**. Loches holds the memory of two exceptional women who were completely devoted to their king: Agnès Sorel, the "Dame de Beauté", who was the first woman to be officially recognized as the mistress of a king of France, and Joan of Arc, who persuaded the Dauphin, Charles VII, to be crowned in Reims.

Azay-le-Rideau is one of the most famous Renaissance châteaux in Touraine. Set on a small island in the Indre, it was erected between 1518 and 1523 for financier Gilles Berthelot. With its harmonious lines and its main staircase, which has a straight banister and is sumptuously decorated with medallions and friezes, this elegant white château embodies all the refinement of the Renaissance. The **Château de Chenonceaux**, also known as the *château des six femmes* (château of the six women), was constructed in 1515 by a wealthy bourgeois named Thomas Bohier, administrator of finance under Francis I. He put his wife, Catherine Briçonnet, in charge of the building's construction. She was the first of six chatelaines to have lived in this unusual residence, built right on the Cher.

The **Château d'Amboise**, a royal residence, was overhauled by artists and craftsmen whom Charles VIII had brought back with him from Italy. He died tragically, leaving his successors to put the finishing touches on his home. This château was the first in the Val de Loire to reflect the influence of the Italian Renaissance. **Chambord**, the most grandiose and fairy tale-like of the Loire châteaux, was erected in the heart of a game-filled forest by Francis I, an avid hunter. Its construction took over 25 years, during which the king always managed to find enough gold to finance the project. The château has 440 rooms, 83 staircases (16 large ones), 800 capitals and some 365 chimneys!

Finally, the classical **Château de Cheverny** was the model for Captain Haddock's Château de Moulinsart in the Tintin cartoons. Riding to hounds is still a great Cheverney tradition. **Blois**, the last stop on this tour, is a remarkably beautiful town whose architecture has been well-preserved and well-restored. The Château de Blois, famous for its Francis I-style staircase, bears witness to several centuries of history and serves as a wonderful résumé of the architecture of the Val de Loire between the 13th and the 17th centuries.

There is a lot to see and do throughout this magical tour. A few words of advice: don't overdose on châteaux; limit yourself to one or two a day. Tour châteaux from different periods so that you can see a variety of styles, and admire the others from the outside. The admission charges range from 30 FF to 55 FF, with the average being about 40 FF; don't forget to plan your budget accordingly.

22. TOUR OF THE LOIRE VALLEY

Total distance: 490 km
Number of legs: 9
Level of difficulty: 🚲 🚲
Diagrams: pp 197, 203, 211, 216
Maps: A24 to A28

Leg from Nantes to Saint-Florent: 55 km

The capital of Brittany from 1213 to 1524, **Nantes** enjoyed a period of great prosperity during the 15th century, under Dukes John V and Francis II. The construction of the Château des Ducs, encircled by moats and ramparts, began in 1466 under Francis II and continued under Anne of Brittany. The château was remodeled several times afterwards. It is legendary for its many famous prisoners (Bluebeard, the Marquis de Pont-Calleck, the Duchesse de Berry, etc.). This former fortress now houses the Musée d'Art Populaire Régional, the Musée des Arts Décoratifs and the Musée de Salorges. The Cathédrale Saint-Pierre-et-Saint-Paul, built in the flamboyant Gothic style, contains the tomb of Francis II and Marguerite de Foix. It is pleasant to stroll through the old pedestrian neighbourhoods between the cathedral, the Église Sainte-Croix and Place du Bouffay (see p 189 for practical information on Nantes).

The superb, covered Passage Pommeraye was inaugurated in 1843. It was designed to embellish the area by linking Rue Crébillon and Rue de la Fosse, and to drive out the "girls" living there. In the shopping arcade that leads down level by level to the Bourse, you can admire a number of old shop signs. On the upper level, there is a peripheral arcade adorned with statues of adolescents by Jean Debay. The surrealist movement was supposedly born in the shadowy light of the little lanes and bistros of the Quai de la Fosse.

Painting buffs won't want to miss the Musée des Beaux-Arts, which boasts one of the richest collections in France. The Jardin des Plantes, a garden near the train station, was founded in 1806 and is another local must.

Nantes is the seventh largest city in France and the capital of the Pays de la Loire region. Although there is a lot of traffic here, you can feel relatively confident cycling out of town, since you'll be riding along streets with a bike lane for nine kilometres. If you are careful to stay in the lane, you should have no problem leaving Nantes.

There are few hotels in Saint-Florent-le-Vieil, so it is advisable to make the necessary arrangements for your stay there before leaving Nantes. To get out of town, go to the Gare Nord (train station). With your back to the station, turn right and take Boulevard Ernest Dalby toward the Jardin des Plantes and Doulon. Ride alongside the railroad tracks then over the level crossing, and continue straight ahead (bicycle shop). Take the bike lane in the direction of Sainte-Luce-sur-Loire (bicycle shop). Head out of Nantes on the D68.

Ride into **Sainte-Luce-sur-Loire**, staying in the bike lane. Follow the signs for **Thouaré-sur-Loire**. Ride around the traffic circle in front of the village church and head for Saint-Julien-de-Concelles, then immediately cross the bridge over the Loire. On the other side, pick up the D751 in the direction of Champtoceaux. Continue on the Vignoble d'Anjou tourist route, which follows the Loire. Take the D751 into **Varenne**. The town, perched on a plateau, has a château surrounded by a pretty park, from which you can enjoy a view of the narrow valley.

Continue along the Vignoble d'Anjou tourist route. The road climbs gently, rising up above the river and running through the vineyards. Then, a fairly steep downhill stretch with several sharp turns brings you back down to the level of the river. Keep following the D751 to the village of **Champtoceaux**, which lies at the top of a steep hill. The tourist office is located in the Jardin de Champalud, a sort of "balcony" overlooking the Val de Loire, and a pleasant place for a stroll. Because of its strategic location, this once fortified town bore

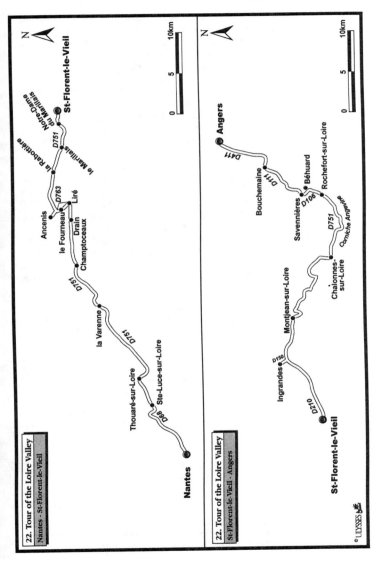

22. Tour of the Loire Valley
Nantes - St-Florent-le-Vieil

22. Tour of the Loire Valley
St-Florent-le-Vieil - Angers

© ULYSSES

witness to many battles. During the Middle Ages, the Bretons and the Angevins fought over it. After the citadel was destroyed by Jean de Bretagne, a village was built farther to the east. You can learn more about the local history by taking the trail that runs around the remains of the fortress. Champtoceaux is also renowned for its white wines.

Continue along the D751 to **Drain** and Liré. This downhill stretch offers a lovely view. At the locality of "Cul du Moulin", the vestiges of two arches from an 18th-century dam are visible on the banks of the river. This dam served as a tollgate for river traffic. Boats had to pass under the arches, and a crew member would go down a little staircase to pay the toll.

Ride into **Liré**, birthplace of Renaissance poet Joachim du Bellay, a member of the Pléiade. For the melancholy, there is a museum in an authentic 16th-century residence on Rue Grand-Logis, which contains etchings, original drawings and reproductions of his works. Head for Ancenis on the D763. After passing through a small wooded area, ride into **Le Fourneau**. Instead of crossing the bridge leading to Ancenis, take a right on the little road that follows the Loire to **La Rabottière**, a former barge port. If you feel like it, you can go take a look at the ruins of the **Château d'Ancenis** and the statue of Joachim du Bellay on the right bank of the Loire.

PRACTICAL INFORMATION ON ANCENIS

Population
7,300 *Ancenois*

? **Tourist office:** Place du Millénaire, 44150 Ancenis, ☎ 02 40 83 07 44

Bicycle shops: Chauvigné, Rue du Château, ☎ 02 40 98 88 70
Évasion 2000, 207 Rue Genhogran, ☎ 02 40 83 33 93

Market
Thursdays

Specialty: wines from the Anjou region

Map
IGN no. 25

Go back over to the left bank at the intersection; continue following the Loire in the direction of Notre-Dame-du-Marillais. At the fork, keep left (no sign). You'll see the clock tower of the Marillais church. Proceed to the village. Take the D751 to **Notre-Dame-du-Marillais**. Cross the bridge, enter the village, and proceed to Saint-Florent-le-Vieil.

Leg from Saint-Florent-le-Vieil to Angers: 65 km

Saint-Florent-le-Vieil, set atop Mont Glonne, overlooks the Loire from a height of 45 metres. On the left as you enter the village, the esplanade of the abbey forms a kilometre-long promenade. This belvedere offers a panoramic view of the Moquart and Batailleuse islands and the Coteau de Varades, just opposite. The abbey church dates from the 18th century. The abbey farm, once fortified, now houses the Centre Permanent d'Initiation à l'Environnement.

PRACTICAL INFORMATION ON SAINT-FLORENT-LE-VIEIL

? **Tourist office**: Place de la Mairie BP 54, 49410 Saint-Florent-le-Vieil, ☎ 02 41 72 62 32.

Ride down to the old town, whose ancient houses are still standing, and follow the signs to the tourist office, located on Place de la Mairie. Be careful on the steep, winding lanes leading down to the wharves.

To leave Saint-Florent-le-Vieil, ride down to the intersection in the lower town. Head toward Le Mesnil-en-Vallée, Chalonnes and the Corniche Angevine on the D751, then pick up the D210 in the direction of Ingrandes and Montjean-sur-Loire. From the road, you can see the village of **Ingrandes** across the way. This old town, which was an important port in the 17th and 18th centuries, is worth a quick detour.

Ride past the campground and continue following the river to **Montjean-sur-Loire**. You'll see a church perched atop its promontory. Don't take the suspension bridge across the Loire. Proceed straight ahead to the old mariners' quarter. Go past the tourist office, cross the Pont-de-l'Île (bridge) and head for Chalonnes-sur-Loire. This truly peaceful island road winds its way through big fields. For about six kilometres, you won't pass a single hamlet, only a few grazing cows. At the tip of the island, take a right onto the bridge leading to

Chalonnes-sur-Loire, then immediately pick up the Route de la Corniche Angevine (the D751 in the direction of Rochefort-sur-Loire).

You'll start heading up a winding, hillside road. This uphill stretch is about four kilometres long. Take your time, and make a stop along the way at the Chapelle Sainte-Barbe-des-Mines, built for miners and their families; the hamlet no longer exists. The road finally reaches a plateau in the midst of a large vineyard. At Haie-Longue, there is a monument to aviator René Gasnier, who made his first flights in 1908. A viewpoint indicator enables you to take in the superb panorama of the valley. The total distance of the Route de la Corniche Angevine is 10 kilometres. It leads to the village of **Rochefort-sur-Loire**, which has old houses and is located along a branch of the Loire known as the Louet. White Coteaux du Layon wines are produced here.

Keep your eyes peeled for the sign for Savennières, on the left, and take the D106. Cross the Louet, then, on the bridge over the Loire, take the D106 to **Béhuard**, a tiny island where you'll find an enchanting village with 15th- and 16th-century houses. Take the time to ride around it, then return to the D106 and proceed to **Savennières**. The village church is one of the oldest in Anjou (10th and 11th centuries). Overlooking the Loire, with an excellent exposure, the vineyard produces an outstanding Chenin Blanc; Savennières wine is the jewel of the Anjou wines.

Take the D111 out of the village, toward Épiré. The road veers away from the railroad tracks then immediately starts climbing toward the La Roche aux Moines estate, the Coulée de Serrant vineyard. This three-kilometre loop, in the vineyard, is sure to interest wine lovers. The road then leads back to the D111. The Coulée de Serrant is an appellation controllée on its own, the exclusive property of the Joly family. Since 1985, the vineyard has been completely organic (no chemical fertilizers, pesticides or any sort of synthetic chemical products).

Proceed to the village of **Épiré**, which you'll reach after a good climb of about one kilometre. Continue toward **Bouchemaine**. At the traffic circle at the bridge, take the D112 across the Maine, in the direction of Ponts-de-Cé. At the first intersection, turn left and follow the D411 to **Angers**. At the traffic circle, continue straight ahead toward the Lycée David. At the light, keep going straight. Ride into the town, still proceeding straight ahead. Do NOT follow the signs for Angers-Centre, which will lead you onto the expressway. Take Rue Eblé to the corner of Rue Évin and Rue du-Petit-Thouars, and turn toward the train station. From there, follow the signs for *centre-ville* and the tourist office, which is located on Boulevard du Roi-René, opposite the château.

Leg from Angers to Saumur: 70 km

You can roam about as you please inside the Angers fortress, admiring the Châtelet, the Gothic chapel, the Logis Royal and the Grande Galerie. The latter contains a precious jewel of Medieval art: *l'Apocalypse*, an impressive 103-metre-long hanging illustrating the text of St. John the Apostle. Wind up your visit with the rampart walk and the Tour du Moulin (tour of the mill), so that you can take in a view of the town.

PRACTICAL INFORMATION ON ANGERS

Population
146,163 *Angevins*

Tourist office: Place Kennedy BP 5157. 19051 Angers Cedex 02, ☎ 02 41 23 51 11, ⚏ 02 41 23 51 10

Bicycle shops: Cycles Bernard, 42 Rue Boisnet, ☎ 02 41 87 59 56
Pineau G., 36 bis Boul. Ayrault, ☎ 02 41 88 30 47
Renault M., 107 Av. Pasteur, ☎ 02 41 43 43 61

Market
Saturdays

Major events: Festival d'Anjou (July); Angers l'été (July and August)

Specialties: Rillaud (delicatessen), Quernons d'Ardoise (blue chocolates), Savennières wines, Layon wines, Cointreau

Map
IGN no. 25

Fans of Gothic art won't want to miss the nave of the Cathédrale Saint-Maurice, a model of the Plantagenet (or Angevin) style, characterized by its amazingly delicate vaults. The sickroom in the Hôpital Saint-Jean, another masterpiece of the Plantagenet style, contains 10 hangings by Jean Lurçat known collectively as *Le Chant du Monde*, a contemporary replica of the castle's *Apocalypse*.

To explore the sections of Angers on either side of the Maine, pick up a copy of the guide *Promenades Historiques* at the tourist office. There are three tours signposted with arrows: the old city and its surroundings, the façades and gardens, and the Quartier de la Doutre, on the right bank. Wine lovers should make sure to visit the Maison du Vin de L'Anjou, near the château. The saga of one of the oldest Angevin enterprises, the commercialization of Cointreau, began in the 19th century.

Take Boulevard du Roi-René out of Angers. At the traffic circle, head toward Cholet on Rue Rabelais and Avenue de Lattre-de-Tassigny. At the light, continue straight ahead toward the Ponts-de-Cé. At the next traffic circle, head for the Château de Brissac. Take a right off of the N160, toward the **Ponts-de-Cé**. Ride straight across the town, which stretches three kilometres, then cross the bridge over the Saint-Aubin. At the traffic circle, head in the direction of **Saint-Maurille** and **Mûrs-Érigné**. Cross the second bridge over the Loire and the bridge over the Louet.

Next, continue toward Soulaines on the D120. At the light, head for Brissac-Quincé, then take an immediate right toward Soulaines. Take the D120 out of Mûrs-Érigné. The road leads down to the Rivière Aubance, making a few sharp turns along the way. Ride into **Soulaines**.

From there, take the D123 toward Brissac-Quincé. Ride into **Saint-Melaine-sur-Aubance**. Continue on the D123, which leads through the Aubance valley to **Brissac-Quincé**. You'll see herds of cattle grazing in big fields and hills covered with vines. The Château de Brissac will then come into view. Take the D55 into the village.

The château, purchased by René de Cossé and still inhabited by his descendants, is incredibly tall. All the rooms (open to the public) are furnished with private collections. In the cellars, you can sample the wines produced on the property. Visitors are also welcome to roam about the 28-hectare estate. The guided tour takes 45 minutes.

Gérard Depardieu fans might be interested to know that the actor owns a vineyard 15 kilometres south of Brissac, in Tigné, a village of 800 inhabitants. To get there, take the D748 to Martigné-Briand, then the D167 to the Château de Tigné.

At the foot of the town of Brissac-Quincé, follow the sign for Ponts-de-Cé, then turn right on the D55, toward Saint-Mathurin. Ride past

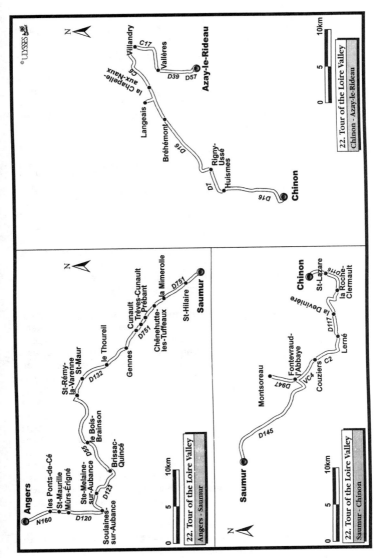

22. Tour of the Loire Valley
Chinon - Azay-le-Rideau

22. Tour of the Loire Valley
Angers - Saumur

22. Tour of the Loire Valley
Saumur - Chinon

the farm, the mill and the Château du Bois-Brainson. The road winds through a region covered with orchards. Continue toward Saint-Mathurin. Keep your eyes peeled; in the vineyard on your right, just before the town of Dion, there will be a sign indicating a dolmen.

Don't cross the bridge leading to Saint-Mathurin. Right before it, turn off toward **Saint-Rémy-la-Varenne**, a village with a noteworthy church, chapel and priory. Take the D132 along the Loire to **Saint-Maur**. The classical Saint-Maur-de-Glanfeuil monastery was founded in 543 and now houses an ecumenical centre.

Continue toward Gennes. Cross the village of **Le Thoureil**, a former river port from which the region's apples and wines were once shipped out. Inside the church, you can admire the statuettes of the 12 Apostles that originally graced the Abbaye de Saint-Maur. This charming town on the banks of the Loire is an excellent place to take a little break. Follow the road along the river and take a look at the pretty lily ponds.

Ride into **Gennes**. The Gallo-Roman amphitheatre in the southern part of the village is fairly well-preserved. It could accommodate up to 10,000 spectators back in the late 1st century. You can examine the relics found on the site at the nearby archaeological museum.

Head toward Saumur and Cunault on the D751. Here, wide stretches of golden sand line the banks of the Loire. **Cunault** was an important pilgrimage site and marketplace in the Middle Ages. The village is built around the immense Église Notre-Dame. Get off your bike so that you can admire the building up close; it is the loveliest Romanesque church in the department. The Logis du Prieur (the priory), located opposite, was built in the 16th century.

Make your way to **Trèves**. Cunault and Trèves were once river ports that specialized in shipping out tufa stone. The 11th-century tower is all that remains of the Château de Trèves. Next, proceed to **Prébant** and **Chênehutte-les-Tuffeaux**. At the Cave aux Moines, you can see snail "corrals" and a mushroom bed laid out in tunnels bored into the tufa. The Romanesque church in Chênehutte boasts a magnificent clock tower. The road then leads through a series of charming villages, all built out of tufa, where almost every family has its own vegetable garden.

Ride through the hamlet of **La Mimerolle**, and continue on the D751 to **Saint-Hilaire**. At the Musée du Champignon, set up inside a cave dwelling, you can see cultivated mushrooms (*champignons de Paris*, wood blewits, shiitakes, oyster mushrooms), as well as 200 kinds of forest mushrooms, ranging from the edible to the most dangerous. You can also sample grilled mushrooms prepared in all sorts of different ways. Plan your schedule around this highly instructive visit. The tunnels are cold and damp, so make sure to cover up well.

Continue to Saumur. On either side of the road, there are cellars, wine storehouses and wine shops that offer tastings. At the traffic circle, follow the sign for Bagneux. At the light, head for the château and the *centre-ville* of Saumur. We recommend taking a small detour to Bagneux, where you can admire a large dolmen, a majestic megalithic monument. Proceed to Saumur in the bike lane. Take the Pont Fouchard across the Thouet and continue to the tourist office, located on Place Bilange.

PRACTICAL INFORMATION ON SAUMUR

Population
32,000 *Saumurois*

Tourist office: Place de la Bilange BP 241, 49418 Saumur Cedex, ☎ 02 41 40 20 60, ✆ 02 41 67 89 51

Bicycle shops: Cycle DMD, 57 Quai Mayaud, ☎ 02 41 67 68 32
Cyclepro, 93 Route de Rouen, ☎ 02 41 67 76 63
Cycles Peugeot, 19 Av. du G.-de-Gaulle, ☎ 02 41 67 36 86

Market
Saturdays

Major events: Fête de la Loire and Salon des Vins de Saumur (May); Festival International des Géants (late May); Carrousel de Saumur (late July).

Specialties: Mushrooms, *pâtés aux prunes* (cakes), *fouets* (breads), Saumur wines

Map
IGN no. 25

Leg from Saumur to Chinon: 45 km

The old quarter of **Saumur** still has narrow streets, lovely old houses with tufa walls and slate roofs, as well as a 12th-century church, the

Église Saint-Pierre. The Musée de la Cavalerie will interest visitors with a passion for things equestrian. Furthermore, a number of riding events are held in Saumur during summer (July and August). Finally, the Maison du Vin provides complete information on Saumur wines, which are among the town's greatest treasures.

To leave Saumur, take Rue Docteur-Péton up to the château. It's a steep climb to the upper part of town. To visit the castle, lock your bike up in the area laid out for that purpose.

The tour of the castle includes a historical presentation on the site. Visitors are free to stroll through the gardens and tour the Musée du Cheval and the Musée d'Arts Décoratifs on their own. The splendid view from the look-out tower, extending for several kilometres, is not to be missed. Open every day but Tuesday.

After touring the castle, go back outside, get back on your bike, then turn left and continue uphill on Rue des Moulins (in the previous century, there were many windmills, or *moulins*, here). The view from the top of the plateau is superb. At the intersection with the D45, ride toward Champigny, which produces a famous Saumur wine, then head out of Saumur on the D145. The road winds through the vineyards. Proceed to Fontevraud-l'Abbaye, riding for about four kilometres along a forest road. Don't be surprised if you bump into soldiers in the middle of manœuvres; duty calls!

Ride into **Fontevraud-l'Abbaye**, and follow the signs for the abbey and the centre of the village. Head up into the village and go under the archway into the courtyard. There's a bike shed on the left.

Within the abbey walls, you'll find the recumbent statues of Richard I, Cœur de Lion (the Lion heart), Eleanor of Aquitaine, Henri II (Plantagenet) and Isabella of Angoulême. Founded by a hermit named Robert d'Arbrissel around 1100, Fontevraud comprised five separate priories and was a vital center of Christianity. A mixed abbey, it was run by abbesses, including several of royal blood. Before becoming a historic monument, it was a prison for 150 years. Open to the public 365 days a year.

Before leaving Fontevraud, stop by the tourist office. From the Église Saint-Michel (founded by Henry II), take the path lined with linden trees; the tourist office is located in the Chapelle Sainte-Catherine, which dates from the 13th century. This former chapel of rest is topped by a Plantagenet-style graveyard lantern. During the last war, it was used as a bike repair shop!

Head back toward the abbey and turn left toward Montsoreau. At the traffic circle, take the D947 and continue to the village of **Montsoreau**. At the intersection, follow the signs for the mushroom bed. If you didn't get to visit the Musée du Champignon, this smaller mushroom bed is sure to interest you.

Continue straight ahead, in the direction of Chinon, in order to reach the Château de Montsoreau, located on the banks of the Loire. There are a number of cave dwellings in the area. The waters of the river used to surround the castle, built in the 15th century. It now houses a museum on the Goums Marocains, cavalry units recruited in Morocco. Closed on Tuesdays.

The village is ranked among the "most beautiful villages in France". Take the time to explore its little hillside lanes and stroll along the promenade leading from the castle to the Église Candes-Saint-Martin, which is lined with old houses.

After exploring the village, head back to Fontevraud on the D947. Take the Route de Couziers, and follow the Circuit de Moustier, the VC4. You might come across some soldiers on manœuvres. Ride into **Couziers**. At the intersection with the C2, head for Chinon. At the fork, veer right toward Lerné. The road is very pleasant and leads through large fields.

Next, take the D117 to Lerné, still following the Circuit de Moustier. The road leads across vast farmlands and small wooded areas to the privately owned farm and Château de Chevigny. Ride into **Lerné**, a village built entirely of pale tufa. Go past the chapel and continue heading for Chinon on the D117. Keep left toward the **Abbaye de Seuilly** and ride up behind the village. Turn right on the D117, in the direction of Devinière. The **Musée de la Devinière** is the birthplace (15th century) of the colourful and witty writer François Rabelais (*Gargantua* and *Pantagruel*). Noteworthy items inside include regional furnishings and literature on Rabelais and his work.

Turn left on your way out of Devinière and take the D117 into the hills. At the intersection with the D24, continue toward Roche-Clermault and Chinon. When you get to the D759, head for **Roche-Clermault**. Go into the village and over the level crossing, then follow the ramparts road. Head toward the upper part of the old town. Ride past the pilgrimage chapel. It's a steep little climb, but the magnificent panoramic view is well worth the effort. You'll see more cave dwellings along the way. Follow the narrow road leading to Chinon, which climbs up into the woods. Opposite the vineyards, turn left (no sign), then start the long downhill ride to Chinon-Parilly.

Ride into **Saint-Lazare** and head for *centre-ville* and the château. Take the bike lane along the road lined with big plane trees. Cross the bridge over the Vienne and proceed to the centre of Chinon.

Leg from Chinon to Azay-le-Rideau: 50 km

PRACTICAL INFORMATION ON CHINON

Population
9,000 *Chinonais*

Tourist office: 12 Rue Voltaire BP 141, 37501 Chinon, ☎ 02 47 93 17 85, ⚏ 02 47 93 93 05

Bicycle shops: Chinon Cycles, 31 Rue du Commerce, ☎ 02 47 98 41 19 Espace ICM, Route de Tours, ☎ 02 47 93 01 07

Market
Thursdays and Sundays

Major events: Fête de la musique (June 21); Festival de Théâtre Musical en Touraine (mid-July); Marché Rabelais (1st weekend in August); Marché à l'Ancienne (3rd Saturday in August)

Specialties: Chinon wines, *confiture de Vin* (wine preserves; Claude Fleurisson)

Map
IGN no. 25

Chinon was once a powerful fortified town surrounded by a huge wall and made up of three castles separated by moats. The imposing ruins on the hill overlooking the village are steeped in history. All that remains of the throne room, where Joan of Arc recognized the Dauphin, is the west gable and the chimney. A medieval atmosphere still pervades old Chinon, especially the collection of buildings known as the "Grand Carroi". Pick up the pamphlet for the self-guided tour of this charming town on the banks of the Vienne. Have you heard about

Chinon's specialty, *Quernons d'ardoise*? They are chocolates of the same shape and colour as a piece of *quernon*, a kind of slate found in Anjou.

Located on the Indre, between Chinon and Tours, the bustling village of Azay-le-Rideau welcomes flocks of visitors during summer. Make hotel reservations.

Ride out of Chinon, heading up to the castle. At the traffic circle, head for Tours and Huismes on the D751. Immediately afterwards, pick up the D16 in the direction of the Château de Langeais, the Château d'Ussé and Huismes. Ride past the Château de la Grille vineyard. The road, slightly hilly, winds through vast farmlands. Ride into **Huismes**, whose church has a lovely turret topped with a pepper-box. Continue toward Ussé. At the intersection with the D7, keep heading down to Rigny-Ussé.

Follow the signs for the **Château d'Ussé**. It was built in the 15th and 16th centuries by the prominent de Bueil family, and has been modified time and again by the numerous families who have owned it since. Each season, an exhibit of period clothing is presented here. The guided tour takes about 45 minutes.

Return to the bridge and cross the Indre. Make sure to look back and admire the lovely view of the château. Proceed to Bréhémont and Langeais on the D16, following the left bank of the Loire. It's a very easy ride, made that much more enjoyable by the pretty little vineyards along the way. To visit the Château de Langeais, cross the Loire at the big intersection and continue to the village. **Langeais** was one of the last castles to be built in the Loire Valley. Visitors can admire its beautifully furnished apartments, as well as its collection of Gothic and Renaissance tapestries, a real treasure. Wax effigies have been used to recreate Anne of Brittany's wedding to Charles VII. Open every day.

Go back to the left bank and continue following the Loire by taking the C6 toward the **Chapelle-aux-Naux**. Ride under the viaduct; the road then veers left, in the direction of Villandry. After passing the locality of La Tuilerie, you'll see the château in the distance. At the stone cross, leave the road and ride into **Villandry**. Follow the signs for the château, then leave your bike in the parking lot.

The Château de Villandry was the last great Renaissance château to be built on the banks of the Loire. Touring its gardens is an unforgettable experience, and merits at least 45 minutes. There are three levels: a "water garden", an ornamental flower garden and an ornamental vegetable garden.

Back on your bike, head left as you leave the château. Take the first left, the D121, which leads to Druye. Ride up the hill toward the village church. At the intersection, proceed to Vallères on the C17, a pleasant little road. Herds of sheep can be seen grazing in the fields along the way. A winding downhill stretch will take you through orchards and vineyards. Ride into **Vallères**, then head for Azay-le-Rideau on the D39. When the road intersects with the D751, continue in the direction of Azay-le-Rideau. This is a busy road, so be careful! Take the D57 to the château and the village.

Leg from Azay-le-Rideau to Loches: 50 km

Leave your bike in the parking lot of the château. **Azay-le-Rideau** is surrounded by water and greenery, making for a true visual feast. Inside, the apartments and rooms are richly furnished. Visitors can admire a collection of Flemish and French tapestries from the 16th and 17th centuries. The guided tour takes about an hour. A sound and light show is presented here every night.

PRACTICAL INFORMATION ON AZAY-LE-RIDEAU

Population
3,053 *Ridellois*

? **Tourist office:** Place de l'Europe 37190, Azay-le-Rideau,
☎ 02 47 45 44 40

To leave Azay-le-Rideau, turn right on your way out of the château and head toward Artannes-sur-Indre on the D84. A small lake has been laid out on the Indre, and you'll enjoy a series of lovely views on your way past. When you reach the D17, stay on course for **Artannes-sur-Indre**. Head for Montbazon. At **Monts**, ride down into the centre of the village and continue toward Montbazon on the D17. Ride under the viaduct, then into **Vontes**. Keep your eyes peeled for Rue de la Gargousserie. When you get there, take a right (in front of the nuclear power station). At the first fork, head left on Rue des Trois-Cheminées. Ride over the highway. Right before Montbazon, on the left, you'll see a narrow road leading to the Château d'Artigny (part of

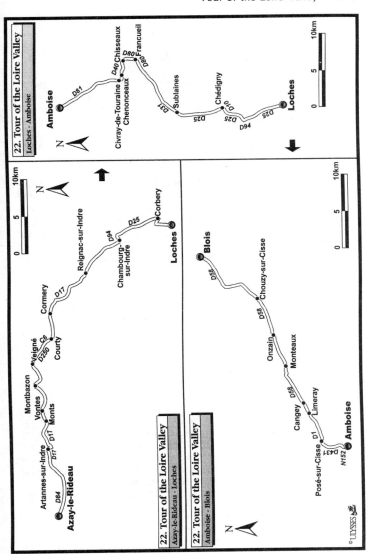

22. Tour of the Loire Valley
Loches - Amboise

22. Tour of the Loire Valley
Azay-le-Rideau - Loches

22. Tour of the Loire Valley
Amboise - Blois

© ULYSSES

the Relais & Châteaux hotel chain), the former residence of François Coty, founder of the famous perfumery that bears his name.

Head down to **Montbazon**. When you reach the N10, turn right, then take Rue de Moulin just before the bridge over the Indre. Don't cross the river. Take the D250 out of Montbazon and continue straight ahead, making no other turns. Take the C6 out of **Veigné**, follow it as far as **Courty**, then head for Veneuil. The road winds its way through vast fields of grain. Ride into **Cormery**, then turn left toward the village. Ride around and take a look at the remains of the big Benedictine abbey, founded in 791. While you're there, try some macaroons, the local specialty.

Take the D17 through the Indre valley to Courçay and Reignac-sur-Indre. The road follows the river, leading through a lovely wooded area. Continue on the D17 to **Chambourg-sur-Indre**. At the village church, follow the signs for Chédigny (D94). Cross the Indre and continue straight ahead to the D25, then head for Loches and Beaulieu. Cross the Pont de Courbery. At the traffic circle, follow the sign for Loches. The tourist office is on Place de Wermelskirchen.

Leg from Loches to Amboise: 45 km

Plan to spend some time exploring **Loches**, a fascinating fortified town dating from the Middle Ages. You can stroll about freely within the citadel, visit the Porte Royale, the Romanesque Église Saint-Ours, the Logis Royal (royal chambers) and the Donjon (keep), and walk around the ramparts. The village of Loches is renowned for its local products: delicatessen, goat cheese, honey, gingerbread, etc., so take the opportunity to stock up. Wednesday and Saturday are market days.

To leave Loches, start at the tourist office and follow the sign for Tours. At the traffic circle, pick up the D764, which leads to Chenonceaux. Cross the bridge, then take an immediate left toward Chédigny and the Indre valley. Follow the D25 out of Loches (the same road you came in on). Ride through the pleasant, rolling countryside. At the D94, turn right in the direction of Chédigny. Ride through the woods, then take the D10 into **Chédigny**. Continue on the

PRACTICAL INFORMATION ON LOCHES

Population
7,100 *Lochois*

? **Tourist office**: Place de Wermelskirchen BP 112, 37601 Loches Cédex, ☎ 02 47 59 07 98, ⚏ 02 47 91 61 50

Bicycle shop: Schmitt, 7 Rue des Moulins, ☎ 02 47 59 02 15

Market
Wednesdays and Saturdays

Major events: Summer solstice, music week (June); Son et Lumière (sound and light show; Fridays and Saturdays during summer); Festival de Théâtre Musical (late July)

Specialties: Local delicatessen products, goat cheese, *Lochoise*-style mushrooms, honey.

Map
IGN no. 26

D25 to Sublaines. The road leads through some enormous fields of grain. At the intersection, at the edge of **Sublaines**, head for Bléré and Amboise on the D31.

Keep your eyes out for the C4, on the right, and head for **Francueil**. Ride down into the village, as far as the D81, then take the road that climbs up to the church. Take the D80 toward Chenonceaux. Cross the Route Nationale and continue straight ahead in the direction of Chenonceaux.

Take the bridge over the Cher, ride into **Chisseaux**, then head for **Chenonceaux** on the D40. Follow the signs for the château. Leave your bike in the parking lot. The **Château de Chenonceaux** gracefully spans the Cher with its six arches. You can take a self-guided tour by following the signs and referring to the brochure distributed on the premises. Don't be surprised if you find people jostling to get inside; this romantic château is very popular with visitors to the Loire Valley. During summer, a sound and light show is presented here at 10pm.

Leave Chenonceaux by following the signs for Amboise. Take the D40 as far as **Civray-de-Touraine**, then follow the D81 to Amboise. Ride past the "Châteaux de la Loire en Miniature" park. Follow the signs for Amboise-centre. The tourist office is located on the Quai Général-de-Gaulle.

Leg from Amboise to Blois: 45 km

Amboise stretches along the left bank of the Loire. At the château, (partly dismantled) visitors can admire the Logis du Roi (King's chambers), the Salle des États (states room), the flamboyant Gothic Chapelle Saint-Hubert, which houses the tomb of Leonardo da Vinci, and the gardens, which afford a magnificent panoramic view of the valley.

Leonardo da Vinci spent the last years of his life at the Manoir du Clos-Lucé, a red-brick, Renaissance-style residence that now contains a collection of models made according to plans drawn up by the brilliant artist and inventor. The theme of the exhibit is "Forty machines that are four hundred years ahead of their time".

Head out of Amboise in the direction of Pocé-sur-Cisse, then cross the bridge immediately and follow the N152. Right after, pick up the D431 and proceed to **Pocé-sur-Cisse**. In front of Pocé church, turn onto the D1 and head for **Limeray**. Continue following the D1 in the direction of **Cagney**. Keep your ears pricked, as you might come across a duck and goose farm.

Take the D58 into **Monteaux**, winding your way through fields of grain. Ride into **Onzain** and follow the signs for Chaumont and Chouzy-sur-Cisse. Proceed straight ahead toward **Chouzy-sur-Cisse** on the D58. Head for Blois. At the cemetery, at the end of the village, follow the signs for La Pinsonnière, La Gallardière and Belair. Don't go over the level crossing. The road climbs gently on its way through the fields.

Continue in the direction of Belair. Ride straight through the Forêt de Blois. You'll come to a major road, the Gaston d'Orléans highway. Take a right (no sign). Ride into **Blois** and follow the signs reading *toutes directions*. At the traffic circle, head toward *centre-ville* and the château (follow the white sign). The tourist office is located on Avenue Docteur-Jean-Laigret, near the train station.

The last stop on this tour, the former *cité royale*, is a lively place perfectly suited to strolling about. Park your bike (or send it to Paris?);

PRACTICAL INFORMATION ON BLOIS

Population
50,000 *Blésois*

? **Tourist office:** Pavillon Anne-de-Bretagne, 3 Av. Jean-Laigret, 41000 Blois, ☎ 02 54 74 06 49, ⇔ 02 54 56 04 59

Bicycle shops: Cycles Leblond, 44 Levée des Tuileries, ☎ 02 54 74 30 13
Cycles Peugeot, 33 A. Wilson, ☎ 02 54 78 12 94

Market
Saturdays

Major events: Foire de Blois (Ascension); sound and light shows at the château (summer)

Specialties: Malice du Loup, Pavé du Roi and Patelins (sweets)

Map
IGN no. 26

this town, steeped in history and full of passion, is best toured at a leisurely pace on foot. That way, you'll have plenty of time to explore the old quarters and tumble down the winding little lanes and numerous stairways. The château de Blois, which has seen its share of modifications, merits a visit. The Cathédrale Saint-Louis is surrounded by a whole network of beautiful medieval streets.

Excursion to the Edge of the Sologne Region: 65 km

From the centre of Blois, ride to the wharves. Cross the bridge over the Loire, in the direction of Blois rive-gauche, Châteauroux and Chambord (straight ahead). Be extra-careful, as the traffic is fairly heavy for about seven kilometres. At the circle, continue toward **Saint-Gervais-la-Forêt**. At the light, head for Vineuil and Chambord on the D33. Go into **Le Chîteau**, proceed to Huisseau-sur-Cosson, then ride across the Parc de Chambord. Enclosed by a 32-kilometre wall, this huge forest park is a reserve for hundreds of deer, buffalo, foxes and boars. Follow the sign for the **Château de Chambord**. Leave your bike in the shed in the parking lot.

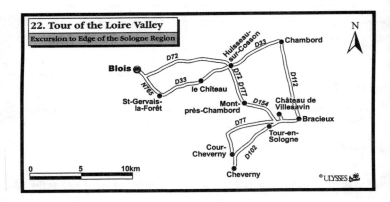

One of the most remarkable things about the Château de Chambord is its roof, whose tall chimneys are richly carved with royal symbols. Inside, an equally remarkable double-helix staircase, designed by Leonardo da Vinci, makes it possible for two people to go up or down the stairs without meeting. Visitors are free to roam about the château as they please. Take the time to stroll along the terraces and in the part of the park that is open to the public. Lookouts have been built so that visitors can observe the wildlife; don't forget your binoculars.

Afterward, take the D112 through the forest to **Bracieux**, a charming village in the Beuvron Valley. Proceed to the centre of the village, which is built around an 18th-century covered market. Follow the D102 out of Bracieux, toward Villesavin and Cheverny. Continue along the road to Cour-Cheverny. You can visit Villesavin on the way back. Ride to **Tour-en-Sologne**, then head for **Cour-Cheverny**. Along the way, the region becomes greener and greener, and the houses disappear behind magnificent trees. Take the D102 across the village, in the direction of **Cheverny**. Ride alongside the château walls, and leave your bike in the parking lot near the church.

The Château de Cheverny is a fine example of the classical architecture of Louis XIII residences. Still inhabited by the descendants of those who built it, this château has preserved its furnishings and sumptuous interior decor. You can also visit the kennel, which houses a pack of 70 Franco-English hunting dogs. The Musée de la Vénerie has a trophy room containing over 2,000 sets of deer antlers.

Head back to Cour-Cheverny. Ride past the park and follow the D765 toward Blois. Keep your eye out for the Chemin de la Chassière on the right leading to the Huards vineyard. Continue on the Voie du Tertre. At the fork, veer left toward Jouvençay, then turn right on the Route de Tour-en-Sologne. Ride past the Huards estate. Take the D77 into Tour-en-Sologne, to the D102, then head for Bracieux and the **Château de Villesavin**. Cross the river and take the D154 to the château. The former residence of Jean le Breton, Seigneur de Villandry, it is small and well-preserved. You can visit a few furnished apartments, where some pieces of pewterware are on display. Behind the château, you'll find a 16th-century dovecote and a carriage museum (Musée de Calèche).

When you leave the château, take the D154 toward Chambord. Ride to the village of **Mont-près-Chambord**, then pick up the D177 in the direction of Huisseau-sur-Cosson. Ride through part of the Forêt de Boulogne, then take the D72 into **Huisseau-sur-Cosson**. Make sure to take a look at the 12th-century church, topped with a pyramidal roof.

Continue on the D72 toward Saint-Claude-de-Diray. Right after the bridge, keep right, staying on course for Saint-Claude-de-Diray, then follow the sign for Blois. Be careful! At the traffic circle, head for Blois-sud. Take the downtown (*centre-ville*) bridge back into Blois.

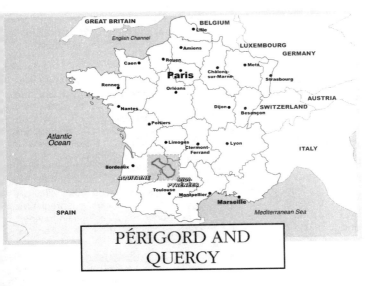

PÉRIGORD AND QUERCY

Périgord and Quercy — here are two provinces of southwestern France with everything going for them (and for you!). This tour is an uninterrupted stretch of little country roads and delightful scenery. In this land of gourmet predilection, of foie gras and truffles, the senses are sharpened in cheerful, sunny markets, their stalls overflowing with fresh produce. The history of the region is inscribed in its architecture, from the smallest, prehistoric cavern to the most sophisticated castle. Nowhere else do history and nature coexist in such perfect harmony. This tour, into the hearts of Périgord and Quercy, proves to be most enchanting. It is a return to the source, as bicycle becomes time machine.

The tour is in the shape of a large loop and begins in the heart of Périgord Pourpre. Périgord is divided into regions according to the hue of local vegetation. Bergerac owes the surname "Pourpre" to the particular way that the sun's brilliance accentuates the purple tint of its vineyards' autumn foliage. Bergerac developed on both shores of the Dordogne, and the city drew its fortune from the river — *Brageirac* means "sand bank, deep bottom" in Old French. Our bicycle tour through the "valley of humanity" begins here, in the adopted home of a famous Parisian poet: Cyrano, henceforth, of Bergerac.

Périgord Noir owes its name to the dense and dark foliage of the region's abundant oak and chestnut trees, which thrive in the area's rich, fertile soil. Its hilly roads run through alternating landscapes of farm fields and small, fragrant woods.

The Vallée de la Dordogne, the domain of prehistory in Périgord Noir, heard the first rumblings of humanity in the territory of Hexagone. Homo sapiens chose this region for its cliffs and their particularly numerous caverns and shelters, in which early humanity protected itself from the elements and developed weapons for hunting. Les Eyzies, at the confluence of the Vézère and Beune rivers, hosts an annual European championship of prehistoric weapons competition. At the Musée National de la Préhistoire, the lifestyle of individuals who lived 30,000 years ago is exhibited. All around the village, the history of these people is told in different grottoes and caves. Les Eyzies is a treasure-trove for palaeontology buffs: the earliest prehistoric sepulchre, original artefacts of "Cro-Magnon man", animal engravings, and wall-paintings, including the famous bison in the cave of Font-de-Gaume.

The tour snakes through the splendid Vézère valley, and leads to the geological site of **La Roque-Saint-Christophe** *(every day; ☎ 05 53 50 70 45)*, a 600-metre-long cave dwelling on five levels, overhanging the valley. At **Montignac-Lascau**, the symbols of prehistory have inspired a modern technological utilization — you can admire reproductions of 17,000-year-old cave-paintings near the caverns that house the originals.

The itinerary quits the Vézère and returns to the meandering Dordogne. Before you reach the river's fertile plain, however, a stay at **Sarlat-la-Canéda** is a must. The sight of radiant sunlight on the old, golden-hued stone walls of this delightful town is sheer bliss. For gourmets and art-lovers alike, Sarlat is a gratifying stop. The emblem of *salardaise* cuisine, the goose, is available in all its forms: foie gras, *confit*, *magret*, and many more!

As the tour rambles along the banks of the Dordogne, medieval "gems" are revealed, hanging from white and ochre cliffs: the village of **Beynac**, signalled by its prominent fortified castle, and, nearby, the alluring sight of **La Roque-Gageac**.

Finally, on the way to the Lot valley, the tour cuts across the **Causses de Gramat**, ridged, dry calciferous plateaus planted with oak and juniper and perforated by chasms, caves, and subterranean rivers. At the **Gouffre de Padirac** *(guided tour, 90 min;* ☎ *05 65 33 64 56)*, you can enjoy a raft ride on an emerald river through the belly of the Earth.

The Alzou, a modest stream, flows below an extraordinary site, clinging onto the cliff: **Rocamadour**. Turn back time to the era of great pilgrimages in the course of an entrancing visit to this holy site.

Revisit the Middle Ages in a stroll through the sinewy streets of old **Figeac**, a charming ensemble of half-timbered houses and yellow sandstone homes with sculpted window frames.

What a pleasure it is to explore the Lot valley by bicycle! A grand view awaits in every curve of road. On either side of the Lot, old villages are enthroned on high cliffs. **Saint-Cirq-Lapopie**, a favourite place of painters and writers, will charm you. This picturesque village, classified a historic monument in its entirety, still moves to the rhythm of olden times.

Cahors, capital of Quercy, is built on an isthmus of the Lot. At its bend, the river quietly flows under the most celebrated Gothic bridge: the Pont Valentré, the emblem of Cahors. As it follows the course of the Lot, the itinerary snakes through vineyards, fiefdoms of the Comtes-Évêques de Cahors. Cahors wine has been pressed uniquely from *côt noir* grapes for more than 2,000 years — do not miss the opportunity to taste this legendary vintage.

Party to the eventful history of three centuries of conflict between the French and the English, late medieval bastions were created here, in a period of demographic explosion, as a response to kings' desires to house and protect the new population. These fortified towns succeed each other all along the last leg of the tour: **Villefranche-du-Périgord** and **Monpazier**, magnificently preserved, and **Beaumont**, are all old French or English bastions.

---

23. GRAND TOUR OF PÉRIGORD AND QUERCY

Total distance:	540 km
Number of legs:	10
Level of difficulty:	🚲 🚲
Diagrams:	pp 223, 237, 243
Maps:	A29 to A32

Due to the extraordinary high number of tourist attractions, Périgord and Quercy are two of the most visited regions of France. If you would like to stay in Le Bugue, Montignac, Saint-Cirq-Lapopie or Villefranche-du-Périgord during the high season (July and August), be sure to make reservations as there are few hotels in these villages. You may have to overnight in neighbouring villages. It is very important to carefully plan your itinerary. To obtain lists of hotels, inns and lodgings, ask at the tourist offices of these villages, or consult travel guides.

Leg from Bergerac to Le Bugue: 60 km

The best way to discover the old city of **Bergerac** is still on foot. The tourist office has a guidebook, *Promenade dans le Vieux Bergerac*, that

---

PRACTICAL INFORMATION ON BERGERAC

Population
28,500 *Bergeracois*

Tourist office: 97 Rue Neuve d'Argenson, 24100 Bergerac, ☎ 05 53 57 03 11, ⇒ 05 53 61 11 04

Bicycle shops
Guy Barbier, 31 Rue Candillac, ☎ 05 53 27 29 40
Périgord Cycle, 11 Place Gambetta, ☎ 05 53 57 07 19
Cycle 2000, 111 Boul. de l'Entrepôt, ☎ 05 53 57 71 99

Market
Wednesday and Saturday

Major events: l'Omelette à l'Aïlé (2,000-egg omelette, May 1st); Fête Nationale (fireworks, sound and light show, July 14th); Les Tables de Cyrano, Fête de la Gastronomie (food festival, around July 14th); Mercredi du Jazz (Jazz Wednesday, all summer); Festival Cyrano (July and August)

Specialty: Cassoulet de Bergerac (bean and duck stew)

Access from Paris: A10, A71, A20, N21; by train: TGV, Gare de Montparnasse-Libourne, transfer for Bergerac.

Map
IGN no. 48

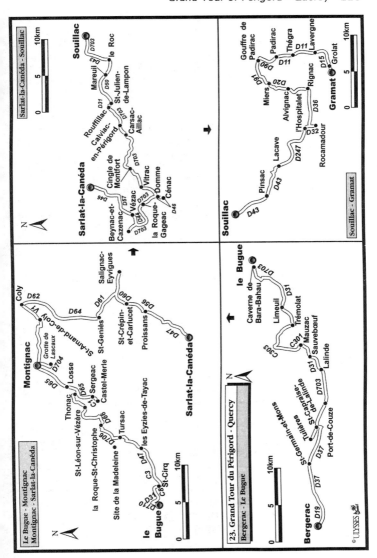

leads you on a tour of the town's restored old quarters. To reach the tourist office, turn left onto Avenue du 108ᵉ Régiment d'Infanterie as you leave the train station. Take an immediate right, onto Boulevard Victor-Hugo, and ride (if you have already picked up your bicycle) to the traffic light. Turn left in front of the parking lot, and proceed to the next stoplight. Turn onto Rue Neuve d'Argenson. The tourist office is on your left, about 700 metres ahead.

To leave Bergerac, from the tourist office, take Rue Neuve d'Argenson, and follow the signs for Agen. In front of the bridge over the Dordogne, turn left onto Rue Albert-Carrigat. Cross Pont Louis-Pimont (use the sidewalk), and take Avenue Paul-Painlevée in the direction of Agen via the N21. After about 3 km, look left for the D19 and take it toward La Conne and Cours-de-Pile. The road is bordered by huge conifer farms and greenhouses.

Enter **Saint-Germain-et-Mons**, and take the D21 in the direction of Mouleydier. At the intersection with the D37, turn right in the direction of Saint-Agne. Keep left at the fork, toward Lanquais. At the crossroad, ride toward Saint-Capraise.

Cross the Dordogne toward **Saint-Capraise-de-Lalinde**. From the D660, take the bicycle path along the canal. A short detour leads to one of the oldest hydroelectric dams in France: take the bicycle path on your left, and ride to **Tuilières**.

Follow the signs to the electric works, the locks, and the fish ladder. After your visit, return to the path along the canal, and ride in the direction of Saint-Capraise, to **Port-de-Couze**. Leave the bicycle path, take a left onto the bridge over the canal, and continue on the D703 to **Lalinde**. Of the original plans of this English bastion, the central square and the Romanesque door are all that remain.

Cross the village of Lalinde, and keep on the D703 toward **Sauvebœuf**. At the exit, take the D31 to **Mauzac**. Just past the village, take the C301, on the left, toward Trémolat and Limeuil. This magnificent, narrow road that gradually rises into the forest, turns into the C303. It then leads through a lovely descent with a few turns — you have entered switchback territory... A parking lot signals the proximity of a magnificent lookout over the Cingle de Trémolat (the river winds large knots, here called "*cingles*", or "cuts"). The superb panorama of this loop of the Dordogne, prettily encircling the fertile land, can be contemplated from a cliff top.

Let yourself coast along the scenic descent to **Trémolat**. This charming village possesses a hotel, Le Vieux Logis (part of the Relais & Châteaux chain), that merits a visit. Originally, this little 17th-century country inn was an agricultural holding. The hotel, with moss-covered roof and abundant charm, has been in the same family for 400 years. The ideally situated heavy church, 12th-century fortress and Benedictine shelter, served as a stopover for pilgrims.

Leave Trémolat on the D30 in the direction of Limeuil and Le Bugue. The road gently undulates, and ends with a short, respectable climb to the lookout over Cingle de Limeuil, at the beginning of the Vézère valley. From the top of the cliff, the road again makes a superb show of the valley, and then pleasantly descends, zigzagging to the old fortified town of Limeuil. This small medieval villages is regarded as one of the most beautiful in France.

Leave Limeuil-Bas in the direction of Le Bugue, on the D31. Then, riding over a small plateau, climb the C101 to Limeuil-Haut. Pause at the Romanesque chapel of Saint-Martin. It was founded by Richard the Lionheart, in memory of Archbishop Thomas Becket, who was assassinated by King Richard's father, King Henry II Plantagenet.

Continue on the D703 in the direction of **Caverne de Bara-Bahau** *(guided tour, 40 min, every day; ☎ 05 53 07 27 47)*, preserve of the bear cave. Approximately one hundred metres from the mouth of the cave, you can admire magnificent works from the repertoire of Aurignacian art: near full-size animal figures, engraved by hand and flint tip, decorate the cave walls. Foresee 40 minutes for the guided tour.

Remount your bicycle, and ride to **Le Bugue**. Follow the signs for the tourist office, situated on Rue du Jardin Public. If this land of rivers peaks your curiosity about aquatic life, you can visit the Aquarium du Périgord Noir (we have left the purple for the black!). An interesting item in the history of Le Bugue is the 1319 decree by the King of France, Philipe Le Long, that the weekly market be held on Tuesday. Hence the Tuesday market has animated Le Bugue for six centuries!

Leg from Le Bugue to Montignac: 50 km

Interspersed along this leg of the tour, are numerous interesting tourist attractions. You may have to plan for more than one day to see all of the sites described in this section of the itinerary.

PRACTICAL INFORMATION ON LE BUGUE

Population
2,800 *Buguois*

? **Tourist office:** Porte de la Vézère, 24260 Le Bugue, ☎ 05 53 07 20 48, ↝ 05 53 54 92 30

Bicycle shop
Jean Marc Giat, Av. de la Libération, ☎ 05 53 07 13 23

Market
Tuesday and Saturday

Major events: Fête de la Saint-Louis (August 25th); Foire de la Saint-Michel, chestnut-tree and nut market (last week of September)

Map
IGN no. 48

Do some stretching before you leave Le Bugue, because a three kilometre climb bids you good morning! To leave the city, from the tourist office continue straight in the direction of Sarlat and Les Eyzies. At the large crossroad, take the road on the left in the direction of Rouffignac via the D710. Cross the centre of town, and look right, just before the church, for Rue Bastière toward Rouffignac and Manaurie via the D31. Now you should be warmed up! Follow the signs to the campground. Continue straight on the D31 to the fork, where you must keep right to continue on the C8 toward Grotte Saint-Cirq. An excellent descent leads to **Saint-Cirq**. To visit the cave, keep right at the fork at the town entrance, and follow the signs for one kilometre. This small prehistoric cavern is decorated with magnificent engravings of bison, reindeer, and horses, as well as the "Sorcier de Saint-Cirq" (the witch of Saint-Cirq), one of the rare representations of a human figure from this era.

After the visit, return to the C1, and descend to Saint-Cirq. Control your speed! Watch for chicks, geese, hens, and ducks scratching in the middle of the road. At the intersection, take the C3 toward Les Eyzies-de-Tayac. The road hugs the Vézère and the railroad tracks, which you cross to enter Les Eyzies.

Enter the town on the D47. **Les Eyzies-de-Tayac** is tucked between high, grey and ochre cliffs. The town has been conferred the title "prehistoric capital of the world", by virtue of its numerous famous caves and shelters. Its Musée National de la Préhistoire is right in the centre of town. In summer, thousands of vacationers crowd to visit the **Grottes de Font-de-Gaume** *(closed Tuesdays, guided tour by reservation, 45 min;* ☎ *05 53 06 90 80)*. If you choose to visit the area in July or August, prepare yourself for long line-ups at cave entrance gates. Know that at Font-de-Gaume there is a limit of 20 visitors at a time and 250 visitors per day, and many organised groups have reserved tickets well in advance. Good planning and some reservations will save you hours of waiting during your stop here. Inform yourself at the appropriate office about the procedures for visiting those caves that interest you.

PRACTICAL INFORMATION ON LES EYZIES-DE-TAYAC

 Tourist office: 24620 Les Eyzies, ☎ 05 53 06 97 05, ⬛ 05 53 06 90 79

Cross the village, and leave Les Eyzies on the D706 in the direction of La Roque-Saint-Christophe and Montignac. On leaving the town, the road climbs through forest. Continue to **Tursac**. A goose farm is a reminder that this is still the land of foie gras. Continue along the D706 toward **Site de la Madeleine**. This prehistoric site is the namesake of a culture: the Magdalenian, the latest period of the Palaeolithic era. A troglodytic village frequented by human beings since prehistoric times *(every day;* ☎ *05 53 50 70 45)* occupies the site. Also of interest are the ruins of a 15th-century castle and chapel.

The itinerary skirts an impressive cliff and invites a stop at Préhisto-Parc for insight into the daily life of the first hunters, Neanderthal and Cro-Magnon man. Hunting scenes, an early sepulchre, and the habitat of Magdalenian families, fishermen, engravers, and painters are all exhibited here in a protected site.

Proceed on the D66 toward La Roque-Saint-Christophe. The road becomes very narrow in certain spots, and the cliff is always within a hair's-breadth! A parking lot and picnic area are maintained at the foot of this site. A stairway leads to the stronghold of **La Roque-Saint-Christophe**, cradle of numerous civilisations and one of the oldest and largest troglodytic cities. Dug into the cliff, it overlooks the valley on five levels that may have been inhabited by up to 3,000 people.

Continue on the D66 toward Saint-Léon-sur-Vézère and Montignac. Cross a narrow bridge, and take time to visit the charming village of

Saint-Léon-sur-Vézère. Its Romanesque church, with its flat-stone roof, is considered one of the most beautiful in Périgord Noir. The cemetery chapel and Château de La Salle, in the centre of the village, date from the 14th century. Continue on the D66, and then the D706, toward Montignac. A long descent through woods leads to **Thonac** (the church's bell-tower wall is remarkable). At the crossroad, take the D65e in the direction of Castel-Merle and cross another little bridge.

To visit the prehistoric site at **Castel-Merle** *(closed Wednesdays, except in July and August;* ☎ *05 53 50 79 70)*, take the D65 on the right. Ride to **Sergeac** through the beautiful countryside, and continue on the C1 toward Castel-Merle. All along these cliffs, are shelters and strata dating from the Palaeolithic to the Iron Age, in which you may find flint, bone, ivory, etc. At the same site, you can visit an English fort that served as a surveillance post over the Vézère during the Hundred Years' War. The duration of this visit is approximately 45 minutes.

Return to the crossroad, and proceed on the D65 toward Montignac. The road here offers an unobstructed vista of the Vézère and **Château de Losse** towering over its waters. Jewel of the Renaissance, the castle belonged to Jean de Losse, governor of Guyenne under the last Valois and the first Bourbons. A guided tour of the furnished apartments of the Grand Logis lasts approximately 40 minutes. There is free access to the park and the gardens. To reach the entrance to the castle, you must re-cross Pont de Thonac and take the D706.

Continue on the D65 to **Montignac**. At the village, turn right. Follow Rue du 4 Septembre to the town centre. The tourist office, at Place Bertran-de-Born, houses a museum dedicated to Eugène Le Roy, a Périgord writer. Ruins of a feudal castle dominate the town. Half-timbered houses from the 12th century and old buildings complete a worthwhile visit to this historic refuge of the counts of Périgord.

Attention! You must procure tickets to visit Lascaux II, at Montignac, at the tourist office. Again, do not be surprised at the wait, as tours are scheduled and entry is limited to 2,000 per day.

Leave Montignac on the D704e. The road gently climbs behind the village and offers a very pleasant vista of Montignac, nestled at the bottom of the valley. Continue climbing to the parking lot (2 km), and

PRACTICAL INFORMATION ON MONTIGNAC

Population
3,000 *Montignacois*

? **Tourist office:** Place Bertran-de-Born, 24290 Montignac, ☎ 05 53 51 82 60, ⊷ 05 53 50 49 72

Bicycle shops
MBK Didier Faure, Rue Joubert, ☎ 05 53 51 90 78
Jean Louis Ricros, 27 Rue du 4 Septembre, ☎ 05 53 51 87 02

Market
Wednesday and Saturday

Major events: Festival de Musique en Périgord Noir (July and August); Festival de Folklore du Monde (3rd week in July)

Specialties: Lascaux (meringue nut cake); stone carvings of Lascaux (reproductions of the bull); brooches (reproductions of prehistoric jewellery)

Map
IGN no. 48

lock your bicycle well in view. Follow the signs to the reception. **Lascaux II** is situated 200 metres from the original cave, closed to the public since 1963, of which it is a replica *(closed Mondays, except in July and August; ticket sales exclusively at Montignac,* ☎ *05 53 35 50 40,* ⊷ *05 53 06 30 94; at the site,* ☎ *05 53 51 95 03)*. Since 1983, visitors view this double, that is, the upper section of the cavern, including the Salle des Taureaux (bull room) and an axial by-path. The atmosphere of the original cave is re-created thanks the scientifically rigorous reproductions of the paintings of Lascaux. Double back to Montignac and, in passing, take note of Château de Puy-Robert (part of the Relais & Châteaux hotel chain). This elegant 19th-century building is surrounded by a magnificent park.

Leg from Montignac to Sarlat-la-Canéda: 40 km

Leave Montignac on the D704 in the direction of Sarlat and Saint-Amand-de-Coly. About four kilometres from the town, take a little road on the left that rises in the direction of **Saint-Amand-de-Coly**. This small village surrounds a fortified 13th-century monastic church.

Artisans gather around the church and music concerts are performed here during the summer season. Cross the village, and take the V1 in the direction of **Coly**.

From Coly (church with bell-tower wall), follow the D62 toward Sarlat. At the fork, proceed on the D64, which follows the Chironde, on the left. Ride through cornfields and little woods to **Saint-Geniès**, a charming village of flat-stone-roof houses. Turn left onto the D61 toward **Salignac**. Ride to the intersection with the D60. From this crossroad, you can turn left toward the Château de Salignac (medieval fortress built on rock), and then retrace your steps to take the D60 toward Proissans and Sarlat.

At **Saint-Crépin** (Manoir de Cipières), follow the D56 toward **Proissans**. The road consists of considerable climbs and descents: switchbacks through vast agricultural fields and forests of holm-oak. From the top of these hills **Sarlat-la-Canéda** is visible. Let yourself coast to the foot of the town, and enter it on the D47. Follow the signs to the historic quarter and the tourist office.

PRACTICAL INFORMATION ON SARLAT-LA-CANÉDA

Population
10,500 *Sarladais*

Tourist office: Place de la Liberté, 24203 Bergerac, ☎ 05 53 59 27 67, ⚹ 05 53 59 19 44

Bicycle shops
Cycles Cum's, 8 Av. Gambetta, ☎ 05 53 31 28 40
Peugeot Cycles, 36 Av. Thiers, ☎ 05 53 28 51 87

Market
Wednesday and Saturday

Major events: La Ringueta, festival of traditional games (Pentecost)

Specialties: *salardaise* potatoes, goose and duck *confit*, nut candy

Map
IGN no. 48

Sarlat holds an important position in the world of cinema. Italian, American, and French directors have shot scenes of films here: *Les Misérables*, *La Fille de d'Artagnan*, *La Promise* (Sarlat becomes Budapest), and many others. Many architectural styles and periods commingle in the heart of the city: timber-framed houses; roofs of flat stone, slate, or tile; sculpted dormer-windows; double turrets; Gothic and Renaissance-style windows.

Leg from Sarlat-la-Canéda to Souillac: 60 km

Be vigilant as you leave Sarlat — for the first time on this tour you will run into heavy automobile traffic. Follow the signs for Bergerac and Cahors, and then proceed in the direction of Beynac and Domme. At the traffic circle, take the D46 toward Vézac and Beynac, and then fork toward Vézac and Beynac-et-Cazenac via the D57. A good climb and descent with a bit of traffic awaits. Leave **Vézac**, and take the D49. Then, at the crossroad, take the D703 toward **Beynac-et-Cazenac** and its majestic castle.

PRACTICAL INFORMATION ON BEYNAC

 Tourist office: 24220 Beynac, ☎ 05 53 29 43 08

A fortified castle arises from the road like a startling apparition. From the village, take the road that climbs a distance of three kilometres toward the castle. It leads to the back of the medieval town. Beynac is considered one of the most beautiful villages in France. You might choose to make a stopover here. At the end of the day, when the sun gleams on the stones of its old houses, the village attains a breathtaking beauty!

After a guided tour of the castle, follow the signs and the little road that descends back toward the village and the D703. Ride back toward Sarlat. At the crossroad and the exit of the city, continue on the D703, and ride toward La Roque-Gageac. Follow the Dordogne to the village of **La Roque-Gageac**, an impressive and quieting sight. Ochre-stone and brown-tile houses are reflected in the river, flowing peacefully through the meadows. A small exotic garden, perched up high just near the church, merits a visit.

Continue on the D703 through fields of corn. To visit the bastion of **Domme**, at the intersection with the D46, cross the Dordogne, and enter Cénac. Take the D49 on the left. The road rises steeply and leads to Porte des Tours. Follow the signs for the town centre and the caves situated at Place de la Halle. A public garden, a lookout and a promenade are maintained at the edge of the cliff. This bastion, founded by Philippe le Hardi in 1283, is worth the detour (6 km round-trip) despite the difficult climb!

PRACTICAL INFORMATION ON DOMME

 Tourist office: 24250 Domme, ☎ 05 53 28 37 09, ✉ 05 53 29 34 62

Check your brakes! Double back to the bridge and cross the Dordogne, riding toward **Vitrac** and Groléjac. From the port of Vitrac, take the D703 in the direction of **Cingle de Montfort** and Carsac. The road hugs the river. Climbs and descents succeed each other all the way to **Carsac-Aillac**. Take the D704, and then immediately turn onto the D703 in the direction of **Calviac-en-Périgord**, **Rouffillac**, and Carlux. From the entrance to Rouffillac, the town's castle is visible on an overhang.

Cross the Dordogne again toward **Saint-Julien-de-Lampon** via the D31. Proceed toward **Mareuil** and Le Roc on the D50. This quiet little road runs through a forest for ten kilometres on the way to Souillac. Enter **Le Roc** on the D43 and turn left at the crossroad (no road sign).

The tour crosses vast cornfields. Cross a bridge, and keep left to enter **Souillac** on the D703, following the signs to the town centre. The tourist office is on the left at the traffic light. Souillac is a small town on the border between Périgord and Quercy. A Benedictine monastery was founded here in 665. The beautiful cupola church of Sainte-Marie was erected in the 12th century, and restored in the 17th century. To stroll about the old quarter, leave the main street.

Leg from Souillac to Gramat: 55 km

To leave Souillac, from the tourist office take the N20 or Avenue de Toulouse toward Rocamadour and Grottes de Lacave. Do not cross the bridge. Take the D43, on the left, toward Pinsac and Grottes de Lacave. Enter **Pinsac** and cross the bridge over the Dordogne. From the

---

PRACTICAL INFORMATION ON SOUILLAC

Population
3,800 *Souillagais*

? **Tourist office:** Boul. L.-J.-Malyx, 46200 Souillac, ☎ 05 65 37 81 56

Bicycle shop
Sport Évasion, 23 Boul. L.-J.-Malyx , ☎ 05 65 37 03 64

Market
Friday

Major event: Fête de Souillac (2nd week of July)

Specialty: Prune de Souillac Louis-Roque (brandy)

Map
IGN no. 48

---

road, you have a lovely vista of Château de Freyne. Continue on the D23 in the direction of Lacave. Cross a little bridge. Enter **Lacave**. To visit the caves *(guided tour, 60 min; ☎ 05 65 37 87 03)*, follow the signs from the crossroad. These magnificent concretion caves are reached by tram and then by elevator. The tour includes 12 eccentrically shaped chambers, among them the "chamber of wonders", illuminated by black light. Count on a full hour to visit this "swallowed city".

To proceed in the direction of Rocamadour, return to the crossroad, and ride straight on the D247. The road comprises a climb of two kilometres and a superb descent. Enter **L'Hospitalet**. Take the D673 on the left and pass Grotte des Merveilles. Just before the esplanade, take the *"voie sainte"* (holy road), on the right, the little road of the riverside dwellers that descends toward Rocamadour (very steep!). For an easier descent, take the D32, which snakes to the bottom of the splendid valley (the tunnel is short).

Leave your bicycle well in view at Porte du Figuier. **Rocamadour**, hanging from the cliffs of Canyon de l'Alzou, is one of the most popular sites in France. Foresee a trek of a few hours to retrace the path of medieval pilgrims. You can take the site's only trail, with its

hundreds of steps or ascend in one of two elevators that lead to the
seven chapels of the holy site. An annual pilgrimage takes place during
the week of September 8th.

PRACTICAL INFORMATION ON ROCAMADOUR

? **Tourist office:** 46500 Rocamadour, ☎ 05 65 33 74 14, ≈ 05 65 33 62 59

Leave Rocamadour, and return to L'Hospitalet via the D32. Continue
on the D36 toward Gramat. Pass the Forêt des Singes, cross the
Route Nationale, and continue to **Rignac** on the D36. Then take the
D20 to **Alvignac**. Coast down a long, pleasant descent. At the
crossroad, continue toward Miers. At the cross, turn right onto the V1
to enter **Miers**, and once in the village, turn left toward the town
centre. Take the D91, in front of the cenotaph, toward Gouffre de
Padirac. Then turn left onto the D60 in the direction of Gintrac. Keep
right at the fork, and, from the intersection with the D90, ride to
Gouffre de Padirac.

This impressive natural site is among the subterranean marvels of
Europe. Do not miss it! Stalagmites, stalactites, subterranean rivers,
a 110-metre underground raft trip, and emerald green lakes make up
a spectacular and unique voyage to the centre of the earth! The guided
tour lasts 90 minutes. Wear warm clothing (13 °C) and rain gear for
the visit to the chamber called "Lac de la Pluie" (rain lake).

Proceed on the D90 in the direction of Gramat. Leave **Padirac** on the
D673, and cross only one part of the village. Be attentive! In front of
Place de l'Église, take the first little road on the right (no sign). Ride to
the old city of **Thégra**. Turn right on the D14. The road descends. At
the crossing, continue toward **Lavergne** on the D11. At the
intersection, proceed on the D677 toward Gramat. Then, at the
cenotaph of Lavergne, turn onto the small, unnamed road on the left.
Follow this road to the main street. Facing the race course, turn right
(no sign).

Cross Grolat, and enter Gramat on the N140. Follow the signs for the
town centre. The tourist bureau is on the right at the large square.

PRACTICAL INFORMATION ON GRAMAT

Population
3,640 *Gramatois*

Tourist office: Place de la République, 46500 Gramat, ☎ 05 65 38 73 60

Bicycle shop
Lagrange, Av. de Belgique, ☎ 05 65 38 71 38

Market
Tuesday, Friday, and Sunday

Major event: Fête Votive (1st weekend in August)

Specialties: game, plums and chestnuts; pewter ware, furniture

Map
IGN no. 48

Leg from Gramat to Figeac: 50 km

Capital of Causse, the small town of **Gramat** holds an important sheep market and, in autumn, a nut and truffle market.

Ride to the tourist office and leave Gramat on the N140 in the direction of Figeac and Cahors. Take the D677 right away, still in the direction of Cahors. After the church, just beyond the bridge over the railroad tracks, fork left to the D14, and ride toward the Parc Animalier de Gramat.

The itinerary between Gramat and Figeac runs through Causse de Gramat, a collection of remote plateaus and hills. Be sure to pack enough water and provisions. Fields enclosed by short stone walls are characteristic of the region. In these pastures, stunted vegetation is feasted on by numerous flocks of grazing sheep.

Cross the village of **Reilhac**. Proceed on the D14. Before the entrance to the village of **Le Cornouiller**, take the D25, on your left, toward Flaujac-Gare. You will see the road sign once you have turned. Continue on the D25, taking no sideroads.

Keep on the D25 toward **Lalinié** and **Saint-Simon**. At the crossroad with the D11, proceed toward **Assier**. Cross the village, and, in front of the church, take the D653 toward Château d'Assier, a jewel of southwestern Renaissance architecture. Galiot de Genouillac, who was born in Assier, served four kings of France. He was responsible for construction of the magnificent church and had the castle built (between 1525 and 1535) in his own honour! It is open to visitors. You will notice that several houses in the village are built directly on the ground.

Proceed on the D11 to **Reyrevignes**. At the crossroad, take the D2 in the direction of Figeac. The road is rather hilly and includes some good descents, one at the entrance to **Lissac** and another upon arrival at Figeac. Careful! Control your speed. Enter **Figeac**. At the traffic circle, follow the signs to the tourist office, situated at Place Vival.

PRACTICAL INFORMATION ON FIGEAC

Population
10,000 *Figeacois*

? **Tourist office:** Place Vival, 46100 Figeac, ☎ 05 65 34 06 25

Bicycle shop
Lacoste Cycle, 4 Rue Sainte-Marthe, ☎ 05 65 34 60 92

Market
Saturday

Major event: Fête de Figeac (1st Sunday in May)

Specialties: Élixir des Cordeliers de Figeac candy, *cabécou* (goat cheese), *estofinado* (recipe with a base of dried fish)

Map
IGN no. 48

Leg from Figeac to Saint-Cirq-Lapopie: 50 km

Built on the shore of the Célé, this medieval-style city is the birthplace of Egyptologist, Jean-François Champollion. A museum is maintained in his childhood home. The Hôtel de la Monnaie houses the tourist office as well as Musée du Vieux Figeac.

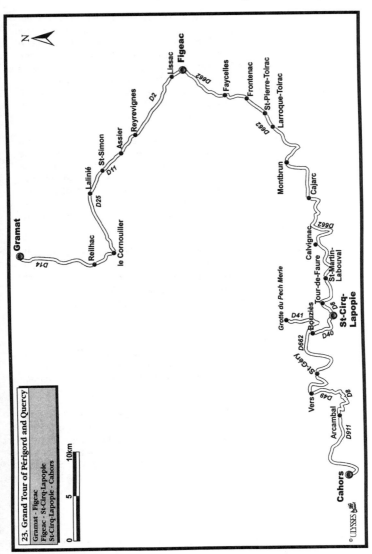

23. Grand Tour of Périgord and Quercy

Gramat - Figeac
Figeac - St-Cirq-Lapopie
St-Cirq-Lapopie - Cahors

© ULYSSES

N

0   5   10km

Gramat
D14
Reilhac
le Cornouiller
Lalinié
St-Simon
D25
D11
Assier
Reyrevignes
D2
Lissac
Figeac
D662
Faycelles
Frontenac
St-Pierre-Toirac
Larroque-Toirac
D662
Montbrun
Cajarc
D662
Calvignac
Tour-de-Faure
St-Martin-Labouval
St-Cirq-Lapopie
D8
D40
Bouziès
D41
Grotte du Pech Merle
D662
St-Géry
Vers
D49
Arcambal
D8
D911
Cahors

From the centre of Figeac, follow the signs for Cahors and Carjac, leaving the town via the D662. Cross a bridge, and continue in the direction of Carjac and Saint-Cirq-Lapopie (pronounced "Saint-Cyr"). At the intersection, follow the signs for the Vallée du Lot via the D662. The road rises gradually, and then descends and narrows considerably through the magnificent village of **Faycelles**. Control your speed. After four kilometres of descent, you reach the Vallée du Lot. The road is closely bordered by the cliff, the river and the railway. Continue toward **Frontenac** and Saint-Pierre-Toirac.

Admirers of old churches can climb a hill to the village of **Saint-Pierre-Toirac**, which is built around a fortified, Romanesque church. The church served as a dungeon during the Hundred Years' War, and the fortification was restored during the wars of religion. An exterior stairway leads to the rampart walk. The house just in front of the church is decorated with lovely passionflowers. Return to the D662. Continue to **Laroque-Toirac**, which has a fortified castle open to visitors.

At the level crossing you will notice the guard's house decorated with flowers; his job is becoming less common in France. Ride over the level crossing and enter **Montbrun**, a little village built into sheer cliff. The valley widens and opens into fields of corn, tobacco, and asparagus. Traverse another level crossing, and enter **Cajarc**. Cross the village.

Proceed on the D662 as it continues through the valley and then climbs a ledge up the flank of the ochre and black cliffs. This leg differs from the preceding one in that it offers many views over the valley. From here, for example, you can see the village of Calvignac, clinging to the cliff on the opposite shore.

Proceed alongside the Lot on the D662 toward **Saint-Martin-Labouval** and **Tour-de-Faure**. Traverse the level crossing and take the D181. Cross a little bridge over the Lot and follow the D8 to Saint-Cirq-Lapopie. The road rises all the while offering a superb view of the old village perched on the cliff. Dismount and follow the signs to the tourist office, situated at Château de la Gardette, right in the heart of the medieval town.

PRACTICAL INFORMATION ON SAINT-CIRQ-LAPOPIE

Population
187 *Saint-Cirquois*

 Tourist office: 46330 Saint-Cirq-Lapopie, ☎ 05 65 31 29 06

 Market
Wednesday

 Major event: Fête Votive (around July 14th)

 Specialty: wood lathe-work (last artisan: François Vinel)

 Map
IGN no. 57

Leg from Saint-Cirq-Lapopie to Cahors: 35 km

You will fall in love with **Saint-Cirq-Lapopie**, known as "the most beautiful village in France", with its timber-framed houses, corbelling balconies, and ogival arches dating from the 13th to the 16th centuries. So as not to miss anything, procure a guidebook from the tourist office. The village abounds with architectural treasures; take extra time to retrace its rich feudal past.

Leave Saint-Cirq-Lapopie on the D8, which climbs behind the village. Facing the large parking lot, take the D40 toward Cahors. You now set out on a rather vertiginous, narrow descent carved into the cliff, with no guard-rail. Control your speed! There is an excellent view of the Lot and the ochre cliffs for approximately five kilometres along this ledge road.

Continue to **Bouziès**. Cross the bridge over the Lot. If you have planned to visit Grotte du Pech Merle, turn right. Ride to the D41, and follow the signs for Cabrerets and Pech Merle (20 km round-trip). At **Grotte du Pech Merle** *(guided tour, 60 min; ☎ 05 65 31 27 05)*, there is an "art gallery" including numerous calligraphic symbols, approximately 60 representations of animals, and 13 human figures, dating from the Solutrean and Magdalenian eras. Pech Merle is in Quercy, while Les Eyzies is in Périgord. Have you made a reservation?

To continue along the tour, return to the D662, and ride toward **Saint-Géry**. The road along the base of the cliff runs through a tunnel in the now very narrow valley. Ride over the level crossing, and enter **Vers**. Cross the village, and continue on the D653 in the direction of Cahors. Immediately fork left to take the D49 toward Arcambal. Cross the Lot. The narrow road climbs through a wood on the edge of the cliff to the village. No question of vertigo here!

The itinerary quits the shore of the Lot to rise into a countryside of grazing horses. Continue to **Arcambal** on the D8. At the fork, keep left. The road descends to the centre of the village. At the intersection, turn right onto the D911, and leave Arcambal via the alley of plane-trees.

Ride carefully! Automobile traffic is heavy all the way to Cahors. Follow the D167 to enter Cahors, crossing the bridge over the Lot (ride on the sidewalk). At the exit, turn left in the direction of downtown via the D663. From the traffic circle at the fountain, take Boulevard Gambetta, on the right, to the tourist office.

PRACTICAL INFORMATION ON CAHORS

Population
20,000 *Cadurciens*

Tourist bureau: Place François-Mitterrand -B P 207, 46000 Cahors, ☎ 05 65 35 09 56, ⊷ 05 65 23 98 66

Bicycle shop
Cycle 7, 417 Quai de Regourd, ☎ 05 65 22 66 60

Market
Wednesday and Saturday

Major events: Printemps de Cahors (photography festival), Cahors Blues Festival (mid-July)

Specialties: Cahors wine, truffles, and nuts

Access: return route to Paris: N20, E09, A20, A71, A10; return train to Paris: Toulouse-Paris Montparnasse line

Map
IGN no. 57

Leg from Cahors to Villefranche-du-Périgord: 65 km

Cahors, an ancient Gallo-Roman town, became a large, prosperous city during the Middle Ages, and today possesses a rich heritage. Cathédrale Saint-Étienne and its cloister, a masterpiece of flamboyant Gothic architecture; the ramparts and Tour des Pendus, and Maison Henri IV are major attractions. There are many ways to discover Cahors' old quarters: by guided tram tour, during a cruise of approximately 90 minutes on the Lot, or, for the more adventurous, on foot with map in hand. The more modern cafés that line Boulevard Gambetta are privileged posts from which to observe *cadurcienne* life while sampling legendary *quercinoise* cuisine.

To leave Cahors, follow the signs to Pont Valentré and cross it on foot. Leave the city on the D8, following the south bank of the Lot in the direction of Luzech. Keep left at the fork. Be careful, traffic is heavy for eight kilometres as you leave the city. Keep on the D8, which is part of the La Route du Vignoble de Cahors. The wine-country landscape begins as you exit **Douelle**. During the course of this leg, wine-tasting opportunities are many. The road is hilly and winds through vineyards to **Luzech**, tucked into a meander of the Lot. This part of the valley, between Cahors and Puy-l'Évêque, was once the fiefdom of the Comtes-Évêques de Cahors.

Continue on the D8 toward **Albas, Anglars, Bélaye** and **Lagardelle**. The road climbs and looks out over vineyards and the Lot, which is relatively wide at this spot. Proceed on the D8 toward **Grézels**. The feudal Château de La Coste, erected in the 13th century, towers above fields of vinery, and houses the Musée Terroir et Vin.

Ride to **Puy-l'Évêque**, and continue toward the town centre. Cross the bridge over the Lot, climb to the village, and continue straight. A very pleasant descent leads through meadows on this lovely, quiet road. At the crossroad, turn right in the direction of **Cassagnes**. The road tracks through undergrowth for about seven kilometres. Leave Cassagnes on the D189. Descend approximately one kilometre to the D673 (no road sign) and turn left. Ride to the junction with the D28 toward **Villefranche-du-Périgord**. The road rises into the woods, finally opening onto very charming dairy farms. Keep on the D28 until the intersection with the D57 toward Villefranche. The road gently slopes down through fields of corn. Enter Villefranche and take the pedestrian walkway, which leads to the tourist office.

PRACTICAL INFORMATION ON
VILLEFRANCHE-DU-PÉRIGORD

Population
850 *Villefrançois*

? **Tourist office:** 24550 Villefranche-du-Périgord, ☎ 05 53 29 98 37

Market
Saturday

Major event: Fête de la Châtaigne et du Cèpe (chestnut and boletus
festival; 3rd Saturday in October)

Specialties: sweet chestnuts, large edible chestnuts, edible flap
mushrooms, and chanterelle mushrooms

Map
IGN no. 48

Leg from Villefranche-du-Périgord to Bergerac: 75 km

The bastion of **Villefranche-du-Périgord**, founded in 1261, is a very
quiet village, surrounded by forests of oak, pine, and chestnut trees
which are particularly glorious in autumn. An important mushroom and
chestnut market is held at Place de la Liberté. Maison du Châtaignier,
Marrons et Champignons promotes the products (chestnuts,
mushrooms) of this beautiful forest, riches that are the base of the
local economy.

Ride to the large crossroad and leave Villefranche-du-Périgord in the
direction of Bergerac on the D660. At the intersection, take the D60
on the right, toward **Prats-du-Périgord**. This old village possesses a
Romanesque church with a bell-tower façade, and a 15th-century
castle. Enter the village, circle the church, and take the little alley on
the right, marked by green signs, toward La Trappe and Mondoux. The
road rises as it leaves the town.

Ride to La Trappe. At the intersection, turn left to proceed on the
Route Principale toward **Meyne**. Pass a small chapel and a cemetery
on your left. Keep left at the fork, and at the intersection with the
D58, ride in the direction of **Le Got**. Continue toward **Peyret**. Traverse
the level crossing, and ride to the D710, onto which you turn right.

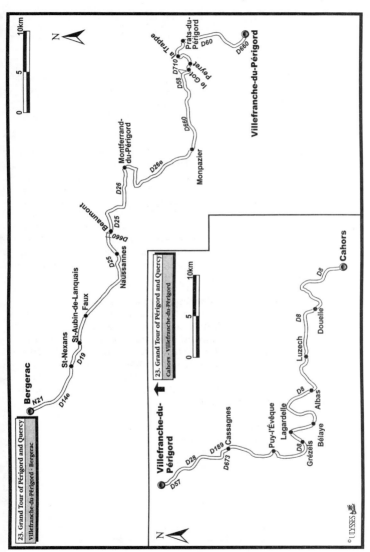

23. Grand Tour of Périgord and Quercy
Villefranche-du-Périgord - Bergerac

23. Grand Tour of Périgord and Quercy
Cahors - Villefranche-du-Périgord

About 500 metres beyond, watch carefully for the D58 on the left toward Monpazier. Then, at the junction, proceed via the D660 to **Monpazier**.

The road rises for about one kilometre. The bastion of Monpazier overlooks the Dropt, a little river that has its source nearby. Follow the signs for the town centre. The fortification, founded by King Edward I in 1283, is the oldest and best-preserved in Périgord. You will fall in love with this town, which I discovered on a particularly serene day.

To leave Monpazier, take the D660 toward Beaumont. Look right for the D26e, which descends in the direction of Saint-Avit-Rivière. Quit the D26e for an old village flanking a hillside that is well worth the detour. This medieval town in hues of orange and ochre boasts lovely houses and a 16th-century market, which is visible from the Route Principale as it descends to the D26. Turn left and ride along the Couze to the junction with the D25. The road climbs for two kilometres, and then gently slopes down. The imposing fortified church of **Beaumont** is discernible. Enter the centre of Beaumont on the D660. This bastion has not stood up well to the test of time. The imposing 13th-century church, flanked by two battlement towers, was a last line of defence against the English.

Cross the town, and ride in the direction of Bergerac. Just outside of town, look left for the D25 toward **Naussannes** and Issigeac. Ride carefully through a steep downhill curve! At the intersection, keep right, continuing via the D19 toward **Faux, Saint-Aubin-de-Lanquais, Saint-Nexans** and Bergerac. The road is straight and includes some good hills. You will pass by magnolia plantations, greenhouses, and tree farms. Enter **Bergerac** on the N21, and continue for two kilometres. Cross the bridge over the Dordogne. Reach the centre of town via Avenue de Verdun, which leads to the station.

GLOSSARY OF BICYCLE TERMINOLOGY

At the train station

train station	*gare*
tickets	*billets*
non-smoking	*non-fumeur*
transportation cost	*coût de transport*
bicycle box	*carton pour le vélo*
how many days?	*combien de jours?*
validate the ticket	*composter le billet*
destination	*destination*
second class	*deuxième classe*
schedule	*horaire*
time	*heure*
baggage (counter)	*bagage (comptoir)*
registration ticket	*étiquette d'enregistrement*
closed	*fermé*
open	*ouvert*
compensation for damages	*réclamation pour dommage*

In the bicycle shop (numbers refer to the diagram on p 247)

bicycling	*faire du vélo*
Excuse me, is there a bicycle shop in town?	*Pardon, y a-t-il un marchand de vélo dans le village?*
I have a flat tire.	*J'ai une crevaison.*
Hello sir (madam), could you look at my bicycle, I have a problem with (or on the same side as):	*Bonjour monsieur (madame), pourriez-vous regarder mon vélo, j'ai un problème avec (ou du côté de):*
rear derailleur (19)	*dérailleur arrière*
front derailleur (6)	*dérailleur avant*
gear cable	*câble de dérailleur*
gear lever (21)	*manette de changement de vitesse*
plate (15)	*plateau*
freewheel (20)	*roue libre*
chain (18)	*chaîne*

rear/front wheel quick-release (1, 12)	*système de blocage rapide de la roue arrière/avant*
hub (14)	*moyeu*
spoke (11)	*rayon*
front fork (10)	*fourche avant*
rear fork (4)	*fourche arrière*
front brakes (9)	*freins avant*
rear brakes (2)	*freins arrière*
brake pads	*patins de frein*
brake cables	*câbles de frein*
brake lever (8`	*manette de frein*
toe clip	*cale-pied*
pedal (17)	*pédale*
crank (16)	*manivelle*
wheel	*roue*
rim (13)	*jante*
fender (24)	*garde-boue*
tire	*pneu*
inner tube	*chambre à air*
pump	*pompe*
bicycle frame	*cadre du vélo*
handlebars (7)	*guidon*
seat (5)	*selle*
seat tube (3)	*tige de selle*
rack (25)	*porte-bagages*
saddlebags	*sacoches*
bottle holder (23)	*porte-bidon*
bottle (22)	*bidon*
bicycle lock	*antivol*
nut	*écrou*
screw	*visse*
tool kit	*trousse à outils*
to grease	*graisser*
to oil	*huiler*
to tighten, straighten	*régler*
to repair	*réparer*
to buy	*acheter*
to rent	*louer*
to screw	*visser*
to adjust	*ajuster*
Thank you very much.	*Merci beaucoup.*
How much will that cost?	*C'est combien?*

Numbers refer to glossary on pp 245,246

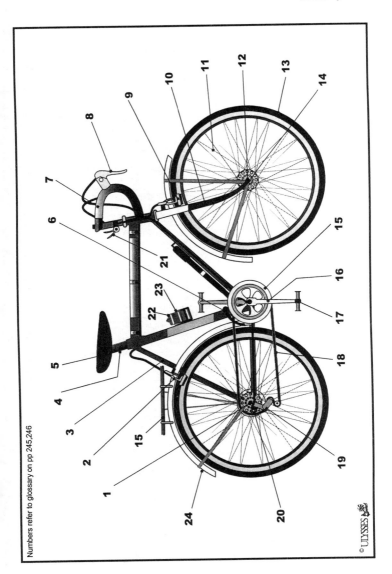

© ULYSSES

INDEX

■ ULYSSES TRAVEL GUIDES

☐ Affordable Bed & Breakfasts in
   Québec .... $12.95 CAN
                 $9.95 US
☐ Beaches of Maine .... $12.95 CAN
                 $9.95 US
☐ Canada's Maritime Provinces . $24.95 CAN
                $14.95 US
☐ Chicago .... $19.95 CAN
                $14.95 US
☐ Cuba .... $24.95 CAN
                $16.95 US
☐ Dominican Republic .... $24.95 CAN
                $17.95 US
☐ Ecuador & Galapagos Islands . $24.95 CAN
                $17.95 US
☐ El Salvador .... $22.95 CAN
                $14.95 US
☐ Guadeloupe .... $24.95 CAN
                $16.95 US
☐ Honduras .... $24.95 CAN
                $16.95 US
☐ Martinique .... $24.95 CAN
                $16.95 US
☐ Montréal .... $19.95 CAN
                $14.95 US
☐ Nicaragua .... $24.95 CAN
                $16.95 US
☐ Ontario .... $24.95 CAN
                $14.95 US
☐ Panamá .... $24.95 CAN
                $16.95 US
☐ Portugal .... $24.95 CAN
                $16.95 US
☐ Provence - Côte d'Azur ..... $24.95 CAN
                $14.95 US

☐ Québec .... $24.95 CAN
                $14.95 US
☐ Toronto .... $18.95 CAN
                $13.95 US
☐ Vancouver .... $14.95 CAN
                $10.95 US
☐ Western Canada .... $24.95 CAN
                $16.95 US

■ ULYSSES GREEN ESCAPES

☐ Cycling in France .... $22.95 CAN
                $16.95 US
☐ Hiking in the Northeastern
   United States .... $19.95 CAN
                $13.95 US
☐ Hiking in Québec .... $19.95 CAN
                $13.95 US

■ ULYSSES DUE SOUTH

☐ Acapulco .... $14.95 CAN
                $9.95 US
☐ Cartagena (Colombia) ...... $9.95 CAN
                $5.95 US
☐ Cancun Cozumel .... $17.95 CAN
                $12.95 US
☐ Puerto Vallarta .... $14.95 CAN
                $9.95 US
☐ St. Martin and St. Barts ..... $16.95 CAN
                $12.95 US

■ ULYSSES TRAVEL JOURNAL

☐ Ulysses Travel Journal ...... $9.95 CAN
                $7.95 US

QUANTITY	TITLES	PRICE	TOTAL
		Sub-total	
		Postage & Handling	$8.00*
		Sub-total	
		G.S.T.in Canada 7%	
		TOTAL	

NAME:_____

ADDRESS:_____

_____

_____

Payment: ☐ Money Order ☐ Visa ☐ MasterCard

Card Number:_____

Expiry Date:_____

Signature:_____

ULYSSES TRAVEL PUBLICATIONS
4176 Saint-Denis, Montréal, Québec, H2W 2M5
(514) 843-9447 fax (514) 843-9448
*$15 for overseas orders

ATLAS

Les cartes réunies dans cet atlas sont des extraits de la série TOP-250 de l'Institut Géographique National de France (IGN). Pour les besoins de ce guide, l'échelle des cartes a été ajustée à 1:350 000.

The maps contained in this atlas are excerpts from the TOP 250 series of the Institut Géographique National (IGN) of France. For the purposes of this guide, the scale has been adjusted to 1:350,000.

LÉGENDE / LEGEND:

0 ___ 5 ___ 10km
1cm = 3,5km

Autoroute (1) - Voie à caractère autoroutier (2)
Motorway (1) - Road with motorway characteristics (2)

Aire de service (1) - Aire de repos (2) - Péage (3)
Service area (1) - resting area (2) - toll-gate (3)

Numéro de sortie d'échangeur
Exit number of an interchange

Route principale à chaussées séparées (1) - Routes principales (2) (3)
Main road with separate roadways (1) - Main roads (2) (3)

Routes secondaires
Secondary roads

Les routes nationales (1) et départementales (2) sont numérotées
National roads (1) and department roads (2) have an official number

N 13 ₁   D 72 ₂

Distances kilométriques (totalisées entre ○ ou villes silhouettées)
Distances in kilometers (between ○ or two outlined cities)

Autres routes : régulièrement entretenue (1), irrégulièrement entretenue (2) - Sentier (3)
Other roads : regularly maintained (1), not regularly maintained (2) - Footpath (3)

Chemins de fer : à 2 voies (1), à 1 voie (2), à voie métrique (3)
Railways : double track (1), single track (2), meter gauge track (3)

Triage (1) - Tunnel (2) - Gare ou arrêt (3), ouverts au trafic voyageur (4)
Marshalling yard (1) - Tunnel (2) - Station or stopping-place (3), open to passenger traffic (4)

Passages : à niveau (1), inférieur (2), supérieur (3)
Level crossing (1), underpass (2), overpass (3)

Limite de camp militaire (1), de zone réglementée de champ de tir (2)
Military camp boundary (1), boundary of firing range restricted zone (2)

Ligne à haute tension (225 kV et plus) - Limite d'État (2)
High-tension line (225 kV and over) (1) - State Boundary (2)

Limite de région (1), de département (2), d'arrondissement (3)
Boundary of region (1), of département (2), of arrondissement (3)

PF   SP

Lieux habités
Populated places

plus de 3 000 habitants (1), moins de 3 000 habitants (2)
over 3 000 inhabitants (1), under 3 000 inhabitants (2)

plus de 100 000 habitants
over 100 000 inhabitants

GRENOBLE

de 25 000 à 100 000 habitants
25 000 to 100 000 inhabitants

LORIENT

de 5 000 à 25 000 habitants (1), de 3 000 à 5 000 habitants (2)
5 000 to 25 000 inhabitants (1), 3 000 to 5 000 inhabitants (2)

¹ Voiron   ² Rillieux

moins de 3 000 habitants : commune (1), hameau important (2)
under 3 000 inhabitants : commune (1), important hamlet (2)

¹ Gonfaron   ² Saretta

Château (1) - Édifice religieux (2) - Refuge (3) - Repère isolé (4) - Ruines (5)
Castle (1) - Religious building (2) - Shelter (3) - Isolated Landmark (4) - Ruins (5)

Concentration industrielle (1) - Fort (2) - Grotte (3) - Phare (4)
Industrial complex (1) - Fort (2) - Cave (3) - Lighthouse (4)

Canaux : navigable (1), non navigable (2) - Marais salants (3) - Marais (4)
Navigable canal (1), non navigable (2) - Salt pans (3) - Marsh or swamp (4)

Aérodromes : internationaux (1), avec piste en dur (2), sans piste en dur (3)
Aerodromes : international (1), hard surfaced runway (2), soft surfaced runway (3)

Zone découverte à marée basse : Plage (1) - Rochers (2)
Area exposed at low tide : Beach (1) - Rocks (2)

Bois
Wood

Les noms de localités imprimés en caractères gras n'ont qu'une valeur touristique indépendante de tout chiffre de population.

Place names in bold characters are of touristic importance irrespective of population figures.

TOP 250-114, ©IGN 1996, Autorisation : 90-7009

1. La Camargue
2. Le Gard
3. Les Garrigues

TOP 250-114, ©IGN 1996, Autorisation : 90-7009

A3

DE-PROVENCE

TOP 250-109, ©IGN 1992, Autorisation : 90-7009

TOP 250-109, ©IGN 1992, Autorisation : 90-7009

A7

FORÊT DOM. DE CHAUX

TOP 250-109, ©IGN 1992, Autorisation : 90-7009

TOP 250-104, ©IGN 1995, Autorisation : 90-7009

A10

23. Le Périgord – le Quercy

A31

A11

TOP 250-104, ©IGN 1995, Autorisation : 90-7009

A13

TOP 250-102. ©IGN 1996. Autorisation : 90-7009

A14

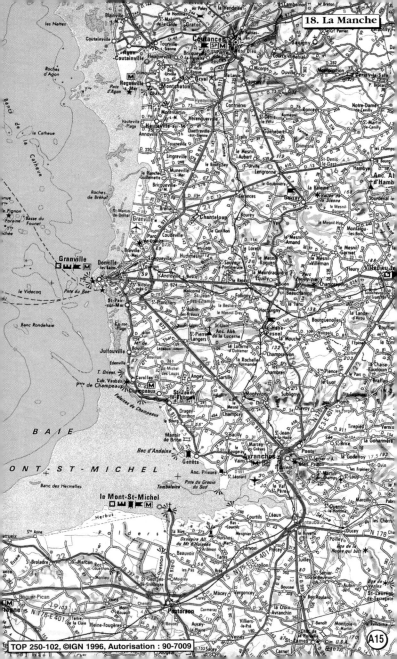

le Mont-St-Michel

TOP 250-105, ©IGN 1996, Autorisation : 90-7009

TOP 250-105, ©IGN 1996, Autorisation : 90-7009

A17

TOP 250-105, ©IGN 1996, Autorisation : 90-7009

A19

A20

TOP 250-105, ©IGN 1996, Autorisation : 90-7009

21. La Côte-sud (Bretagne)

TOP 250-105, ©IGN 1996, Autorisation : 90-7009

A21

TOP 250-105, ©IGN 1996, Autorisation : 90-7009

A23

TOP 250-106, ©IGN 1996, Autorisation : 90-7009

TOP 250-106, ©IGN 1996, Autorisation : 90-7009

TOP 250-106, ©IGN 1996, Autorisation : 90-7009

A26

22. La vallée de la Loire

TOP 250-106, ©IGN 1996, Autorisation : 90-7009

A27

TOP 250-106, ©IGN 1996, Autorisation : 90-7009

A28

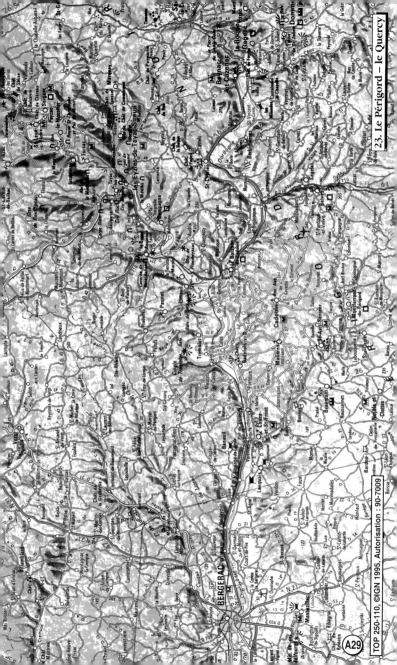

TOP 250-110, ©IGN 1995, Autorisation : 90-7009

A29

TOP 250-110, ©IGN 1995, Autorisation : 90-7009

A30